On Rowan Williams

On Rowan Williams

Critical Essays

EDITED BY **MATHESON RUSSELL**

CASCADE *Books* • Eugene, Oregon

ON ROWAN WILLIAMS
Critical Essays

Copyright © 2009 Wipf and Stock Publishers. All rights reserved. Except for brief quotations in critical publications or reviews, no part of this book may be reproduced in any manner without prior written permission from the publisher. Write: Permissions, Wipf and Stock Publishers, 199 W. 8th Ave., Suite 3, Eugene, OR 97401.

Cascade Books
A Division of Wipf and Stock Publishers
199 W. 8th Ave., Suite 3
Eugene, OR 97401

www.wipfandstock.com

ISBN 13: 978-1- 55635-973-6

Cataloging-in-Publication data:

On Rowan Williams : critical essays / edited by Matheson Russell.

xxiv + 238 p. ; 23 cm. Includes bibliographical references and index.

ISBN 13: 978-1- 55635-973-6

1. Williams, Rowan, 1950–. 2. Church of England—Bishops. 3. Theology. 4. Christianity and politics. I. Russell, Matheson. II. O'Donovan, Oliver. III. Title.

BX5199 W65 O55 2009

Manufactured in the U.S.A.

Contents

Acknowledgments • vii
Foreword: Australia on Rowan Williams / Oliver O'Donovan • *ix*
Introduction • *xiii*

1. The Ecclesiology of Rowan Williams / Rhys Bezzant • 1
2. The Hidden Center: Trinity and Incarnation in the Negative (and Positive) Theology of Rowan Williams / Andrew Moody • 25
3. Disruptive History: Rowan Williams on Heresy and Orthodoxy / Benjamin Myers • 47
4. *Krisis? Kritik?*: Judgment and Jesus in the Theology of Rowan Williams / Michael Jensen • 68
5. Dispossession and Negotiation: Rowan Williams on Hegel and Political Theology / Matheson Russell • 85
6. The Humanity of Godliness: Spirituality and Creatureliness in Rowan Williams / Byron Smith • 115
7. Desire and Grace: Rowan Williams and the Search for Bodily Wholeness / Andrew Cameron • 141
8. Rowan Williams on War and Peace / Tom Frame • 163
9. The Beauty of God in Cairo and Islamabad: Rowan Williams as Apologist / Greg Clarke • 186

Bibliography of Rowan Williams • 205
Contributors • 233
Index • 235

Acknowledgments

During the Summer of 2006, on the lawn of Wycliffe Hall, Oxford, the idea was hatched to commission a group of emerging Australian theologians to write essays on the thought of Rowan Williams. I would first like to thank Michael Jensen for daring to contemplate such a project with me and for encouraging the project along the way with good humor and considered advice. His willingness to be a sounding board at each of the stages of this process has been deeply appreciated.

An editor is at the mercy of his contributors to a large degree, and this editor is extremely grateful to his contributors for their conscientious efforts, for the remarkably humble and appreciative spirit in which they greeted comments on their drafts, and for their patience with requests for still further revisions on already revised drafts. They have made my first attempt at editing a book a surprisingly enjoyable and satisfying experience.

Compiling a bibliography of the kind included in this volume is a time-consuming task. In this case it was made much easier by the generosity of Mike Higton who selflessly agreed to share the fruits of his own scholarly labor in the form of an already extensive bibliography of Rowan Williams' books, articles, lectures, and other work. This contribution I gladly acknowledge, and I offer him my heartfelt thanks for it. I am also grateful to Ben Myers, whose voracious consumption of theological literature seemed to bring to his attention (and hence to mine) an unceasing stream of new items to be included in the bibliography. I owe a debt of thanks as well to Michael Jensen for hunting down bibliographic minutia at my request among the many libraries of Oxford University.

Finally, I would very much like this collection to stand as a tribute to two Anglican clergymen, Robert Forsyth and Andrew Katay, whose years of

Acknowledgments

ministry at both St. Barnabas Anglican Church, Broadway, and the Sydney University Evangelical Union were formative and liberating for more than one of the authors represented in this collection. They remain for me a model of Christian faith and intellectual curiosity—each separately, and both together.

Foreword
Australia on Rowan Williams

Rowan Williams and Australian Anglicans, Australian Anglicans and Rowan Williams: it was not a foregone conclusion that these should seem to represent antipodean poles spiritually as well as geographically. Indeed, for one who can claim only slight acquaintance with the distinctive shapes, traditions, and engagements of Australian Anglicanism it remains something of a mystery how they ever came to appear so. That they *need* not be so, these essays powerfully attest. The authors, speaking out of the wider Australian Anglican experience, but with the confessionally evangelical traditions of Sydney well-represented, show that key questions posed by Williams' contribution to Anglican thought can be addressed through the precious gift of theology, sharing the good news of Jesus Christ through interpretation, reflection, and mutual questioning. In sympathy with many of the critical points the authors have to make to Williams, I am even more sympathetic with their refreshing confidence that these are points that can be raised by Christian theologians to a Christian theologian within the precious charism they share, rejoicing in the common "joy of speaking about one who is the secret of all hearts," to recall that fine phrase Andrew Moody quotes from Williams' Enthronement Sermon. So they bring us closer to the evangelical heartbeat of the man, and prove, to those tempted to doubt it, the theological resilience of the younger generation of Australian Anglicans.

Williams the theologian-Archbishop: but is the Archbishop an accident that (unfortunately, perhaps) befell the theologian? That view has had its advocates, especially in the English universities. Serviceable to scholarship through solid historical treatises like *Arius,* serviceable to the pastorate through the occasional radical gesture, what a pity that Williams had to lead the church! Those of us who regularly heard him preach, or discussed with him the task of theological teaching, knew very well that this could not be the true shape of the man and his work. He left Oxford for Monmouth quite simply because he received the church's call; and he could not claim to be a theologian if he had turned that call down. The authors of these essays are quite right to treat the theologian-Archbishop as an integral whole, a personality whose theology is performed in his office as well as in his library.

Williams' reflective, poetic, and very dialectical conception of the theologian's task is at some distance from the well-marshaled presentation of doctrines that a traditionally-schooled evangelical mind expects. One of the achievements of these authors is to overcome this superficial difference, recognizing how deeply rooted in doctrine Williams is and winnowing his doctrine out for careful appreciation. He constructs his doctrine of redemption around the Trinity, reconciliation, and the church, rather than around justification. Does this imply that he "undercuts" the Protestant element in the Anglican identity? Any answer to this must take note, I should think, of the leading presence of William Tyndale, England's most creative Reformation theologian, in Williams' gallery of *Anglican Identities*. Apparently, it takes a Rowan Williams to find this towering evangelical figure interesting!

The authors write, for the most part, with a studied determination to see this dialectical thinker from all sides, not to pin him to the floor with a one-sided caricature. Only one engagement voices a complete rejection, and as that concerns Williams' record on foreign policy and military matters, it may be worth a comment here. There is a certain truth in Bishop Frame's complaint, especially with regard to the younger Williams, that he could treat international questions all too lightly as a matter for theological comment without troubling with the complex realities—some of his political *obiter dicta* had a carefree, throwaway style he would never have adopted in relation to a text of Athanasius!—and brought too much within the narrow pastoral strategy of teaching Westerners to question themselves. One does not have to think self-questioning unmerited or uncalled-for to see that it can get in the way of a hard and objective look at what other peoples and places are suffering and doing. There is also, however, a proper theological reticence about pretending to know what is factually the case; and the later Williams has displayed that reticence—no more satisfactorily, from

Frame's point of view. What Frame could, perhaps, properly look for from a theologian responding to crises as they unfold is a discursive exploration of what might follow for Christian faith if certain things were the case. Paul Ramsey, himself the prince of such reasoning, used to take an example from Archbishop Michael Ramsey to illustrate just what Christians might say, and what they might not say in such moments. But Ramsey was able to ride on the coat tails of a late-Thomistic casuistry, which was simply not Williams' intellectual world. It is better, perhaps, simply to accept that each has his gift.

Williams' intellectual world has a strong trace of the *via negativa* about it, a point which is explored from several points of view in the collection. One could see the authors handling Williams' negative theology in a manner not unlike that of Williams himself in handling the neo-Enlightenment style of a generation ago. Michael Jensen rightly focuses attention on Williams' critique of our common senior friend and colleague, Maurice Wiles. Moving through Wiles' skeptical questions and doubts and doing them full justice, Williams demands of him one further step, a step promised but not finally accomplished. In what was at once a friendly challenge and a joyful recognition, he took the opportunity of a farewell speech for Wiles' retirement in 1991 to sum up the hidden, unarticulated *motif* of his work in the words, "Woe to me if I preach not the Gospel!"

Oliver O'Donovan
New College, Edinburgh

Introduction

Rowan Williams' stature as a first rate scholar is unquestionable. Within the academy, he is regarded almost universally with enormous respect. Within the church, things are not so cut and dried. It is not yet clear what his legacy will be; and when it comes to assessing his efforts as spiritual head of the worldwide Anglican Communion, the jury is still out. To some Williams is a hero, to others a villain, and to many in between he is an ambiguous and elusive figure, at once irreducible to any of the well-worn factional stereotypes and yet somehow quintessentially Anglican.

Where then does this preacher, activist, and intellectual stand? How does he understand what it is to be Christian? And how does his theology inform his leadership of the church, his politics, and his public interventions? As a theologian, church historian, poet, and social commentator, Rowan Williams has published over twenty books and one hundred and fifty scholarly essays. His theological interests are far too broad to be fully adumbrated in a book this size. Nonetheless, in this collection of essays several of the most fundamental themes that typify his theological viewpoint are expounded and critically examined.

Even into his mid-twenties it was no sure thing that the bright and talented young theologian and pastor would make the Church of England his home. Rowan Williams grew up in a non-conformist church in Wales before being introduced to the Anglican tradition of worship as a teenager. During his student years, both the Roman Catholic and the Russian Orthodox churches held considerable appeal. But, for all its flaws, what allowed Williams to make his peace with the Church of England and to embrace it were its vision of catholicity and the central place it afforded to the sacraments. These emphases reflected what, for Williams, *every* church

Introduction

properly is and ought to be: not coextensive with the universal church but nonetheless a genuine part of it, and not an authority over the faithful but a community open to the judgment of God. Indeed, the sacraments belong at the heart of church life because in these acts the church itself is no longer at the center but God is: nothing else but this can "authorize" a church.

In the first essay in the collection, Rhys Bezzant explores the shape of Williams' ecclesiology, unpacking its guiding threads: the "gift" character of the church, the centrality of the sacraments, and the church's missional vision of a renewed humanity. Bezzant's survey of these themes helps us understand the sometimes-surprising stances the Archbishop has taken on certain issues facing the church today. But Bezzant is not uncritical of Williams' ecclesiology. Indeed he raises a number of critical questions, some of which recur throughout the collection.

The first recurring critical theme raised in Bezzant's essay concerns the Archbishop's prioritizing of *process* over *state*: we dare not think of ourselves as justified and at peace, Williams argues, since this will lull us into a soporific state and close us to the transformative work of the Spirit. The critical issue here is whether legitimate suspicion towards the ideological uses of Christian rhetoric is handled with sufficient balance or whether in fact it is allowed to dominate in such a way that it forces us to downplay or even exclude certain elements of the historical gospel, elements not only of central theological significance but also of considerable pastoral significance, e.g., our having peace with God, our finding rest in him.

The second theme is that of covenantal theology and eschatology. The sacraments themselves are intelligible only within the context of a specifically Jewish theological imagination, in which the people of God stand under condemnation (exile) and await the coming of God to effect their forgiveness, liberation, return, and renewal. The sacraments of baptism and communion proclaim that the decisive sacrifice has been made, that forgiveness is available and that a "new creation" community has been founded—a new creation, however, whose fullness we await to be manifested when Jesus comes again in glory to judge the living and the dead. In contrast, Williams' eschatology seems to reflect a historicizing revision of this traditional narrative, in which the day of the Lord is de-emphasized or reinterpreted as occurring in the unfolding history of the church. It needs to be considered how this inflects his understanding of Christian thought and practice.

Introduction

The third and final recurring theme is that of Trinitarian doctrine. It is undeniable that Williams' entire (un)systematic theological imagination is oriented by the doctrine of the Trinity. It has been an abiding point of interest in his patristic scholarship as well as his contributions to contemporary theology, and it informs all of his ecclesial, inter-faith, and social-critical interventions. No consensus exists among the authors in the present collection on the validity and value of Williams' Trinitarian theology. It is portrayed variously as deeply orthodox and the source of his greatest insights, and as methodologically incoherent and sociologically misapplied. Whatever the case, Williams' theology cannot be appreciated at all without concerted engagement with this theme.

It is his Trinitarian theology that is the explicit topic of the second essay in the collection. As a doctoral student, Williams researched the work of the twentieth-century Russian Orthodox theologian, Vladimir Lossky. "It was Lossky," he remarks in an interview, "who rubbed my nose in the whole idea of theology of negation and what it did and didn't mean."[1] Taking one of Williams' early essays on Lossky's *via negativa* as his point of departure, Andrew Moody embarks on a study of the complex relationship between apophaticism and Trinitarianism in Williams' theology. One of Williams' great talents is the ability to read the history of the Christian dogmatics in such a way that thinkers who are supposed to be poles apart come to appear as entirely compatible interpreters of catholic orthodoxy. From Augustine to St. John of the Cross, Aquinas to Hegel—many commentators have perceived here irreconcilable differences; but it seems they have simply not been looking hard enough. In particular, Moody shows how, for Williams, each of these thinkers is attempting to negotiate the same interface: the interface between the doctrine of the Trinity, with the theological grammar it articulates, and the non-epistemic movement of faith, that movement of response elicited by the gratuitous self-giving of God. For Williams, the apophatic character of Christian language about God is not *in tension with* but is *a function of* God's ecstatic and kenotic being, i.e., God's triune being-in-otherness. There is no ultimate knowledge of God *because* God is love, ceaselessly self-transcending, and open, and in this sense "personal."

But Moody identifies a further, more radical moment of negativity in Williams' theology, a moment that is figured as a "ray of darkness," a

1. Todd Breyfogle, "Time and Transformation: An Interview with Rowan Williams," *Cross Currents* 45 (1995) 308.

Introduction

"bottomless black pit," or a "void." This he sees as a potentially *nihilistic* affirmation, an admission that Jesus in the final analysis represents an assault on our reason, a silence into which we are liable to project our own fantasies of God's character and will. And Moody finds it hard to reconcile this with Williams' Trinitarian apophaticism, which is more or less continuous with the traditions of Christian orthodoxy (although not entirely beyond contestation). This more radical moment of negativity becomes an explicit theme for attention in the essays to follow under the headings of "disruption," "*krisis*," and "dialectics," and in each case it is given a comparatively more positive assessment than Moody gives it.

In the wake of the quasi-scientific pretensions of Enlightenment "doctrinal criticism" and its dismantling by both neo-conservative and postmodern critiques, an abiding concern of recent theological scholarship has been the rethinking of the nature of doctrine and the task of theological thinking. The third and fourth essays in the collection take us to the heart of these debates. Ben Myers presents a sustained argument for a constructivist understanding of Christian doctrine. If doctrine is anything, it is what *we* work out in our necessarily *historical* context in response to the event of Christ and in the crucible of contemporary challenges and concerns. With Williams, Myers is unconvinced by the received accounts of doctrinal development that see the task of theology as a quest to faithfully restate in the contemporary context that which is the inherent meaning-content of the original gospel proclamation. This assumes, he argues, that the meaning and significance of the gospel is already fully present and fully interpreted in the beginnings of Christianity. But this flies in the face of the historical facts of doctrinal development. One need only to observe the process of the ecumenical councils of the fourth and fifth centuries to see that what counts as true and orthodox needed to be creatively *grasped* and could not be ensured by simple *repetition* of historical formulae (this is the fundamental thesis of Williams' *Arius: Heresy and Tradition*).[2] What's more, Myers seeks to expose the more subtle anti-historicism of the so-called "post-liberal" Wittgensteinianism of George Lindbeck. Here too the essential kernel of Christian doctrine, which is purportedly found in the "grammar" of Christian dogma and Christian practice, is regarded as timeless and beyond negotiation. And yet, in truth, the stable core of Christian life and thought

---

2. Williams, *Arius: Heresy and Tradition* (London: Darton, Longman and Todd, 1987).

Introduction

is nothing stable at all; the heartbeat of Christian history is the irrepressible and unsettling presence of the gospel events themselves in the thought, imagination, and practice of the church. If there is any unity at all to the fragmented history of Christian doctrinal development, any "orthodoxy" to speak of, it is something won in each generation when the identity of the Christian community is negotiated through a return to that disruptive founding event. This, to be sure, cannot occur outside of a tradition that re-presents those events to us; but it is nonetheless a risky venture that is productive of something that is new every morning. Nothing short of this is required for Christian truth and genuine faithfulness to God.

To find oneself broken against the rock of Christ—this is the "disruption" that Myers speaks of. It is taken up again in Michael Jensen's essay under the heading of "*krisis*" or "judgment." As he notes, the idea of standing "open to judgment" is one of the most striking leitmotifs in the writings, lectures, and sermons of the Archbishop (indeed, this phrase is entirely fitting as the title to a collection of his sermons and addresses published in 1994).[3] Jensen's essay begins by drawing our attention to the fact that Williams distances himself from the critical methodologies embraced by the academy in the 1970s and 80s. Taking Williams' painstakingly attentive and gracious critique of Maurice Wiles as his text, Jensen explores his methodological concerns. Williams demurs on both theological and philosophical grounds. Philosophically, Wiles, who represents the old guard, puts too much faith in his ability to inhabit unequivocally the position of judge, sitting on the tribunal of reason and bringing to light what is legitimate and illegitimate in the development of Christian doctrine. Williams reveals himself to be a student of the postmodern critics of Enlightenment rationalism when he asks whether we truly possess the wherewithal to deliver such neutral assessments of doctrinal pronouncements. Would not such a presumption fail to reckon with our historicity? At the same time, theologically, we ought to remain aware that our status as finite and fallible creatures necessitates that we humbly open ourselves to a critical reversal: that we be ready to stand in the position of the one who is judged, that we allow the Christian witness to the event of Christ to *judge us*. This, at bottom, is what Williams means by "the priority of *krisis* over *Kritik*."

---

3. Williams, *Open to Judgement: Sermons and Addresses* (London: Darton, Longman and Todd, 1994).

Introduction

Jensen's essay circles towards its carefully articulated critical observations on Williams' stance in a manner that self-consciously imitates Williams' essay on Wiles. It would be uncharitable, however, to read this as parody. On the contrary, Jensen is signaling his intention to do Williams the justice of reading him with no less sensitivity and critical attentiveness than he gives to Wiles. What's more, the basis of his reflection is a shared conviction: discipleship in essence means to stand under the lordship of Christ. This is what motivates him to press the point: does *krisis* really have the priority in Williams' theology? Without insisting upon it, Jensen wonders whether Williams' hermeneutic lacks the resources to determine whether the judgment he finds in the gospel narrative is really the voice of Jesus or whether it is not simply more ideology ("liberationist," "feminist," or some other) whose legitimacy we have merely assumed and which we retrospectively project onto the gospel. Is the judgment effected by the gospel underwriting our critique of modernity, or is it the other way around? If the latter, then perhaps *Kritik* has not truly been relegated to second place after all.

My own essay considers once again Williams' impulse to "tarry with the negative," this time in connection with his reading of Hegel. Arguably the greatest of the German Idealists—certainly the most influential—Hegel is a cardinal reference point for modern theology, and Williams is more convinced than most that his work *deserves* to enjoy the kind of influence that it does. His argument here runs on several fronts at once. On one hand, contrary to deflationary readings and "process" readings, Williams argues that Hegel's Trinitarian theology is far more orthodox than is usually assumed, and that, what's more, it is the grammar of orthodox Trinitarian doctrine that is, for Hegel, the very grammar of *thinking*. What Hegel provides us with, therefore, is a way of seeing the practice of rational reflection through the lens of the cross. On the other hand, it is Hegel to whom we must turn if we are to avoid the aporias of postmodernism, with its problematic and unsustainable ethical stance and its political dead-ends. In this connection, Williams is indebted to the work of Gillian Rose, whose reading of Hegel provides him with a fresh and productive angle from which to approach Hegel—a Hegel rescued from the crude, strongly teleological interpretations of a previous generation (according to which rational necessity is supposed to "lead history by the nose"), and a Hegel exonerated from the postmodernists' charge of being the paradigmatic philosopher of system and totality.

Introduction

This recasting of Hegel sets the terms for Williams' constructive social theory. The main sections of the essay reconstruct this social theory in some detail by examining its basic concepts of "dispossession" and "negotiation." It is *this* theory, I suggest, which undergirds the critique of modernity that the Archbishop has developed in numerous contexts. In essence, the theory presents "thinking" (which here refers to what Habermas would call "communicative action") as a kenotic movement, a self-giving that rediscovers the self in the other. My interests are increasingly recognized as intertwined with yours, and through our collaborative negotiations, difficult and inexhaustible though they are, a new social reality is able to emerge that mirrors more and more the life of God, in which truth and justice coalesce. The thinking Williams does in conversation with Hegel (and Rose) provides him with a sophisticated and formidable, although not incontestable, critical social theory. But the essay concludes with an attempt to expose some limitations in this account insofar as it aspires to be a *political theology*—that is, insofar as it concerns the political vocation of the church vis-à-vis secular society. Once again the pivotal issue is eschatology. It is suggested that, perhaps surprisingly, a *more orthodox* eschatology is what is required in order to untie a knot in Williams' political theology: only an eschatology that is content to locate the kingdom of God in a divinely inaugurated future age (i.e. a "day of the Lord," a day of universal resurrection and judgment) can liberate the contemporary church to enact the kind of self-giving communicative action envisaged by Williams.

The practices of prayer and other spiritual disciplines have always been central to Williams' understanding of the Christian faith and his experience of it. It is no coincidence that his first book is a study of Christian spirituality from the New Testament to St. John of the Cross. But, in keeping with his broader theological outlook, the thrust of Williams' interpretation of Christian spirituality is squarely grounded in a Trinitarian doctrine of God and a kenotic Christology, and this gives it a distinctive twist. As Byron Smith explains in his chapter, what true spirituality looks like, for Williams, is shown to us by the incarnate Word of God. In him we see one who is liberated by his knowledge of God as creator and loving sustainer to be a creature who lives in utter dependence upon the God of grace. What Christ, viewed as *the true human*, reveals is the following. True godliness, far from being a flight from creatureliness, consists in a joyful receiving of our creatureliness as God's gift. And, in our thankful acceptance of our

Introduction

dependent and finite life, we can know the freedom of the sons of God. Sin, by contrast, is the attempt to be like God *qua* self-grounding ground of projects, meanings, and relationships. But because this is what we are not and cannot be, it marks a lapse into an illusory sense of self. Moreover, by taking ourselves to be independent and unconstrained, we ironically find ourselves diminished and dehumanized.

What Smith perceptively highlights, however, is that, for Williams, this "flight" from ourselves is to be analyzed in terms of the economy of fear and vulnerability: precisely because we are dependent and vulnerable, we seek to protect ourselves—if not in fact, then through escapist constructions of reality, i.e., through fantasies of invulnerability and certitude. As Williams understands it, *this* is the tendency that the practices of Christian spirituality are supposed to work against. At their best, the practices of prayer and contemplation focus us on the reality of God's creative love and the truth of our creatureliness. They remind us of what Christ has shown: that the perfect love of God casts out fear and that a life of contented creatureliness is possible, in which we embrace our interdependence upon God and others. Instead of reinforcing the self-evasions of our escapist fantasies, then, true Christian spirituality marks the site of their deconstruction.

The theme of vulnerability and grace continues in the next essay. Indeed, Andrew Cameron's essay could be seen as a case study in how the analysis of vulnerability and grace traced in Smith's essay is employed by Williams in a specific arena, in this case the arena of sexual relationships. In the sexual relationship (ideally), we discover ourselves to be desirable through the desire the other expresses for us. In this connection, Williams' felicitous phrase, "the body's grace," refers not merely to the "gift" of the other's body, but to the "gift" of *finding oneself to be loved* through the giving of the other's body. It is the other's recognition of me as desirable/loveable that is the true gift, enabling me to know myself as one who is loved and thus to enjoy human existence in one of its most exalted and precious modes. And, as Cameron explains, Williams sees this logic expressed at its purest in homosexual love, since here desire is separated from any hint of instrumental interest, e.g., the desire to reproduce; that is to say, what is expressed is an unequivocal desire for me and not a desire for some other end to which I am the means. The culturally sanctioned forms of heterosexual marriage, therefore, are external to the inner logic of sex, and indeed, for

Introduction

Williams, can be read as "an attempt to control and minimize the risk" of human sexuality.

Cameron is convinced that Williams articulates something fundamental about the meaning of sex, something that explains why it is a realm of experience in which we feel so spiritually and existentially (and not merely physically) vulnerable and exposed. He is also convinced that Williams' account captures something of the theological significance of sex, i.e., the way in which it mirrors the joy of knowing ourselves loved by God, with a love that is not needy but rather totally gratuitous and exuberant. Cameron questions, however, whether this is *all* we need to say *theologically* about sex. Are there not further dimensions, for example, to those biblical images and metaphors that draw an analogy between erotic human relationships and the relationship between the creator and his creation? In developing this line, Cameron foregrounds in particular the theo-logic of the celibate relationship, a relationship that provides an alternative, or rather, a complementary paradigm for gendered relationships in the household of God. Just as Williams provides a "thick," existentially satisfying account of sexual relationships, so Cameron attempts to construct an existentially and theologically satisfying account of celibate relationships in an effort to redress a common deficiency in conservative sexual ethics. Once the theological account of gendered relationships is expanded in this way, Cameron argues, does not the conservative ideal of a community consisting of heterosexual married couples and celibates living side by side look somewhat more "plausible, livable, and indeed satisfying"?

Williams has been a frequent commentator on British foreign policy and international relations in both scholarly and popular forums. If his sexual ethics have engendered controversy, his public pronouncements in this arena have done so just as surely. He is a clergyman with a long history of activism, and no one could accuse him of merely entertaining an armchair interest in such matters. Tom Frame does us a great service by gathering in one place a survey of Williams' interventions and positions on such diverse issues as the Falkland Island conflict, nuclear deterrence, the Iraq wars, and the September 11 attacks. It would be fair to say that Frame is unsympathetic with Williams' intellectualist and incessantly self-critical style of reflection on issues of war and peace. In the essay, he repeatedly calls upon Williams to face up to the realities and complexities of hard and soft power. Where the moral duties and responsibilities of nation-states to

Introduction

their citizens are at stake, Frame argues, Williams' rarefied analyses offer little policy direction and perhaps even culpably distract from fundamental policy considerations. A starker juxtaposition of "realist" and "idealist" approaches to war and peace within a theological setting could hardly be imagined. No doubt Williams would be unsatisfied with the theological *niveau* of Frame's analysis, just as Frame is unsatisfied with Williams' grasp of the intricacies of strategic and tactical decision-making. In the end, it becomes clear that Frame's fundamental worry is that Williams has nothing to say that could influence the world of strategic studies, "where decisions affecting whole nations are made and human lives are held in the balance." One wonders, however, whether Williams would accept his premise.

An Archbishop, it seems, is invited to speak in the most unlikely places. In 2004 and 2005, Williams spoke at two Islamic universities, in Cairo and Islamabad respectively. In the final essay in this collection, Greg Clarke examines these addresses in the context of a broader discussion of Williams' theological aesthetics. What gives Williams' public speeches the engaging quality that they possess, he argues, is his underlying conviction that the beauty of the world—whether in art, ethics, or the natural world—is made intelligible by the doctrine of the Triune God, the one free and self-sufficient life whose super-abundance generates all that is, beyond the flat logic of necessity. In this perspective, the world is strictly speaking superfluous, held in being purely by the creative, selfless love of the creator; it has no "use" but exists for the "useless" purpose of reflecting the glory of the Lord. Clarke shows how this theological aesthetics, an aesthetics with kinship to both Hans Urs von Balthasar and David Bentley Hart, is mobilized by Williams to draw outsiders into the Christian story and to bridge the not insignificant gulf between Christian and other religious and non-religious worldviews. Once again, however, the author senses an effacement of eschatology in Williams work. And the essay ends with a proposal to develop Williams' theological aesthetics in a way that does not shy away from the rich eschatological imagery of the Christian aesthetic imagination.

As Williams reminds us, it is the tensions and contradictions in any living tradition that harbor the greatest potential for self-criticism, repentance, and new life. If this is so, then the tensions between the evangelical, liberal, and conservative Anglo-Catholic impulses within the Anglican Communion must be brought to the surface and worked through. Latent tensions will not do; the truth must be spoken in love. Politicized tensions will not do; groups within the Body of Christ who share a theological standpoint cannot merely throw their weight around and think that this will lead to genuine spiritual transformation. Tensions become productive for the collective work of discipleship when they explicitly become the material for what Williams calls "the labor of social meaning," or what we might somewhat tendentiously translate as "the work of reformation." Therefore, if some of the contributors to this collection articulate critical positions vis-à-vis Rowan Williams, let this be seen as a gesture of fellowship, a gesture of mutuality and love. Let them be seen as workers together with him in the field.

1

The Ecclesiology of Rowan Williams

RHYS BEZZANT

It has been said that Rowan Williams' ecclesiology is Rowan Williams' theology.[1] Though he has not composed a comprehensive systematic theology,[2] Williams' disparate writings (scholarly monographs, sermons, dedications, forewords, afterwords, journal articles, opinion pieces in church newspapers, speeches, letters, and book reviews) nevertheless adumbrate systematic concerns, and because they are in the main occasional in nature they inevitably refract current issues, questions, debates, or schisms addressed in the church. It seems that ecclesiology is precisely everywhere even if only suggestively in his written work.

Williams' concern for the church is seen not just in his theological opinions. He also exemplifies in his own career path a commitment to ecclesial life. His decision to relinquish his chair as Lady Margaret Professor of Divinity in Oxford to take up a calling as the Bishop of Monmouth in

---

1. Theo Hobson, *Anarchy, Church and Utopia: Rowan Williams on Church* (London: Darton, Longman and Todd, 2005) 1.

2. "He [Williams] is confessedly happier with narrative than with system." Geoffrey Wainwright, "Rowan Williams on Christian Doctrine," *Scottish Journal of Theology* 56 (2003) 73.

South Wales (his native county and country) in 1991, with its seat in the less than salubrious port-town of Newport, demonstrates this. His ministry was later stretched when he accepted the additional role of Archbishop of Wales (1999); he was translated to Canterbury in 2002, amidst cries of dismay particularly from the evangelical wing of the Church, in England, and abroad. Williams' broader concern for social justice is attested through a conversation in 1984 between ethicist Oliver O'Donovan and theologian John Macquarrie, who, upon the announcement of Williams' appointment to Oxford, remarked that Rowan Williams would make an excellent Oxford don, "if only he's out of jail at the time."[3] Williams had just been arrested for trespassing on an American air force base in England to protest the strategy of nuclear deterrence.

Deep streams of Williams' theological thought come to the surface as he engages with contemporary issues, often creating unexpected crosscurrents that prove difficult to traverse. This survey will sketch an outline of the Archbishop's ecclesiological practice and thinking in reference to some current challenges within the Anglican Communion, from the viewpoint of a fellow Christian and fellow Anglican, who has been nurtured in the evangelical wing of the Australian church.

Ecclesiological Case Studies

The Windsor Process

Williams' translation to Canterbury came at a critical juncture in the life of the international Anglican Communion. Despite the conservative Resolution 1.10 on human sexuality, which had been overwhelmingly endorsed by the Lambeth Conference of Bishops in 1998, the integrity of the Communion has been more recently challenged by the decisions of the Diocese of New Westminster in western Canada, the Diocese of New Hampshire in the US, and the Diocese of Oxford in the UK to affirm at some level the validity of same-sex relationships. These breaches of the resolution emboldened breaches of Anglican polity by, for example, the Dioceses of Uganda, Singapore, and Brazil, who affirmed the propriety either of extra-territorial

---

3. Oliver O'Donovan, "Archbishop Rowan Williams," *Pro Ecclesia* 12 (2003) 5–9.

ordinations, or of entering without permission into an episcopal relationship with a parish or clergyperson in another diocesan's jurisdiction.

To find some constructive way forward through such internecine debates, a new process was instituted by the Archbishop of Canterbury as an adjunct to the established mechanisms for coordinating the ministry and life of the international Anglican Communion.[4] This new strategy consisted of four initiatives: the Listening Process established at the Lambeth Conference in 1998, both to learn more of the struggles of homosexual Christians and to appease those bishops present who were alarmed by the conservative turn of the resolution on human sexuality; the Lambeth Commission on Communion, called by Archbishop Rowan in October 2003, which was responsible for producing the report on the future of the Communion; the Panel of Reference to advise Canterbury and disputants as to the mind of the Communion; and the Covenant Design Group. This last working party has the responsibility of drafting a document that would find a real basis of unity among as many dioceses and provinces as possible, and of creating a structure, if not federal, then at least more intentional than the bonds of friendship between world-wide Anglicans left over from the British Empire. Together these initiatives have become known as the Windsor Process.

It has been necessary to expedite this process given the break-down of order within the Episcopal Church in the United States in the last five years, with parishes removing themselves from a bishop's ministry, the General Convention suing parishes, churches being planted across diocesan boundaries, and multiple Anglican organizations and networks being constituted or realigned. Williams recently addressed the General Convention's House of Bishops meeting in New Orleans, encouraging gratitude for the

---

4. These established mechanisms, the Instruments of *Communion* (formerly known as the Instruments of *Union*), comprise the office of the Archbishop of Canterbury as senior bishop of the Communion, the decennial Lambeth Conference of bishops founded in 1867, the Primates' Meeting for prayer and consultation, and the Anglican Consultative Council, comprising in contrast to the previous instruments laity, women, and priests, and meeting every three years under Canterbury's presidency. Though providing international leadership and coordination, these bodies do not function as the organs of a federal constitution, and have proved inadequate to resolve the present crisis. Williams defends the consultative nature of Lambeth Conferences as a means of securing "catholic" representation in the local church without binding sanctions: Williams, "Authority and the Bishop in the Church," in *Their Lord and Ours: Approaches to Authority, Community and the Unity of the Church*, ed. Mark Santer (London: SPCK, 1982) 102–3.

gift that each is to the other as the basis for being church and to temper appeal to legal solutions:

> We are indebted to one another. I am indebted for your existence. Because I would not be myself without you. And a society, a community, a city that can get to that level of recognition, is one that lives from a deeper place than one that simply talks about contract or even respect. And it's this perspective which I believe, this perspective above all that the church brings to bare. Because the church is a community which lives from and in gratitude.[5]

He has also had to write to an individual diocesan to affirm that the basic unit of the church is the diocese and not the province to encourage parishes to remain within their diocesan jurisdiction, though he affirms the necessary canonical and organizational functions of the province.[6]

Significantly, Rowan Williams' role in the present fissiparous disputes has been to broker conversation, to correct theological and historical misunderstandings, and to provide some kind of missiological edge for the Communion.[7] He is not a member of the Lambeth Commission, nor of the Panel of Reference, and has played no formal part in the drafting of a potential covenant for the Anglican Church. He does of course have formal responsibilities in each of the Instruments of Communion, as Archbishop, as Primate of all England, as President of the ACC, and as convener of the Lambeth Conference. It is this last role which has proved especially vexing for Williams in recent months, as he has issued invitations to attend this non-legislative meeting, due to convene in 2008, with demurring on both sides of the theological and ethical divide.[8]

---

5. Williams, "Sermon Preached at the Ernest N. Morial Convention Center New Orleans," September 21, 2007, http://www.anglicancommunion.org/acns/news.cfm/2007/9/21/ACNS4320.

6. Williams, "Letter from the Archbishop of Canterbury to Bishop John Howe of Central Florida," October 21, 2007, http://www.virtueonline.org/portal/modules/news/article.php?storyid=6935.

7. Williams, *Arius: Heresy and Tradition*, 2nd ed. (London: SCM, 2001) 86–91. Williams' response to the present crisis in the Communion no doubt draws sustenance from his reading of the "paradigmatic" Arian crisis of the fourth century, in which the "limits and power" of competing parties, and the authorities of episcopal experience and philosophical formulation, are contrasted.

8. See Williams, "Lambeth Invitation 2008," *Anglican Episcopal World* 125 (2007) 40.

Fresh Expressions

While the structural crisis within the Communion has received most attention, other shifts have been playing out across the globe. The face of the Communion has changed dramatically in the course of the last thirty years, with the further decline in the fortunes of the church in the West, contrasted with the spectacular growth of the Anglican Church in Africa and Asia.[9] Despite the West's struggle with the forces of secularism and materialism, there have been notable signs of the work of the Spirit, not least those "fresh expressions" so-called, both within the Anglican Church and in other denominations. The Archbishop of Canterbury has taken a lead to sponsor and encourage new models for expressing the life of the church, famously describing the Anglican Church as a "mixed economy," in which the control and command, top-down approach of hierarchical church life is coupled with the spontaneous and bottom-up growth of new congregations, orders, and ministries, often in an unplanned and organic way: "We may discern signs of hope [in Wales]. These may be found particularly in the development of a mixed economy of church life. . . . There are ways of being church alongside the inherited parochial pattern."[10] It has come as a surprise to many to discover Williams, the self-confessed catholic Christian, espousing such a seemingly radical departure from normative expressions.

The book *Mission-Shaped Church*, compiled by the Bishop of Maidstone, Graham Cray, has been the lightning rod for debate in the English church and beyond concerning the place of Anglican life in local communities and the nation. The establishment of the Church in England (though not in Wales, Williams' own native land), whereby nominations for bishop must pass through the hands of the Prime Minister, is perceived as working to maintain the status quo at the cost of the church's prophetic and missiological edge in the nation.[11] The movement for fresh expressions, on the other hand, is implicitly a challenge to the established ecclesiology of the church and its practices, and perhaps even a challenge to the nation's

---

9. It has been said that the typical Anglican communicant is now black, poor, female, and African!

10. As quoted in Graham Cray, ed., *Mission-Shaped Church: Church Planting and Fresh Expressions of Church in a Changing Context* (London: Church, 2004) 26.

11. It is of course conversely true that the position of the bishops in the House of Lords provides the Anglican Church with a voice, prophetic or not, on all major bills coming before the House.

cozy self-perception as Christian, a perception that would eschew any need for creative reformulations of church life. It is perhaps at this point that Williams' own anti-establishment, perhaps anti-English sympathies interact with his commitment to, and delight in, the received liturgical order of the Western rites. In commenting on the diversity of concepts of church, Williams remarks:

> "Church" as a map of territorial divisions (parishes and dioceses) is one.... But there are more and more others.... The challenge is not to force everything into the familiar mould; but neither is it to tear up the rulebook and start from scratch (as if that were ever possible or realistic).... If "church" is what happens when people encounter the Risen Jesus and commit themselves to sustaining and deepening that encounter in their encounter with each other, there is plenty of theological room for diversity of rhythm and style, so long as we have ways of identifying the same living Christ at the heart of every expression of Christian life in common.[12]

Theo Hobson sees this affirmation of fresh expressions as a significant way in which Williams can continue to express his ecclesiological radicalism:

> He attempts to incorporate it [radicalism] into his episcopal role. As a bishop he becomes more intent on nurturing innovation within the church. As we have seen, he has always held that a key part of the bishop's role is looking for fresh opportunities, making connections with the surrounding culture—what might be called "outreach," or in business jargon, "research and development."[13]

Although it would be easy to besmirch Williams' ecclesiology here as opportunistic, he himself unifies theologically both old and fresh expressions through the slogan: the church is "event before institution,"[14] with "permissive rather than prescriptive" structures to sustain the encounter with Jesus.

---

12. Williams, "Foreword," in *Mission-Shaped Church*, vii.

13. Hobson, *Anarchy, Church and Utopia*, 62.

14. Williams, "Keynote Address: Mission-Shaped Church Conference," June 23, 2004, http://www.archbishopofcanterbury.org/sermons_speeches/2004/040623.html. This formulation is reminiscent of modern theories of revelation and language: see Hobson, *Anarchy, Church and Utopia*, chapter 1, for an excellent description of the philosophical influences at work in Williams' oeuvre.

Relations with Rome

Williams faces, thirdly, the ecclesiological challenge of sustaining ecumenical dialogue between the Anglican Communion and the Roman Catholic Church. In his undergraduate days, Williams had to make the decision whether to offer for ordination, and if so, to whom. The discipline of the contemplative life proved attractive to him in its Roman Catholic expression. The lure of formal liturgy had enticed him since first experiencing Anglo-Catholic worship at All Saints' Oystermouth, near Swansea in South Wales, as an eleven year old coming out of the Presbyterian tradition. Although from a Whiggish perspective it was almost inevitable that he would take Anglican orders, more surprising was his doctoral research on modern Russian Orthodox theology, specifically the work of Vladimir Lossky (1903–58), who made the concept of *theosis* (divinization, or perhaps entire sanctification) central to theological systematizing.

Williams finds himself in an awkward position in ecumenical relationship with Rome. While building upon forty years of dialogue in the Anglican Roman Catholic International Commission (ARCIC), and more recent exchange through the International Anglican Roman Catholic Commission for Unity and Mission (IARCCUM), a joint commission of bishops established in 2000, he nevertheless has been a supporter of the ordination of women to the priesthood, and began involvement in 1990 with the leadership of an Anglo-Catholic lobby group, Affirming Catholicism, which pressed for the reappropriation of tradition through affirmation of gender-inclusive structures of ministry. This has led to tensions, albeit polite, with Rome. In a recent interview with Paul Handley, the Archbishop outlined his approach to negotiating with Rome:

> One of the things that I've been talking a bit about recently with the bishops of the Church of England is the need for the whole women-bishop discussion to keep resourcing itself from ARCIC, as well as other places, so we don't lose sight of what there is in the bank about agreed theology. I think we're in a reasonable position to say, yes, we do want to stick with ARCIC, but, when we made the first agreements about ministry, I don't think anyone could have predicted at that point just how important the gender issue was going to be in the relations between the Churches.[15]

---

15. Williams and Paul Handley, "Less a Roman Holiday, More an Italian Job," *Church Times* 7497 (November 17, 2006) n.p. Online: http://www.churchtimes.co.uk/content.asp?id=28990.

While underestimating the strength of concern from the Roman side would be naïve, the difficulties that face the Anglican side are no less daunting. The question of who speaks for Anglicans, indeed what being genuinely Anglican entails, is problematic in ecumenical dialogue. Williams' own commitment to conciliarity has an impact not only on the Windsor Process, but also in speaking with other communions and denominations. In answering the question why he remains an Anglican, Williams replied:

> I'd say that I don't believe the essential theological structure of the Church is pyramidal: that it has one absolute touchstone embodied in a single office. I'm certainly prepared to believe that there's a role for the Petrine ministry of conciliation, interpretation, and mediation in the Church. I don't see that as an executive centre; so I'd start from what would historically be called a conciliarist position. And the thing that always held me back from becoming a Roman Catholic at the points when I thought about it is that I can't quite swallow papal infallibility.[16]

Though couched in the cautious language of diplomacy, the recent greetings extended between the Archbishop of Canterbury and Pope Benedict XVI on Williams' visit to Rome in November 2006 betoken the ecclesiological issues at stake. Pope Benedict began:

> Over the last three years you have spoken openly about the strains and difficulties besetting the Anglican Communion and consequently about the uncertainty of the future of the Communion itself. Recent developments, especially concerning the ordained ministry and certain moral teachings, have affected not only internal relations within the Anglican Communion but also relations between the Anglican Communion and the Catholic Church. We believe that these matters, which are presently under discussion within the Anglican Communion, are of vital importance to the preaching of the Gospel in its integrity, and that your current discussions will shape the future of our relations. It is to be hoped that the work of the theological dialogue, which had registered no small degree of agreement on these and other important theological matters, will continue to be taken seriously in your discernment.

The Archbishop of Canterbury responded, using vocabulary that acknowledges the equality of the institutions:

---

16. Ibid.

It is in that same *fraternal spirit* [noting the warmth of Archbishop Michael Ramsey's reception some forty years earlier in Rome] that I make this visit now, since the journey of friendship that they began is one that I believe that we should continue together. I have been heartened by the way in which from the very beginning of your ministry as *Bishop of Rome*, you have stressed the importance of ecumenism in your own ministry . . . I say this, conscious that the path to unity is not an easy one, and that disputes about how we apply the Gospel to the challenges thrown up by modern society can often obscure or even threaten the achievements of dialogue, common witness and service. In the modern world, no part of the Christian family acts without profound impact on our ecumenical partners; only a firm foundation of *friendship in Christ* will enable us to be honest in speaking to one another about those difficulties, and discerning a way forward which seeks to be wholly faithful to the charge laid upon us as disciples of Christ.[17]

The Joint Declaration at the end of their meeting acknowledges continuing challenges:

> our long journey together makes it necessary to acknowledge publicly the challenge represented by new developments which, besides being divisive for Anglicans, present serious obstacles to our ecumenical progress. It is a matter of urgency, therefore, that in renewing our commitment to pursue the path towards full visible communion in the truth and love of Christ, we also commit ourselves in our continuing dialogue to address the important issues involved in the emerging ecclesiological and ethical factors making that journey more difficult and arduous.[18]

Williams does maintain skepticism towards centralizing authority in the church, though this may be due to its capacity to distort our responsibility towards each other,[19] rather than his hesitation with clerical authority *tout court*. He is equally concerned about any ecclesial life at the local

---

17. Williams, "Address of the Archbishop of Canterbury to the Holy Father," 2006, http://www.vatican.va/holy_father/benedict_xvi/speeches/2006/november/documents/hf_ben-xvi_spe_20061123_archbishop-canterbury_en.html#ADDRESS_OF_THE_ARCHBISHOP_OF_CANTERBURY. Italics mine.

18. Williams and Pope Benedict XVI, "Common Declaration of Pope Benedict XVI and the Archbishop of Canterbury, His Grace Rowan Williams," November 23, 2006, http://www.vatican.va/holy_father/benedict_xvi/speeches/2006/november/documents/hf_ben-xvi_spe_20061123_common-decl_en.html.

19. Williams, "Eine Kirche, eine Hoffnung," *Oekumenische Rundschau* 55 (2006) 535–44.

level that fails to recognize mutual accountability between congregations, thereby remaining immature.[20] He cites Luther as an example of someone whose understanding of authority within the church disallows both ends of the spectrum (Roman Catholics and Anabaptists),[21] and sees the distinctive Anglican position creating unity out of the recognition of ministry patterns, not doctrine alone.[22]

Ecclesiological Themes

Church as Gift

One of the most outstanding contributions of Rowan Williams to modern ecclesiological debates and common to the presenting issues of Communion conciliarity, church planting, and ecumenical relationships, is his insight that the church comes to us as a *gift*. While in classic Reformed thought the Word precedes and generates the church, this, although not denied by Williams, is not his center-stage formulation. Rather, he wants to highlight the utter dependence of the people of God on the gracious action of God, and in this way to defend God's initiative in the world. The church has a divine origin, and ought not to be understood as the accidental or merely historically contingent reactions to the ministry of the incarnate Christ. In contrast to much twentieth-century theology, particularly the ecclesiology of the ecumenical movement, Williams does not aim to see the church so dispersed in the world that its own distinctive presence in the world is denied. The study commissioned by the World Council of Churches, called "The Missionary Structure of the Congregation," adopted the slogan "Let the world write the agenda."[23] This is not Williams' preferred option.

When we understand the church as gift, we renounce all attempts at totalizing or at manipulating as inconsistent with the sheer existence of the

---

20. This becomes a lead concept in Williams' definition of catholicity; see Williams, "Authority and the Bishop in the Church," 93.

21. Williams, *Why Study the Past? The Quest for the Historical Church* (London: Darton, Longman and Todd, 2005) 68.

22. Ibid., 81–82.

23. Colin W. Williams, *The Church*, New Directions in Christian Theology Today (Philadelphia: Westminster, 1975) 32.

church, its presence with or without my involvement. Ministry within the church can also be described using the category of gift:

> Action in the church must be regulated not by abstract rule but by the goal of reinforcing and affirming the other believer in such a way that the community overall is affirmed and strengthened and moved on towards the Kingdom. In other words, my act must be a *gift* for the deepening and strengthening of another's faith. . . .[24]

The church itself is to be conceived using this terminology:

> So believing in the Church is really believing in the unique gift of the *other* that God has given you to live with. The New Testament sees the Church as a community in which each person has a gift that only they can give into the common life. We Christians are so used to the imagery the Bible uses, especially the great metaphor of Christ's "Body," that we forget just how radical and comprehensive is the vision of a community of universal giftedness. The ancient world had sometimes used the image of the body to describe a society in which there were different *functions*, a very natural use for such language. But it was left to Christians to reconceive this in terms of different gifts, and to draw out the further revolutionary implication, that the frustration of any one member is the frustration of all—because then there is something that is not being properly given.[25]

To understand the church and its ministry in terms of divine origin expressed through gift is to learn patience with its current distortions, humility in its disagreements, and surprise at God's leading. Though the Windsor Process may seem slow and ponderous, no doubt in Williams' eyes he is exercising a servant ministry, refusing to manipulate or exert power, but offering leadership by asking combatants to listen and speak. Though the cultivation of new offshoots of church life under the epithet "fresh expressions" may appear to be at odds with his own ecclesiastical preferences, at a deeper level his attitudes are consistent with the deeper theological premise that where God's Spirit surprisingly works, there must we as human beings begin the harvest. Indeed, to minister in a postmodern world is to privilege at some level the local over the universal.

---

24. Williams, *On Christian Theology* (Oxford: Blackwell, 2000) 285.
25. Williams, *Tokens of Trust: An Introduction to Christian Belief* (Louisville: Westminster John Knox, 2007) 106.

The Sacraments as Center

The incarnational principle has been a significant leitmotif amongst Anglican intellectuals since the late-nineteenth century, with the publication of *Lux Mundi* (1889), displacing the atonement principle in many accounts of Christian faith. Building on the emergent scientific worldview of evolution and Romantic literary sensibility, the *continuities* between grace and nature are stressed in the incarnational view, allowing for organic and divine development within the created order. To highlight the incarnation of the Lord Jesus was to assert this principle. The *discontinuity* between God and a sinful humanity was overcome not primarily through an atoning or propitiating death, but through the bodily ministry of Christ, the union of the divine and the human in the person of the Son, and his restoration to bodily life in the resurrection. The death of Christ would typically be presented in Abélardian fashion as an example or type, rather than in Anselmian categories of satisfaction and honor.[26]

Wherever we turn in the writings of Rowan Williams, we discover the priority of the incarnational principle, and the centrality of the sacraments in his conception of Christian faith and experience. Perhaps this is not so surprising given his own Anglo-Catholic theological convictions, however it does provide additional ecclesiological resources upon which to draw for the pressing issues with which he has contended. Christology funds ecclesiology.[27] This becomes the starting point for all conversation: "the essential identity and unity of the Church just is the sort of sacramental givenness of the eucharist and the ministry."[28]

Though Williams naturally gravitates towards this position, he does warn of dangers inherent in applying the incarnational principle too wantonly,[29] and failing to allow it to stand over and against the world:

> The question, "Do you believe in 'the Incarnation'?" is a quite futile one in itself unless it has something to do with the serious question "How do you proclaim, and how do you hear proclaimed, the judgement of Christ?" Anglican theology, with its long-standing enthusi-

26. Wainwright, "Rowan Williams on Christian Doctrine," 80.
27. Williams, *Why Study the Past?* 41.
28. Williams and Handley, "Less a Roman Holiday, More an Italian Job," n.p.
29. Rupert Shortt, *Rowan Williams: An Introduction* (London: Darton, Longman and Todd, 2003) 111: Shortt makes the case that it is too easy for "incarnationalists" to "sacralise the existing order."

asm about the incarnational principle, has often risked blurring the outline of this second question, because the *image* of incarnation, the fusion of heaven and earth, the spiritualizing [sic] of matter, has proved so wonderfully resourceful a tool for making sense of a sacramental community with a social conscience and a cultural homeland. This is not wholly mistaken; but the slippage into ideology is perilously close . . ."[30]

Consequently, the church's visibility is an important theme for Williams, as it can protect from assimilation to the world: "The Church signifies (means, points to) the humanity that could be, that could exist in this tension between security and powerlessness, so that it is indeed in one sense *the* place where Spirit is seen. It is 'seen' in prayer and sacrament."[31]

A further consequence in affirming the sacramental center of the church is, for good or for ill, to promote clericalism. Priestliness is a category for corporate understanding: "Being in the Church is being in the middle of this sacrificial action, the act of Christ's giving; it is being in the climate, the landscape, of priesthood."[32] Indeed, the sacramental heart of the church occupies the entire fifth chapter of a recent book by Williams, *Tokens of Trust*, which is designed as an introduction to Christian faith.[33]

It is through the sacraments that a central theme of all Williams' theology is conveyed: the common *experience of participation*. While there may be cause to defend *structural* unity in the church, whether that involves negotiations between parties in the Anglican Communion, the Anglican Church in its relationship with Rome, or finding a basis between fresh expressions and inherited models, the *spiritual* unity of the church is to be found through sacramental experience of grace:

> Williams believes that participating in the sacraments, especially Baptism and the Eucharist, is the concrete expression of common experience for Christians and it is therefore the means by which accommodation of differences is most easily accommodated in the church. The experience may have different interpretations, but it is

---

30. Williams, *On Christian Theology*, 85.
31. Ibid., 124.
32. Williams, "The Christian Priest Today," in *Glory Descending: Michael Ramsey and His Writings*, ed. Douglas Dales (Grand Rapids: Eerdmans, 2005) 164–65.
33. Williams, *Tokens of Trust*, 105–35.

universally acknowledged by Catholics as an affirmation of the work of Jesus.[34]

Williams himself summarizes what he regards as being at stake in the centrality of the Eucharist when reviewing Zizioulas' book, *Being as Communion*: "Only a eucharistically centered ecclesiology can do justice both to the indispensability of historical continuities and the reality of the eschatological presence of the Spirit's action."[35] It is not merely the sheer number of words interpreting the sacraments that testifies to their importance for Williams.

Renewed Humanity as the Goal

Driving the Archbishop of Canterbury's ecclesiological vision is the belief that the Spirit of God is presently renewing humanity, overcoming violence and alienation, and aiding those who belong to the church to take responsibility for our world. The church is the "most comprehensive human society" and "the new human race."[36] The contemporary expression of the church is contingent, and requires vigilance and hearkening to the Spirit's voice to conform more adequately to its ultimate destiny, which is (borrowing as he does from Paul's letter to the Ephesians) "peace and praise."[37] The Spirit continues to reveal God's mind to the church, and this process of revelation promotes the maturity of the church as it owns its place in the world and in the story of salvation. Williams' thesis is that:

> Revelation . . . is essentially to do with what is *generative* in our experience—events or transactions in our language that break existing frames of reference and initiate new possibilities of life. . . . [A]ny such puzzlement over "what the Church is meant to be" *is* the revelatory operation of God as "Spirit" insofar as it keeps the Church engaged in the exploration of what its foundational events signify. To identify Word and Spirit as simply two stages of a single process of divine communication somewhat misses the point of the necessary

---

34. Bryce McProud, *Common Experience and the Accommodation of Differences: The Foundation for Unity in Rowan Williams' View of the Church* (Eugene, OR: Wipf & Stock, 2005) 26.

35. Williams, "Book Review: John D. Zizioulas, *Being as Communion: Studies in Personhood and the Church*," Scottish Journal of Theology 42 (1989) 101–5.

36. Williams, *Why Study the Past?* 2.

37. Williams, *Tokens of Trust*, 8.

distinction between the event that defines the field and the terms of the interpretative enterprise, and the enterprise itself.[38]

This dynamic view of the church replaces that older taxonomy that defined the church in terms of its marks or notes in a more static way.[39] He speaks approvingly of Bonhoeffer's ecclesiology, which resists abstract definition and encourages engagement:

> So if we ask about the nature of the true Church, where we shall see the authentic life of Christ's Body—or if we ask about the unity of the Church, how we come together to recognise each other as disciples—Bonhoeffer's answer would have to be in the form of a further question. Does this or that person, this or that Christian community, stand where Christ is? Are they struggling to be in the place where God has chosen to be? . . . Typically, Bonhoeffer does not give us any quick answers about the problems of unity today or the problems of moral discernment that cause such agony to our various churches. . . . Nor should we expect such an abstract answer from any source, Bonhoeffer or elsewhere. He will always tell us simply to look for Jesus in Gethsemane and stay there.[40]

Williams also relativizes the importance of the church and in so doing outlines its instrumental missionary character:

> The Church exists for the sake of the kingdom of God. . . . This means that it is essentially missionary in its nature, seeking to transform the human world by communicating to it in word and act a truthfulness that exposes the deepest human fears and evasions and makes possible the kind of human existence that can pass beyond these fears to a new liberty. The Church, in claiming to exist for the sake of opening the world to a fuller life in which God can be discerned as the controlling meaning of things, claims to have something to contribute to all human cultures . . .[41]

To allow the church to be defined as the dynamic pilgrim people of God journeying through history is to find some common ground with post-

---

38. Williams, *On Christian Theology*, 134, 144.

39. Williams, *The Church*, 20.

40. Williams, "Sermon delivered by the Archbishop of Canterbury, Rowan Williams, in honour of Dietrich Bonhoeffer," February 5, 2006, http://www.britischebotschaft.de/en/news/items/060206.htm.

41. Williams, *On Christian Theology*, 31–32.

Vatican II Roman Catholic interlocutors,[42] as well as with post-modern anti-institutionalists. Glancing expectantly forward to the emergence of new life allows for a process of constant revision to the status quo. The last word has not been spoken as to the shape of the church, or for that matter as to the shape of the world. The realignments within worldwide Anglicanism may all be energized in Williams' mind by the hope of eschatological renewal of the people of God today.

Ecclesiological Critique

No Condemnation for Those in Christ

The character of our union with Christ, often overlooked amongst evangelical theologians, is conversely highlighted in the theology of Rowan Williams. His presentation of the incarnation as the center of theological reflection gives a model for the conjunction of the human and the divine, which is carried over into other areas of theory and practice. His sympathy for mystic theologians, like Teresa of Avila or John of the Cross, furthermore bears witness to the ways in which he privileges the vision of God over the reign of God,[43] or of union *with* Christ over justification *by* Christ in his theological method:

> Contemplative prayer classically finds its focus in the awareness of God at the center of the praying person's being—God as that by which I am myself—and, simultaneously, God at the center of the whole world's being: a solidarity in creatureliness. It is the great specific against the myth of self-creation and isolated self-regulation. St John of the Cross speaks of the vision of God in the *state of union* as a vision of the creator . . .[44]

Indeed, one has to look assiduously in his writings to find any sustained explication of theology of the atonement.[45] In *Tokens of Trust*, designed to

---

42. Frank D. Rees, "Three Ways of Being Church," *International Journal for the Study of the Christian Church* 5 (2005) 41–57.

43. See this distinction expounded in H. Richard Niebuhr, *The Kingdom of God in America*, First Wesleyan ed. (Middletown, CT: Wesleyan University Press, 1988).

44. Williams, *On Christian Theology*, 76. Emphasis mine.

45. Wainwright, "Rowan Williams on Christian Doctrine," 80. Gary Williams elsewhere comments: "The forensic pattern of guilt and deserved retribution dealt with by substitution

provide education in "the essentials of what Christians believe,"[46] there is a whole chapter devoted to the sacraments but only cautious and contorted theology of the atonement:

> In rejecting what Jesus has to give, we show where we are heading. In that sense, at least, he is carrying the burden of our sin—bearing the results of what we habitually do. St Paul says that he "becomes" sin—that he becomes a sort of embodied image for what we are; and that he takes on himself the curse that is laid on us (2 Corinthians 5.21 and Galatians 3.13).[47]

This needs to be held next to a statement a few pages earlier in which we are warned that to "speak of original sin isn't necessarily to speak as if there were a great metaphysical curse hanging over the human race; it's just to observe that our learning how to exist is mixed in with learning what does *not* make for our life or our joy."[48] His understanding of *union* with Christ does not find its counter-concept in our sinful and cursed *union* with Adam.

Williams is suspicious of "final resolutions of our condition,"[49] something borne out in the apparent evasiveness of his language[50] and a constant theme in his writings.[51] For example, the Lord Jesus himself is unique only because he "'uniquely' reveals the God whose nature is not to make the claim of unique revelation as total and authoritative meaning"![52] The Protestant understanding of the doctrine of justification by grace through faith as a forensic declaration contrasts with Williams' reserve towards just such a punctiliar and resolved status for the church. Williams' ecclesiology thankfully does not collapse the church into the world.[53] However, in his writings

---

is central in Scripture, but Williams replaces it with a victim theology, where the atonement is about men inflicting wounds, not God bearing his own judgement in Christ." Garry J. Williams, "The Theology of Rowan Williams," 2002, http://www.latimertrust.org/download/lt-study55.pdf.

46. Williams, *Tokens of Trust*, vii.
47. Ibid., 86–87.
48. Ibid., 82–83.
49. Williams, *On Christian Theology*, 164.
50. Wainwright, "Rowan Williams on Christian Doctrine," 78: "I am somewhat disappointed by the insufficient concreteness of Williams' ecclesiology."
51. Shortt, *Rowan Williams*, 19.
52. Williams, *On Christian Theology*, 105.
53. Williams holds that the language of *hagioi*, *ekklesioi*, and *paroikoi* all suggests an al-

the church's distinctness is not expressed through its unique and privileged status as a result of divine justification. *Pace* Williams, the life of the church is not entirely "becoming"—it has received the final declaration of "no condemnation" (Rom 8:1) as an important complement to its being *in Christ*.

The case may be made that acknowledging the church's favored status *coram deo* could undermine any motivation towards continual repentance or growth in humility, or potentially lead the church to excuse its past failings without contrition. To this my response is that we must apply corporately Paul's point concerning individuals in Romans 6: grace does not necessarily lead to license. Nor does such a forensic aspect of ecclesiology undermine the most helpful contribution made by Williams, namely describing the church in dynamic and not merely static categories. I agree with Williams that the church "as a distinct institution is provisional, existing until the natural order of human society has been fully penetrated by the saving presence of God."[54] What must also be affirmed, however, is that the eschatological intrusion of God's kingdom into contemporary society is expressed (using forensic categories) through the revelation of the righteousness and the wrath of God (Rom 1:16–18) as foretastes of the coming world (Rom 5:9–11). The expressions of the life of the church may be "provisional," even while the foundations of her life are firm (Eph 2:20).

We Live by Faith and Not by Sight

A useful trope since the Reformation in analyzing the nature of the church has been the distinction between its visible and invisible states. This has enabled theologians to acknowledge the difference between the church's organization and its inner life. The Scriptures provide us with encouragement to serve our brothers and sisters "whom we have seen" (1 John 4:20); we are bidden not merely to recite the acts of God but also to take the visible elements of bread and wine and to "do this in remembrance of me" (1 Cor 11:24–25); and Jesus rebukes Phillip by appealing to an argument of visibility: "Whoever has seen me has seen the Father" (John 14:9). Williams frequently speaks of the importance of the visibility of the church as "sign"[55]

---

ternative rendering of authority for the church in the world of imperial Rome. See Williams, *Why Study the Past?* 32–34.

54. Williams, *On Christian Theology*, 225.
55. Ibid., 124.

to ground its life in nature, history, and matter. In leading the morning Bible studies from the book of Acts for the 2005 meeting of the Anglican Consultative Council, he repeatedly affirmed ecclesial visibility:

> The Church is the community that makes Christ visible. (Monday, 20 June)
>
> [The incarnation is] the pivot on which the whole history of the universe turns. (Monday, 20 June)
>
> So this reading [Acts 4] is a very powerful affirmation of the visibility of Jesus Christ in his Church. (Tuesday, 21 June)
>
> It is the dying, forgiving Stephen, where God is seen. (Wednesday, 22 June)
>
> Stephen, the martyr, who in his death and in the forgiveness that flowed from him as he died became a sanctuary, a holy place where God's glory was visible. (Thursday, 23 June)[56]

It is however striking that in these very instances from the book of Acts where Williams highlights the *visibility* of the church, he seems to ignore the *audibility* of the church around which the relevant passages actually revolve. The early chapters of Acts contain speeches that are necessary to interpret what has most recently been seen in the passion and resurrection of the Lord Jesus, and the descent of the Spirit. Indeed, the account of the stoning of Stephen is provoked by his *speech* wherein he reminds his hearers that God must be not be localized in ritual or in a house made by human hands (Acts 7:48),[57] and as they rush to kill him they block their *ears* (Acts 7:57). To make Stephen himself "a sanctuary, a holy place" is to miss entirely the point of Stephen's speech! This speech is furthermore Stephen's defense before the high priest against the charge that he has spoken "blasphemous words against Moses and God" (Acts 6:11). In the book *Anglican Identities*,[58] it is equally remarkable that, portraying significant leaders

---

56. Williams, "Archbishop of Canterbury's Daily Bible Studies," in *Living Communion: The Official Report of the 13th Meeting of the Anglican Consultative Council, Nottingham 2005*, ed. J. M. Rosenthal and S. T. Erdey (New York: Church, 2006) 35, 36, 39, 44, 47.

57. Williams fails to see the anomaly of describing Stephen as a holy place, when Stephen has just preached against seeking holy places! Williams also speaks on Saturday, 25 June, of the "loss and suffering" that promote the growth of the church, while ignoring the frequent refrain in the book of Acts that the "Word of the Lord" is responsible for its growth.

58. Williams, *Anglican Identities* (Cambridge, MA: Cowley, 2003). Williams is keen to defend this omission by arguing that the chapters in this book appeared previously as separate papers, and the book itself was not conceived as a comprehensive whole. It would however not have been a difficult task to rectify the imbalance through writing new material.

within the Anglican Church throughout the centuries, not one eighteenth-century revivalist is presented.

It appears to me that Williams repeatedly undercuts the Protestant conviction that the Word, both the person of Jesus and the proclamation of Jesus, creates the church. The call of Jesus must necessarily precede the faithful response of his people. Jesus speaks in order that we may hear and believe (Rom 10:14).[59] To privilege seeing over hearing is not only to ignore, for example, Augustine's carefully crafted summary of the sacraments as "visible words," it is to relegate the importance of verbal proclamation in the life and mission of the church to the second division of theological truth and practice.[60] Luther defends the priority of the Word:

> there is no more terrible disaster with which the wrath of God can afflict men than a famine of the hearing of his Word. . . . Likewise there is no greater mercy than when he sends forth his Word. . . . Nor was Christ sent into the world for any other ministry except that of the Word. Moreover, the entire spiritual estate—all the apostles, bishops, and priests—has been called and instituted only for the ministry of the Word.[61]

The sacraments do of course in Anglican formulation represent means of grace, and the Lord's Supper does "proclaim the Lord's death until he comes" (1 Cor 11:26), but this is not to be understood without reference to the oral liturgical context that both Jesus and Paul affirm. To restore some balance to Williams' ecclesiology, the nature of the life of faith as response to a prior promise (Rom 4, Heb 11), the covenantal (or promissory) structure of both Old and New Testaments, and the Scriptures' description of the faculty of sight as sub-optimal must at some level be acknowledged. We are reminded that now we "see in a mirror dimly" (1 Cor 13:12), but the Word of God is "sharp," "piercing," and "judging" (Heb 4:12).

---

59. It is worth pointing out that the Greek of Romans 10:14b renders the relative pronoun relating to the Lord as the direct object of our hearing, and not as the indirect object, which is often mistakenly used in translation.

60. This is seen explicitly in Williams' statement: "It [the church] is 'seen' in prayer and sacrament; that is to say, prayer and sacrament (and I include the reading and preaching of Scripture under this head) *name* and interpret the deepest direction and growth of human life as being *in* Christ and *towards* the Father." Williams, *On Christian Theology*, 124.

61. Martin Luther, "The Freedom of a Christian," in *Luther's Works: Career of the Reformer*: 1, vol. 31, American Edition, ed. H. J. Grimm and trans. W. A. Lambert (Philadelphia: Fortress, 1957) 346.

The Spirit of Truth Will Guide You

Williams makes much of the ways in which the life of the Trinity shapes our understanding of ecclesiology.[62] Not only does the Incarnation speak of God's vulnerability, and the cross and resurrection of hope despite tragedy, God's internal sociability impacts our ecclesial life.[63] Though near fatally opaque in its construction, Williams here wants to pick up on elements of the Father's relationship with the Son and transpose them into a humanly existentialist key:

> The Spirit as that which forms or sustains the new world of perception through the constant recreation of the Church as it is judged by its foundational charter in the paschal event is the condition of the Christian reading of the cross . . . God is constitutive of the identity of Jesus; God is also constitutive, in a different sense, of the process of the Church continually coming to judgement—the encounter of believers with the encounter of Father and Son . . . Not only Jesus' distance from the Father, but our distance, our critical "absence," from Jesus is included in the eternal movement of God in and to himself. Without this, we should indeed be able to do no more than look at Jesus as exemplar, with the ideological risks that implies, making the life of God once again undialectically external in its realization to our present history.[64]

Furthermore, as previously intimated, the Spirit's role in Williams' mind is not to be confined to "*communication*, in a narrowly 'linear' sense,"[65] but rather in the expansive context of liberation:

> The Spirit's "completion" of Christ's work is no longer to be seen epistemologically, as a supplement or extension to the teaching of Christ, or even as that which makes it possible to hear and receive the Word. It is, rather, a completion in terms of liberation and transformation: it is *gift*, renewal and life. It is not possible to speak of Spirit in abstraction from the Christian form of life as a whole: Spirit is "specified" not with reference to any kind of episodic experience but in relation to the human identity of the Christian. . . . The sign of Spirit is the existence of Christlikeness (being God's child) in

---

62. Williams, *On Christian Theology*, 288.
63. Williams, *Tokens of Trust*, 137.
64. Williams, *On Christian Theology*, 164–65.
65. Ibid., 116.

the world. And the connection of Spirit with ecclesiology belongs here.[66]

In traditional Protestant thought, the close relationship between the Spirit and the Word is affirmed in scriptural summary ("the sword of the Spirit which is the word of God," Eph 6:17) as well as circumscribed theologically as distinct though not separate means of God's action in the world: the Word is the instrument of the Spirit's agency. The Spirit's work does not presume any prior inadequacy of the Word, but achieves the "efficacious confirmation of the Word" in human life.[67] Such a conception is challenged when Williams avers that Christ's work is "incomplete" until the Spirit "liberates" and "transforms." Indeed, the Spirit's work in the passage quoted above is expressly *not* to be understood as localizing the efficacy of the Word, or making possible hearing and receiving the Word, or providing a foundation for our Christian experience, but rather as linking virtue or Christlikeness with participation in the world's liberation. The Spirit is detached from the specifics of an individual's experience of the *Word* and made a category to bridge the experience of an individual and the *world*, thus releasing the Spirit's work from soteriological controls. It is of pastoral concern to me to note this categorical reassignment, because it allows for a church without moorings in the Word, and for the church's global mission to be described without Christological shape.[68] Calvin writes: "It is this inviolable decree of God and of the Holy Spirit which our foes are trying to set aside when they pretend that the church is ruled by the Spirit apart from the Word."[69]

---

66. Ibid., 123–24.

67. John Calvin, *The Institutes of the Christian Religion*, ed. J. T. McNeill and trans. F. L. Battles (Philadelphia: Westminster, 1960) I.ix.3.

68. Williams holds in high regard the Orthodox theologians who promote pneumatology as constitutive of ecclesiology, especially Lossky. See the summary of Orthodox debates concerning pneumatology in John D. Zizioulas, *Being as Communion: Studies in Personhood and the Church* (Crestwood, NY: St Vladimir's Seminary Press, 1985) 123–26. Zizioulas uses similar language to summaries his case for the priority of pneumatology over Christology in systematic formulations: "Unless the Church lets Pneumatology so condition Christology that the sequence of 'yesterday-today-tomorrow' is transcended, she will not do full justice to Pneumatology; she will enslave the Spirit in a linear *Heilsgeschichte*" (ibid., 180). As previously noted, Williams affirms Zizioulas' understanding of the Spirit's relationship with the eucharist in particular: see Williams, "Review: *Being as Communion*," 102.

69. Calvin, *Institutes*, IV.viii.13. More generally, coordinating Spirit and Word in Christian history has provided checks and balances against formalism at one end of the spectrum and unbridled enthusiasm at the other.

More expansively, Williams along with other theologians wants to ground the theological rationale of the church in the "communal existence of Father, Son and Holy Spirit."[70] This is often achieved in ecumenical conversation through the bridging category of *koinonia*.[71] Such appeal to social Trinitarianism to justify or support ecclesiological convictions must be approached with care, for the application of Trinitarian theology in the New Testament to ecclesiology is sparse.[72] It is true that John describes how the eleven are to love each other as the Father loved the Son (John 17:26), and indeed that the eleven are sent into the world just as the Father sent the Son into the world (John 17:18), but in neither instance is a substantial case for a fully-orbed ecclesiological schema mounted. Avery Dulles points out in any case that:

> [t]he fellowship of Christians cannot exactly replicate that of the divine persons. As human beings, we are distinct substances, and our relationships are, unlike those in the Godhead, accidents. We can acquire or lose these relationships without ceasing to be ourselves. . . . Contemporary ecclesiologists who adhere to a Trinitarian model of the church do not all agree about what kind of unity this model requires. Different models of the Trinity call for different ecclesiologies . . .[73]

It is no doubt true that some of our ecclesiological questions are not answered with any degree of certainty in the scriptural deposit, leaving us to use wisdom to decide on a course of action under the rubric of *adiaphora*. However, with Amy Plantinga Pauw,[74] my appeal is for "theological modesty" when applying Trinitarian formulations from the New Testament and church history to contemporary ecclesiological debates. The doctrine of the Trinity attempts to describe the immanent life of the Godhead in order to affirm the deity of the Son and of the Spirit and their role in salvation history. The development of ecclesiological norms, on the other hand, is better

---

70. Williams, *On Christian Theology*, 226.

71. Ibid., 227.

72. For just such a caution against the ecclesiology of Miroslav Volf, see Paul S. Fiddes, *Participating in God: A Pastoral Doctrine of the Trinity* (London: Darton, Longman & Todd, 2000) 66.

73. Avery Dulles, "The Trinity and Christian Unity," in *God the Holy Trinity: Reflections on Christian Faith and Practice*, ed. T. George (Grand Rapids: Baker, 2006) 73, 75.

74. Amy Plantinga Pauw, *"The Supreme Harmony of All": The Trinitarian Theology of Jonathan Edwards* (Grand Rapids: Eerdmans, 2002) 117.

established from those scriptural texts and themes which bear more closely on the common life of God's people, and not from philosophical constructions devised outside of the Scriptures and designed for Christological defense. Not every development in the life or structure of the church ought to be justified with respect to the life of the Trinity *ad intra*, or to the liberation that the Spirit brings. McGrath opines:

> I am concerned that much Trinitarian theological reflection has lost its moorings in Scripture. . . . I wish to raise the question of whether one can speak of the doctrine of the Trinity as playing a foundational role in theology when it is, in my view, something that we infer from other foundations. . . . How can we ground a concrete reality in a theological abstraction that itself is the outcome of theological reflection on divine revelation? . . . I insist that one of the most fundamental and essential distinctives of the evangelical approach to theology is its insistence that we must nourish and govern theology at all points by Holy Scripture, and seek to offer a faithful and coherent account of what it finds there. This means that evangelicalism aims to keep as close as possible to the conceptualities and vocabulary of Scripture.[75]

My most serious reservation concerning Williams' *ecclesiology* is thus triggered by his adventurous use of the doctrine of the *Trinity*, and reflects, on my part, a deeper methodological disquiet.

In sum, Rowan Williams' ecclesiology is a fascinating rehearsal of the theological themes of gift and process, with the sacraments as their conjunction. While concerns have been raised here from an Evangelical perspective over the Archbishop's priorities and formulations regarding the church, his unenviable role as broker of new Anglican ecclesial identity as we enter the new century certainly deserves our respect. He has served the worldwide Communion well by reminding us of the exalted place of the church in God's redemptive purposes, allowing God to set the agenda through it for the world, and prompting us to recall the provisional, and sinful, life of the church as we meet it. We must approach the doctrine of the church both critically and scripturally, neither lionizing nor demonizing the institution that sustains our corporate experience of God.

---

75. Alister E. McGrath, "The Doctrine of the Trinity: An Evangelical Reflection," in *God the Holy Trinity: Reflections on Christian Faith and Practice*, ed. T. George (Grand Rapids: Baker, 2006) 26–27, 28, 32.

2

The Hidden Center:
Trinity and Incarnation in the Negative (and Positive) Theology of Rowan Williams

ANDREW MOODY

> ... we are given the joy of speaking about one who is the secret of all hearts, the hidden centre of everything—and so one who comes to us always, yes, as a stranger, "as one unknown"...[1]

What does it mean to say we "know" God? What does it mean to say that God has been "revealed"? Is he truly revealed in Jesus? Exhaustively? Exclusively? Such questions as these haunt the writings and sermons of Rowan Williams from start to finish, framing his myriad interests in spirituality, Christology, hermeneutics, soteriology, anthropology, ecumenism, art, and his studies in historical and contemporary theology. Above all, such questions are raised in the context of Williams' profound fascination with Trinitarian theology, with the result that Trinitarianism is both the answer

---

1. Williams, "Enthronement Sermon, Canterbury Cathedral," http://www.archbishopof-canterbury.org/sermons_speeches/2003/030227.html.

and the question. In that Williams finds it difficult to simply answer "yes" to these questions, he is a negative or apophatic theologian. In that the God he regards *as* hidden is the Triune God revealed in Christ, his is a Trinitarian and Christian apophaticism. How and whether those two things can exist together will shape our enquiry in this essay.

Williams learned his appreciation for the *via negativa* through his doctoral studies of Orthodox theologian and Russian exile, Vladimir Lossky.[2] For Lossky, writing out of a tradition shaped by Dionysius the Areopagite and Gregory Palamas, true knowledge of God can only be attained apophatically because God is ineffable—absolutely unknowable as to his essence and beyond rational comprehension in the energies by which he reveals himself to us.[3] Theology that takes us closer to God is that which leads us *through* all that is positive and partial, crucifying our intellects so that ultimately we contemplate that which transcends all understanding;[4] and theology that does this most of all is Trinitarian theology: "The Trinity is a cross for human ways of thought."[5]

Almost all of this is true for Williams too. In short, Williams sees the entire theological enterprise in apophatic terms. Apophaticism is the defining theme of Christian spirituality through the ages;[6] it is the heart of every

---

2. See Williams' comments in his interviews with Rupert Shortt, in Rupert Shortt, *God's Advocates: Christian Thinkers in Conversation* (London: Darton Longman & Todd, 2005) 14; and with Todd Breyfogle, in Todd Breyfogle, "Time and Transformation: A Conversation With Rowan Williams," *Cross Currents* 45 (1995) 293–312. "It was Lossky who rubbed my nose in the whole idea of the theology of negation and what it did and didn't mean" (308).

3. Lossky, *The Mystical Theology of the Eastern Church* (London: James Clarke, 1957) 70.

4. Lossky, *Orthodox Theology: An Introduction* (Crestwood, NY: St. Vladimir's Seminary Press, 1978) 31–33.

5. Lossky, *Mystical Theology*, 65, 66. The phrase turns up in several places: Williams, "The Via Negativa and the Foundations of Theology: An Introduction to the Thought of V. N. Lossky," 96, 109; and idem, "Eastern Orthodox Theology," 579. Mike Higton discovers another reference in Williams' thesis; Higton, *Difficult Gospel: The Theology of Rowan Williams* (London: SCM, 2004) 48–49.

6. Williams observes that of all the main features in Lossky's work—(i) unequivocal immanent Trinitarianism; (ii) a positive evaluation of the body; (iii) insistence on the immanence and transcendence of God; (iv) regard for supra-intellectual *ekstasis* as the only way to encounter God—the only one unambiguously and uniformly affirmed in the tradition is the last; Williams, "The Via Negativa and the Foundations of Theology," 105. The implication seems to be that apophatic mysticism has the highest claim to be what Christianity is about—even above Trinitarianism. A similarly ambitious claim is made in Williams, *Wound of Knowledge*, 180.

authentic encounter with God;[7] it is central to the task the theologian;[8] and applies to God himself: "the great 'negative theologian', who shatters all our images by addressing us in the cross of Jesus."[9] Like Lossky, Williams also regards the Trinity as having a special place in negative theology. While he has little sympathy for Lossky's Palamite essence-energy distinction,[10] he nonetheless employs the same hidden/revealed dichotomy through the paradigm of dialectic. God is unknowable yet *revealed* in his unknowableness so that his revelation leads us on to a mystical knowledge that is beyond concept and rationalizing. And, as with Lossky, it is the doctrine of the Trinity that most clearly reveals how unknowable God really *is*: first as it thwarts human attempts to wholly understand it and secondly in the way it disturbs the logic of individuality with other-person centeredness. In Williams' own words, Trinitarian theology represents a "prohibition against would-be final accounts of divine nature and action."[11]

Trinitarian theology is thus that which both proves the necessity of negative theology *and* tethers Williams' apophatic approach to Christianity (i.e., stops it from being *simply* apophatic). As Williams insists repeatedly in his writings, the negative theology he has in mind is not merely some abstract *aporia* or shapeless void imagined by Arians or postmodern theorists.[12] Christian apophasis is something more concrete, having to do with *truths* made difficult or held in dialectical tension,[13] and dealing with the

---

7. "the only possibility of knowing God is to face, at least sometimes, the silence, the absence between the cherubim [of the Ark]." Williams, *Ray of Darkness*, 85.

8. "part of the theologian's task in the Church may be to urge that we stand aside from some of the words we think we know . . ." Williams, *On Christian Theology*, 85. "The theologian's task is to remind the Church of [its relationship to the initiative of God], *and* of that concurrent and inevitable temptation to treat dogma as a solution, a closure" (ibid., 86); "we are indeed compelled to a 'negative' theology in the traditional sense . . . suspicious of its recurring temptation to theoretical resolution and conceptual neatness" (ibid., 146).

9. Williams, *Wound of Knowledge*, 149.

10. Ibid., 56–57.

11. Williams, "Trinity and Pluralism," in *On Christian Theology*, 178.

12. For the former, see Williams, *Arius*, 242–43; and idem, *Wound of Knowledge*, 52; for the latter, see idem, "Hegel and the Gods of Postmodernity," 77. See too, idem, "Trinity and Ontology," in *On Christian Theology*, 160; and idem, *The Dwelling of the Light*, 55.

13. Williams draws approving comparisons between Hegel and John of the Cross, Lossky and Yannaras, with the former's project depicted as the struggle to "conceive a structured wholeness nuanced enough to contain what appeared to be contradictories." Williams, "Hegel and the Gods of Postmodernity," 76–77.

action of God in actual history. Above all it is that which is revealed in the life, death, and resurrection of Jesus Christ.

Of course to speak of God revealed in history is *already* paradoxical (and in this sense again apophatic). Along with the mainstream of classical theology—and against certain modern theologians[14]—Williams insists on the independence of God from creation and history. God *in se* has no history; there is no drama or *dramatic personae* in God,[15] no "transactions in eternity."[16] Whatever "personhood," "subjectivity" or "agency" mean in God they mean something different from what they signify when applied to contingent beings like us. How then can God be revealed in something limited, particular, and mortal as the person of Jesus Christ? The way Williams answers these questions branches out into the most important (and problematic) themes in his theological world.

A Positive Apophasis

Perhaps the most basic response Williams makes to this puzzle of ineffability and incarnation is to observe that *if* God is so wholly other and transcendent then the *only* possibility of knowing him is in history. Williams rejects "mythological" theologies which purport to supply insights into the (metaphysical) physiology of the divine existence or presume to describe the immanent Trinity in the sort of terms just proscribed—historical, dramatic, and so on. "[T]he divine substance, what-it-is-to-be-God, is beyond any kind of intellection."[17] God is not to be found "in speculation about what sort of individual might possess an assortment of very unusual metaphysical characteristics,"[18] or in theories about essences or energies.[19] In contrast to such metaphysical speculation Williams insists that "paradoxically, the

---

14. Such as Jürgen Moltmann and David Brown. See Williams, "The Nicene Heritage," 47. And (at this point) Hegel too; see Williams, "Trinity and Ontology," 160–61. The issue is the freedom of God—does God in some sense "need" the world to be himself? Williams denies that history has any "constitutive role in the life of the Trinity" (ibid.).

15. Williams, *Dwelling of the Light*, 49.

16. Williams, *Arius*, 241. See also Williams, "Balthasar and the Trinity," 47.

17. Williams, *Wound of Knowledge*, 61.

18. Williams, "Trinity and Revelation," in *On Christian Theology*, 146.

19. Williams commends Gregory of Nyssa's apophatic insistence regarding the unbridgeable gulf between the human intellect and the divine nature. Williams, *Wound of Knowledge*, 61–62.

denial of a 'history' of transactions in God focuses attention on the history of God with us in the world: God has no *story* but that of Jesus of Nazareth and the covenant of which he is the seal."[20]

Such comments as these immediately raise questions as to whether there is any correspondence between the life of God *ad intra* and what we seen revealed through Jesus Christ. Do we see any glimpse of what God is *in se* or only what he is *pro nobis* (however that might work)?

Yet Williams—quite deliberately—wants also to say that there are deep patterns of similarity between the inner life of God and what is revealed amongst humanity and (supremely) Jesus Christ. He writes in *The Dwelling of the Light* of the "shocking" way Jesus "translates into human terms what and who God the Son eternally is." The shock comes, writes Williams, "from realizing that this means that God's life is compatible with every bit of human life."[21] Later in the same book, in his exegesis of the icon of the Pantocrator, we find something similar as Williams celebrates the unique insights found in Jesus and his mediation of a truth that searches far beyond whatever can be intimated by mere concepts and propositions.

> The being of God, about which we can say nothing adequate at the level of theory and abstraction except the most tantalizing generalities and negations ("all-powerful," "beyond time and change" and so on), is, as far as we are concerned, fully laid open to us in Jesus. To be in relation with Jesus is to be "in the truth," even when we cannot formulate this in tidy philosophical language. And this also tells us that there is something in the being of God that is appropriately expressed in a vulnerable life, in the self-forgetfulness that brings ultimate truth to us in the limits of suffering and mortality. The nature of God is both irreducibly mysterious and completely expressed in God's putting himself unreservedly at our disposal and our mercy in becoming embodied in a human life.[22]

Williams' understanding of *how* Jesus reveals God involves a mixture of analogy and dialectic. In terms of the first, Williams—as we shall shortly see—believes that there is a real and meaningful connection between words such as "love" or "gift" or "subjectivity" when applied to humans and when applied to God, such that it is legitimate (though never simple) to discuss

---

20. Williams, *Arius*, 244. See also Williams, "Trinity and Ontology," 159: "we cannot say what God is in himself; all we have is the narrative of God with us."
21. Williams, *Dwelling of the Light*, 12.
22. Ibid., 71–72.

God using these words. Although Williams never offers a theology of *analogia entis*, and occasionally even dismisses the concept,[23] he does nonetheless allow that "certain configurations of finite agencies . . . [are] more clearly transparent to the simple act of divine communication."[24] While there is always a danger in *assimilating* God to creaturely conceptions of, say, "love,"[25] there is that in God which we can only call "love."[26]

Williams may be shy of calling this correspondence *analogia entis* but he is perhaps more sympathetic to an *analogia personarum*.[27] Harkening back once again to his earliest research, Williams expresses his attraction to Lossky's apophatic conception of the *imago Trinitatis*, wherein what is common to God and humans is found "not in any quality that we and God have in common" but in the "ineffability of the human person" that makes "talking about the person . . . as difficult as talking about God."[28] Both divine and human persons *as persons* are ultimately impossible to understand, isolate, or finalize given that what it means to be personal is to exist in the dynamic of *inter*-personal relations. Thus he writes that "If we are to speak of God in terms of Jesus, we must say that in God there is that which makes possible the identity-in-difference—indeed, identity in distance or in absence—of Jesus and who or what he calls Father: something approaching the 'externality' of creator and creation, yet decisively not that, but a mutually constitutive presence, an internal relation of terms."[29]

Just as the Son receives what he is from the Father (and in this receiving makes the Father who *he* is) so Jesus receives what he is as human

---

23. See for example his dismissal of the "facile synthesis" of the *via eminentiae* in Williams, "The Via Negativa and the Foundations of Theology," 98. See also his characterization of negative theology as prohibiting "any ultimate return to an analogy of being between God and the subject." Williams, "Hegel and the Gods of Postmodernity," 72.

24. D. Z. Phillips, *Religion and Morality* (Basingstoke: Macmillan, 1996) 144, cited in Higton, *Difficult Gospel*, 46.

25. For example, Williams, "What Does Love Know? St Thomas on the Trinity," 260–72, 271.

26. In his introduction to the Trinity presented at al-Azhar al Sharif, Cairo, Williams speaks of a "perfect circle of giving and receiving," adding that "the only word we can use for that relationship of pouring out and giving is love." Williams, "Address At Al-Azhar, Sharif, Cairo, Saturday 11 September 2004," http://www.archbishopofcanterbury.org/sermons_speeches/2004/040911.html

27. The expression, as used by Donald MacKinnon, occurs in Williams, "Trinity and Ontology," 159.

28. Breyfogle, "Time and Transformation," 308.

29. Williams, "Trinity and Ontology," 158.

from the same Source—hence the suggestion of some analogy with "creator and creation." At the same time, Williams follows Athanasius in making the Father (*as Father*) dependent on the Son and, along with much modern theology, retranscribes this interdependence into strongly relational and personalist—as opposed to ontological—language. Here to be a "person," whether human or divine, *means* to be defined and constituted by relations: by giving and receiving and by transcending "the life of conscious 'natural' individuality closed upon itself."[30] Williams offers this pattern of self-transcendence (*ekstasis*) and self-forgetting (*kenosis*) as "the reality underpinning apophatic theology,"[31] both for the believer and for the members of the Trinity themselves. "God is the supreme paradigm of the personal, a life wholly lived in *ekstasis* and *kenosis*, since the divine hypostases which are God are wholly defined by relations of love, gift, response. It is from the paradigm of the divine hypostases that we come to grasp our own vocation to personal being."[32]

This concept of personhood and relationality as apophasis is crucially important to Williams and is a recurrent theme in some of his most profound and technically challenging analyses. In "Balthasar and the Trinity" Williams traces how *ekstasis* and *kenosis* define the life of God in both eternity and history; the Father kenotically pours out all that he is in the begetting of the Son. The Son reciprocates with a kenotic conforming of himself to the self-bestowing Father both in heaven and on earth. As Williams summarizes it: "The obedience of the Son to the Father in the time of his incarnate life is nothing other than the reproduction in time of the eternal Son's conformity to the 'character' of the Father's self-bestowal ... [I]t is just this interweaving of eternal and temporal movement towards the Father on the part of the Son that underlies the whole enterprise of [Balthasar's theology of] 'theodramatics.'"[33]

Following through the implications of Balthasar's own kenotic theology, Williams interrogates another aspect of his theology, namely the way Balthasar connects the Father to the analogy of masculinity and the Son to femininity.[34] For Balthasar the Father is "masculinely" active and the Son

30. Williams, "Eastern Orthodox Theology," 579.
31. Ibid.
32. Ibid.
33. Williams, "Balthasar and the Trinity," 39.
34. Ibid., 44–47.

"femininely" receptive but, as Williams points out, this dynamic is also subverted by the contention that "the Father is [also] passive or dependent on the other two Persons."[35] The "fundamental insight" here for Williams is that Balthasar shows how the very heart of divine life is a complication of doing and being done to, mutual action and response, rather than "some purely active self-donation on the part of the primary agent, the Father."[36] Somehow there is between the Persons of the Trinity a real difference or "excess" which enables them to act freely toward each other—even "worship" each other. In terms that resonate with what we have already seen in Williams' comparison of the "externality" in God and that between creation and God, Balthasar too finds "the otherness of the divine Persons [to be] . . . the foundation for analogical otherness of God to creature."[37] Williams finds this analogy of difference between creation and the Trinity "immensely suggestive."[38]

In separate explorations of Augustine and Aquinas[39] Williams again works to show how mutuality and relationality can be uncovered even in these theologians, who are so often cast as the whipping boys for modern Trinitarianism. Augustine is roundly berated by social Trinitarians and Eastern-influenced theologians for reducing the Trinity to a (solitary) super-mind, yet Williams' more nuanced reading unpacks a dynamic wherein the divine self-knowledge/love envisaged by Augustine arises from "recognising in someone else a pattern (*forma*) of justice or goodness that we already know within ourselves."[40] Although Williams writes that there is "no simple answer" to whether Augustine's scheme implies one or three consciousnesses,[41] he is sure that Augustine's model of divine wisdom and loving can only exist as "something like a relation between subjects." Again reprising the theme of otherness and mutuality: "The Father knows the Son because he knows himself as (and only as) the Son's begetter; the Son knows the Father because he knows himself as (and only as) the one generated by

---

35. Ibid., 45.
36. Ibid., 46–47.
37. Ibid., 44.
38. Ibid., 49.
39. Williams, "Sapientia and the Trinity"; and idem, "What Does Love Know?"
40. Williams, "Sapientia and the Trinity," 322.
41. Ibid., 330.

the Father ... God [is] understood as self-gift, as movement into otherness and distance in self-imparting love."[42]

Williams discovers something similar in Aquinas. The supposed subordinator of divine plurality who reduces the Trinity to a mere afterword on the divine oneness[43] becomes, on Williams' reading, another exponent of difference, otherness, and even "ecstatic movement."[44] Williams sees Aquinas' intellectual analogy as a way of showing motion without (spatial) movement and demonstrating otherness without positing separate individuals;[45] "God's inner *verbum* is an inner differentiation, as ours is."[46] In a summary of Trinitarianism that could just as easily have been found in his works on Augustine or Balthasar, Williams writes:

> In God, the doctrine tells us, that is, in the reality that is formative of the entire universe, there is perfect reflection or participation, and there is endless invitation, the stimulus of difference; as if (you can say no more) God is utterly familiar to God and utterly strange to God ... [Divine Loving] knows a bestowal and a self-emptying so complete, in the relation of Father and Son that there can be no "terminus" to the act of self-giving.[47]

Williams' project of discovering difference, otherness, mutuality, and dynamism in historical Trinitarian theologies reaches its high water mark in his 2002 treatment of the *Romanzas* of John of the Cross.[48] Dissatisfied with much traditional theology that confines Trinitarian apophaticism to the ineffable essence, Williams defines John's agenda as demonstrating that the "negative moment" should also "reach into our discourse about the persons" and relations[49] and, with this in mind, works to extract an extremely intricate rendition of the Persons and their relationship to the creation. In *Romanza 1* this involves John's vision of the Father and Son as lovers

---

42. Ibid., 322.

43. See, for example, Catherine Mowry LaCugna, *God for Us: The Trinity and Christian Life*, 1st ed. (San Francisco: Harper, 1991) 143ff.

44. Williams, "What Does Love Know?" 271.

45. "God must be sufficiently other to God for the metaphor of 'intellection' to make sense; God must be sufficiently free in his loving of his own love for the language of gratuity to make sense" (ibid.).

46. Ibid., 262.

47. Ibid., 271.

48. Williams, "Deflections of Desire: Negative Theology in Trinitarian Disclosure."

49. Ibid., 116.

united by a single love that is at once their essence, an "excess" of what each desires in the other and an active equal agent (the Holy Spirit). There is mutuality but not the closed mutuality (simply Father and Son) of mutual reinforcement; the Spirit's presence opens up "further otherness"[50] and the whole scheme suggests movement and growth in desire. In the subsequent *Romanzas* Williams traces the way the "excess" and growth of desire of the Father and Son for each other give rise to the creation event. In tones that find resonance in Richard of St Victor or even Jonathan Edwards,[51] the Father's desire for the Son causes him to create a world which can join in his love for the Son, while the Son proposes to hold the bride in his arms so that she might be "burned by his Father's love." The vision Williams discovers here is a wondrous baroque labyrinth of desire and love wherein the "human relation with God lives in a tension between the nuptial and the filial."[52] The love and desire of the divine and created subjects for each other are "deflected" so that, for instance, the Father loves the Son in the Son's love for the creation while the Son loves the Father in sharing the Father's love for him with his bride and so on.

From these observations of "deflection" and "desire" in the divine life and our incorporation into that, Williams distils a form of spirituality and a theology of personhood. For the divine Persons, the eternal process of desire and fulfillment that occurs through their loving each other through each other gives rise to ecstasy. There is no thwarting of fulfillment or gap between desire and fulfillment even though there is always more otherness and desire; "the endlessness of self-bestowal . . . never reaches a terminus, never exhausts the otherness of the other."[53] Yet for finite humans caught up in this deflection, the process is painful—*kenotic*—and the gap between desire and fulfillment is perceived as a lack. We search for a terminus to our longings in God but the triune God is not a fixed object that can be apprehended *like that*. He is infinite and infinite motion, and will not "stand

50. Ibid., 118.

51. Richard uses the principle of desire for the beloved to be loved by a third to prove the necessity of a Trinity for perfect love: see Richard of St Victor, "Richard of St Victor: The Twelve Patriarchs; the Mystical Ark; Book Three of the Trinity," in *Classics of Western Spirituality* (1979) 392. Jonathan Edwards famously declares that "God created the world for his Son, that he might prepare a spouse or bride for him to bestow his love upon; so that the mutual joys of this bride and bridegroom are the end of creation." Cited in Paul Helm and Oliver Crisp, *Jonathan Edwards: Philosophical Theologian* (Aldershot: Ashgate, 2003) 152.

52. Williams, "Deflections of Desire," 119.

53. Ibid., 134.

still" for us.⁵⁴ The supreme example of this occurs on the cross, where Jesus' experience of the Father's love is experienced in abandonment; the Father's love *in* the Son for the world produces an absence in the immediate relation between the two in Gethsemane and Calvary. "The Son's love must enact the Father's, not simply reflect it back to him."⁵⁵

Whatever additional questions we might want to ask regarding *why* the Father's love for the world in the Son has to manifest as abandonment and whether these readings truly reflect the way Augustine, Aquinas, and John of the Cross *actually* see the Trinity,⁵⁶ Williams' way of drawing connections between God and humanity is undeniably provocative. The idea that the creation is an excess of the love of the Father for the Son (and vice versa) and that we are caught up in the way the Persons love each other is a kind of apophaticism that finds deep resonance in biblical theology. One begins to wonder what light this vision of personhood might throw, for example, on the corporate views of humanity found in Romans 5? How might the experience of deflected love as absence help us to produce a Trinitarian reading of Hebrews 5:8 or the Farewell Discourse? Might Williams' way of thinking about divine and human relatedness unlock new understanding in passages like 1 Corinthians 15:28 or Revelation 3:21 or give genuine substance to that (so often) hopelessly vague term "perichoresis"? If part of the theologian's task is, as Williams insists,⁵⁷ to open up new lines of enquiry, then his Trinitarian theology succeeds admirably.

---

54. Ibid., 121, 128.

55. Ibid., 122.

56. It is surprising to observe how closely Williams' reading of these pre-moderns corresponds to the Trinitarianism he finds in Hegel: the "elaboration of belief in God as love"; the affirmation of "the thinkable character of contingent particulars, and precisely in so doing, to think what is not any particular but that which 'holds' the flow of one particular into another," thereby retranscribing "the doctrine of divine simplicity into the terms of a process" such that if "the divine predicates are thought as they should be, they 'yield' the divine simplicity as a dialectical unity." Williams, "Logic and Spirit in Hegel," 119. Williams observes that "St Thomas can sound remarkably like Hegel after you have read Balthasar!" Williams, "Balthasar and the Trinity," 49. We might add that Augustine and John of the Cross sound a lot like Hegel after you have read Williams!

57. Williams, "Beginning with the Incarnation," in *On Christian Theology*, 86.

The Spiral or the Void?

Up to this point we have seen how Williams' Trinitarian apophaticism is generated out of quite positive ideas concerning God. God really *is* "love"—even though we can never finalize what that means, even though what "love" means is a complex reality of giving and emptying that reaches far further than we can see. Our human language *does* signify something real *in God*—whatever "love" means in the Trinity it is not *less* than we can conceive but far more. Here the image of revelation that comes to mind—an image actually employed by Williams—is that of the hermeneutical spiral where we know *something*—"*what* we are interpreting is unquestionably this historical narrative and not another,"[58] it is "not a theology of agnosticism"[59]—yet we are never complete in our knowledge. Rather the Spirit works to produce an "unending rediscovery of Christ,"[60] a "spiral" that "never reaches a plateau."[61] The same positivity can be discerned in greater detail through the dialectic of identity and difference that expresses divine love. Williams' Hegelian approach to the Trinity looks to the reconciliation of opposites and the elaboration of complex process. It considers concrete particulars—and "that which 'holds' the flow of one particular into another."[62] It retranscribes "the doctrine of divine simplicity into the terms of a process" such that "divine predicates 'yield' the divine simplicity as a dialectical unity."[63] In other words, the dialectical form of the *via negativa* begins with cataphasis and then shows the paradoxes and instability in the relationship between and within positive truths.

Yet relational dialectic isn't the only kind of apophasis Williams discovers in the revelation that comes through Jesus Christ. He also seems to envisage a kind of meta-dialectic—not between concrete particulars but between revelation and something much more radical. In a Christmas opinion piece for the Guardian in 2000, Williams speaks of the "terrible aptness" and "rhetorical rightness" of a "God who speaks in a child's cry" to a "world

---

58. Williams, "Trinity and Revelation," 142.
59. Ibid., 146.
60. Ibid., 143.
61. Ibid., 142.
62. Williams, "Logic and Spirit in Hegel," 116.
63. Ibid., 119.

of competition, frenzied chatter and control obsession."⁶⁴ He presses us to face the possibility that, "silence, stumbling apparent crudity, tell you more about God than the languages of would-be sophistication. As if the best theology were the noise of someone falling over things in the dark."

In *Ray of Darkness* Williams makes the same point again. Here the baby Jesus "challenges us with his silence" as he "confronts us with the alarming, mysterious, shattering strangeness of God" and "passes annihilating judgment on our efforts to be right and secure."⁶⁵

More often however, it is the image of the cross that Williams employs to the same effect. At one point Williams recalls the image of a one-thousand-year-old crucifix from Cologne cathedral. In this "figure of extraordinary stillness," in the "curve and sag of the heavy corpse" with its closed eyes and averted face, Williams finds his revelation. "Nothing is explained," he writes, "It is a plain fact in wood. 'We have the news which has no value as a response to everything.' We have the news of the death of God in the world of religious meanings—or rather, God can only live in the grammar of religious talk when that talk expresses God's freedom from it."⁶⁶

Here, then, the revelation of Jesus is a revelation that negates any confidence in the possibility of our knowing truth about God. As Jesus dies on the cross it is the archetypally apophatic revelation, the "ray of darkness" that Jesus accepts and retransmits to us as a sign of God's presence.⁶⁷ Jesus becomes something like a Zen koan—an unconquerable assault on our reason that moves us beyond reason itself.⁶⁸ Williams ushers us toward a theology so completely chastened in regard to theological concepts that it throws up its hands and turns to God in doubt and crisis. Writing again in *Ray of Darkness*: "You must recognise that God is so unlike whatever can be thought or pictured that, when you have got beyond the stage of self-indulgent religiosity, there will be nothing you can securely know or

---

64. Williams, "Telling the Christmas Story Like It Is," *The Guardian*, December 23, 2000. Williams' suggestion that the incoherence of the baby Jesus reveals God is helpfully traced in Higton, *Difficult Gospel*, 50–51. See also Williams, *Ponder These Things*, 38.

65. Williams, *Ray of Darkness*, 35–37.

66. Williams, "The Finality of Christ," in *On Christian Theology*, 106.

67. Williams, *Ray of Darkness*, 103, cf. 82–83.

68. See Lossky here too: *Mystical Theology*, 39-40.

feel. You face a blank, and any attempt to avoid that or shy away from it is a return to playing comfortable religious games."[69]

Again, "Christians who claim to find God uniquely and definitively in Jesus, and especially in the Cross of Jesus are claiming that the roots of their faith are in massive and total negation of false God-images and religious securities."[70]

Or once again, "We have been going round and round the paths, and suddenly we see that our path goes round a hole, a bottomless black pit. In the middle of all our religious constructs—if we have the honesty to look at it—is an emptiness. It makes nonsense of all religion, conservative or radical, and all piety."[71]

Working on a more technical level, Williams sees the same tension between revelation and darkness at work in the formulation of orthodoxy and dogma. Williams argues that the creeds themselves proclaim the same repudiation of certainty, the same rejection of the "tyranny of concepts,"[72] that his own apophaticism embraces. In an extended response to R. C. Moberly's claim that the proclamation of Christ as *verus Deus, verus homo* is the basis for dogma,[73] Williams protests that doctrine is not to be discovered through a "wistful searching for the pre-dogmatic Jesus of history,"[74] nor should its truth be seen as concern for "rationality or comprehensive elucidation,"[75] nor should it be seen as something "'done with' or settled."[76]

---

69. Williams, "The Dark Night," in *Ray of Darkness*, 82.

70. Ibid., 83.

71. Ibid., 81.

72. Williams, *Wound of Knowledge*, 53. "The Athanasian God 'transcends his transcendence' to be encountered in the . . . weakness of the flesh of Christ" (52). "The one truth of which we *can* be sure is that God escapes all definition in his freedom" (53).

73. Williams, "Beginning with the Incarnation," 79–92.

74. Ibid., 82. Williams makes similar comments in an earlier response to Maurice Wiles: "A good deal of recent criticism of classic incarnational doctrine seems to be based on the complaint that there is not enough evidence to justify dogmatic conclusions. . . . But what if the entire enterprise is not about *historical* evidence and (incommensurable) dogmatic conclusions at all?" Williams, "Doctrinal Criticism: Some Questions," 257. "His . . . is a parabolic story, yet it is remembered in diverse and less than wholly coherent narrative forms, whose historical foundation is uncertain." Williams, "Does it Make Sense to Speak of Pre-Nicene Orthodoxy?" 17.

75. Williams, "Beginning with the Incarnation," 82.

76. Ibid., 84. Observe Williams' rather idiosyncratic definition of "heresy" as "an undeveloped, arrested, inadequate form of belief," as to living orthodoxy that "continues to be made." *Arius*, 24, 25.

What is left after all this negation is the idea that dogma actually *keeps* things from being settled—keeps supplying "large and strange images"[77] that escape our understanding and so "bring the [church's ideologies] to judgement."[78] The creeds and dogmas function in the light of the cross, where God destroys human imaginings of what he is like and offers, *ex nihilo*, the gift of the risen Christ—"a life lived 'away' from a centre in our own resourcefulness and meaningfulness."[79] He writes approvingly of the way Nicaea and Chalcedon eschew "cosmogenic fantasy"[80] and adopt the "least conceptually extravagant, and least mythologically extravagant language."[81] Nicaea teaches us that "between what is seen in history and what is seen in silence, there is no gap to insert speculative dramas for heavenly individuals, because in the incarnate Word the history and the unsayable resource of divine act are no longer to be pulled apart."[82]

The Positive Value of Negative Theology

Of course it is not possible to achieve anything approaching an *overall* assessment of Williams' apophatic Trinitarianism without inquiring as to why negative theology is attractive in the first place. More specifically, as

77. Williams, "Beginning with the Incarnation," 84.

78. Ibid., 85.

79. Ibid., 83.

80. Williams, "The Nicene Heritage," 47.

81. Williams, "Doctrinal Criticism: Some Questions," in *The Making and Remaking of Christian Doctrine: Essays in Honour of Maurice Wiles*, ed. Sarah Coakley, David A. Pailin, and Maurice F. Wiles (Oxford: Clarendon, 1993) 251.

82. Williams, "The Nicene Heritage," 48. The difficult question this leaves us with, however, is how the positive aspects of Jesus' life and ministry—his power, love, radical demands, offer of forgiveness, and so on—are meant to be seen in the light of this deeper apophasis. It may be that this is a straightforward contradiction, that Williams unapologetically wants us to *simultaneously* (dialectically) believe that Jesus reveals God and also that we know nothing of God (except that it is *Jesus* who tells us nothing). Alternatively there might be a degree of hyperbole here. Williams may mean that our understanding of Jesus' love (for example) is so incomplete that it is *as if* the concept itself were useless. As Williams paraphrases Denys: "All . . . images are provided by God in his creative goodness, and to some measure true; yet all must be 'denied' in their human and limited sense, so as to lead us back to silence and unknowing." Williams, "Religious Imagery," 282. Another possibility is that Williams is following Lossky who describes positive theology in terms of a ladder of theophanies that we must ascend and *transcend* until we come at last to the God who is beyond all analogy and concept—even beyond goodness and existence; see Lossky, *Mystical Theology*, 39–40. Trying to work out exactly what Williams thinks here is immensely difficult and leaves the impression that there may be no single answer for the reader on this point.

Williams himself notes, we need to ask what apophasis is being used *for*.[83] What is the practical goal toward which the apophatic enterprise is working? In William's case, there are intellectual, social, and spiritual reasons for the appeal.

The first attraction for Williams is that apophasis serves as a necessary part of all human thinking because existence itself is paradoxical. As he writes in *A Ray of Darkness,* paradox crops up everywhere in life. When we speak of simultaneously hating and loving someone or "killing with kindness" and so on, "even in banal contexts, we are aware of the fact that our pigeonholes for things, people, emotions and perceptions are often lagging well behind the fluidity of the real world, with its subtle rapid interactions and puzzling quality."[84]

Here, apophasis—or "paradox" as he calls it here—is simply about being honest regarding the nature of reality and the limitations of our understanding. It acts as a placeholder for that which cannot be simply or neatly expressed, so that we "stop ourselves . . . pretending that some awkward or odd feature of our perception isn't really there." And that which is necessary in ordinary human affairs is, of course, far more so when it comes to our relationship with God, "the ultimate situation for paradoxes."[85]

A second reason why Williams thinks we need negative theology is to forestall or disarm the tendency of religion to claim final knowledge and the power that goes along with that.[86] For Williams, the perennial danger is the desire of the church (or any religious institution) to avoid the truth of its own contingency and to claim finality: "That the Church repeatedly seeks to secure a faith that is not vulnerable to judgement and to put cross and conversion behind it is manifest in every century of Christian history. But in so doing, it cuts itself off from the gift that lies beyond the void of the

---

83. Williams notes that one of the most significant features of Lossky's work was his acknowledgment of the diversity in negative theology and the insistence that the "scholar must 'in every work regard the writer's end', must attempt to discern what it is that apophasis is being used for." Williams, "The Via Negativa and the Foundations of Theology," 96.

84. Williams, *Ray of Darkness,* 100.

85. Ibid.

86. "[C]ommunities of religious meaning do not live in a timeless world of ideas or vision, they have political and structural histories, and their self-identification in relation to the sacred is invariably bound up with ways in which power and control are exercised." Williams, "Beginning With the Incarnation," 98.

cross, and imprisons itself in the kind of self-understanding it can master or control."[87]

To counter this besetting sin, the job of the true theologian is quintessentially apophatic—to expose and disinter those uneasy paradoxes and problems that the church would prefer to keep buried, to remind her that she cannot own or capture God with her dogmatic conceptions, and to undermine her cozy myths and privileges. Theology is a vehicle for the operation of the Spirit's breaking and reshaping of us.[88]

The third application of apophasis seeks to achieve the very same end in the life of an individual. For Williams, the heart of Christian spirituality—whether glimpsed in the writings of Irenaeus, the mysticism of pseudo-Dionysius, the *Anfechtungen* of Luther, or most definitively in the cross itself[89]—is the crisis of faith. Christians only actually deal with God as they move beyond easy certainties and realize existentially (and desperately) that they know nothing of God. Only here in the "dark night of the soul," as we feel threatened with our own dissolution, do we actually trust and meet and get to know God. "Christians who claim to find God uniquely and definitively in Jesus, and especially in the cross of Jesus, are claiming that the roots of their faith are in a massive and total negation of false God-images and religious securities. They thus have some ground for interpreting darkness and doubt in their own life in a similar way—as God himself sweeping aside all that is between themselves and him, to give himself to them as he is."[90]

How do we respond to this? First by acknowledging that much of it is undeniably true. Williams is right to argue that we don't really know very much at all about God or ourselves at all. Before we have gone very far in any direction we come to questions that are at best paradoxical, sometimes antinomous, and occasionally fundamentally impenetrable. What does it really mean to say that God made the world by speaking? What does decision mean for God? What is the divine essence? What is my own essence? How is Jesus God and man at the same time? We may well be able to say

---

87. Ibid., 83.
88. Williams, *On Christian Theology*, 124–25, 143–46.
89. See the overview of Christian spirituality through the centuries in Williams, *Wound of Knowledge*.
90. Williams, *Ray of Darkness*, 83.

something about these questions, but we flatter ourselves appallingly if we believe that we know *much*.[91]

Williams is surely also correct to indicate the tendency of humans—including Christians and the church—to delude ourselves about our level of knowledge and the security of our conceptions of God. The hubristic refusal to let God be God that drives humanity into folly and darkened understanding (Rom 1:18ff.) never goes away but crops up again and again, showing itself in our quest for knowledge that puffs up (1 Cor 8:1), in the self-injurious protection of our own sinfulness (1 Tim 4:2) and in our love for human approval (John 5:44). The church never outgrows its need to be rebuked and challenged, nor do we as individuals ever reach a stage at which we can claim to know anything in more than a dim reflection. We are and remain proud and contingent, yet perpetually tempted to deny both.

Some Questions for Williams

Yet there are also some questions we need to ask Williams at this point. Most directly and fundamentally, we might ask whether he provides us with a sufficiently clear explanation of the relationship between apophatic theology and positive faith. As we have seen, Williams appears to give us two different models here: the spiral—envisaging concrete particulars and nameable patterns (Jesus, love, giving, Trinity, etc.) that cannot themselves be adequately conceptualized; and the void—the more radical dialectic between knowledge and *absolute* ignorance. Of the two, the latter scheme is surely the more problematic. Depicting Jesus as providing knowledge and telling us nothing (without really showing how those things can fit together) threatens to be merely incoherent and tends to forestall further enquiry into what it means to partially know or profess a reasonable faith.[92] But Williams' use of the *first* model also leaves us with questions. Isn't it slightly misleading to describe this scheme as apophatic when we are still

---

91. And we might add that what we do know is always incomplete—"we walk by faith not by sight" (2 Cor 5:7). The fundamental human challenge from the tree of knowledge onward is how we respond to that which eludes—or is withheld—from us.

92. We might add that it potentially gives humans another means of shutting God up. When we don't like what he has to say we choose ignorance; when we do, we claim knowledge. Isn't this precisely the danger that accompanies the invocation of the silent Jesus in the crib or on the cross?

locating our questioning within identifiable truths?[93] Isn't this at least as *positive* as it is *negative*?

Perhaps Williams would respond that it is a matter of context, that the theologian's job is to work *within* the church and that the theologian—like apophasis itself—subsists within and reacts to *given* dogma.[94] But in a pluralist (or worse, crassly relativist) age doesn't the theologian also have an equal duty to actively defend the privileging of these Christian doctrines as normative as well as showing the difficulties that lie within them? Isn't Williams underestimating the threats to the church when he so strongly emphasizes apophasis? Has he paid due attention to the potential for churches and Christians to *avoid* God using negative theology?[95] The New Testament exhortations to guard the good deposit, preserve the apostolic tradition, recall past examples, shun those who pervert the gospel and to select leaders who are able to grasp and communicate the deep truths of the faith do not deny Williams' basic point that we must continually be reformed and challenged in our limited understanding of those truths; yet they certainly convey a concern for theological *conservation* that is less pronounced in Williams' writing.

Another potential problem with Williams' apophatic theology is how, in the midst of it, we recognize what represents the *avoidance* of God or, positively, what the Spirit is moving us *toward*. Williams is somewhat vague about how we are to test the church's health (or the merits of any particular negative critique) and sometimes gives the impression that the only criteria that really matter are sociological or communitarian: "The important thing about [Jesus' life] is that it has created a different sort of community."[96] Christianity "simply incarnates the primordial and original traditions of humankind."[97] "[Scripture's] unifying themes are established

---

93. Williams describes Jesus as the "field and terms of the interpretive enterprise" (Williams, *Dwelling of the Light*, 6–7), and—albeit less confidently—acknowledges the "specially protected status [of Nicaea and Chalcedon] because they articulate the conditions for all other theological definition" (Williams, "Beginning with the Incarnation," 89).

94. "I assume that the theologian is always beginning in the middle of things. There is a practice of common life and language already there . . ." Williams, *On Christian Theology*, xii.

95. See n. 92. Williams acknowledges the danger of evasion-by-negation (see, for example, Williams, *Ray of Darkness*, 100) but seems less concerned about it and vague about its diagnosis and remedies.

96. Williams, "Trinity and Pluralism," 172.

97. Ibid., 175 (quoting Panikkar).

according to what is understood as unifying the community."[98] "The work continues for the theologian and the Church . . . of discerning and naming the Christ-like events of liberation and humanization."[99] But here again, how are we to judge what is good for community as we are in the midst of it?[100] How is our evaluation by *this criterion* to escape the very tendencies against which apophasis is leveled in the first place? What of our propensity toward self-protection and flattery, our tendency to cook-up high-sounding defenses for base motives, our readiness to disregard anomalous evidence that the revolution is not proceeding as planned, the pride and tribal-instincts which make us defend our own errors against critics? Has Williams been *consistently* radical enough in his critique of humanity and the church here?

A final question for Williams must be whether the austerity and conceptual minimalism that arises out of his apophaticism prevents him fully enjoying the fruit of his most exciting Trinitarian analyses. Reading across a range of Williams' works it seems evident that there is disjunction between that which Williams is happy to proclaim from the lips of others and that to which he is prepared to offer in his own name. The former Williams *appreciates* as he appreciates poetry, music, sculpture or icon;[101] the status of the latter is less clear—is it simply Williams' *own* theo-poetry or is it an affirmation of that which he takes to be normative doctrine?[102]

Examples of this can be seen in Williams' writings on the Trinity and the Incarnation. Those ideas Williams draws out of John of the Cross or the icons are luminous and brilliant; those written at his own behest are far more cautious. The *Romanzas* dramatize a loving exchange between

---

98. Williams, "The Discipline of Scripture," in *On Christian Theology*, 56.

99. Williams, "Trinity and Revelation," 143. Andrew Goddard, "English Evangelicals and the Archbishop's Theology," http://www.fulcrum-anglican.org.uk/news/2003/20030901goddard.cfm?doc=131 records a legitimate concern that Williams is tending to blur the lines between the Spirit's work in revelation and illumination. This focuses our attention on the deeper issue of how we work out where the Spirit *intends* to work. While both evangelicals and Williams look to the Spirit for constructive disturbance and reform, there seems to be a significant—and absolutely crucial—difference in thinking about how we place ourselves *in the Spirit's path* or where we look to see him at work.

100. We might recall Zhou Enlai's famous "too early to say" assessment of the French Revolution.

101. For Williams' thoughts on the analogy between art and theological truth: see Williams, "The Judgement of the World," in *On Christian Theology*, 41; idem, "Trinity and Revelation," 133–34; idem, *Dwelling of the Light*, xiv–vi, xix, 6; idem, "The Finality of Christ," 106.

102. The fact that it is consistently more circumspect seems to indicate the latter.

Father and Son, speaking of the Father's plan to give his Son a bride, of the Son's delight and purpose to glorify the Father, of the real visitation by a divine Person to woo his wife. Yet Williams *himself* seems to find it difficult to say that the Word and Christ are the same person.[103] Williams derides the identification of "Jesus as human subject with the second person of the Trinity"[104] and warns against trying to apply "the name 'Jesus Christ' to the pre-existent Word."[105] He rejects the idea that "the 'theistic' God (i.e. a divine individual living outside the universe) turns himself into a member of the human race"[106] and insists that Chalcedon was never meant to signify a "heavenly being coming down from his native habitat."[107] When Williams speaks positively about the Incarnation it sometimes sounds so de-mythologized as to approximate adoptionism: "his life is unreservedly and uniquely a medium for the unconstrained love that made all things . . . Jesus embodies God the Word or God the Son as totally as (more totally than) the musician in performance embodies the work performed."[108] "Because the eternal word and wisdom of God has completely occupied his human mind and body, we say that in him this word and wisdom has 'become flesh.'"[109]

---

103. The contrast on this point comes out most strongly in Williams' Christmas Sermon in 2007: Williams, "Archbishop's Christmas Sermon, Canterbury Cathedral, Tuesday 25 December 2007," http://www.archbishopofcanterbury.org. After giving a short précis of the *Romanzas,* Williams observes that the story doesn't begin with sin and fall but with the deeper purpose of God that "there should be persons . . . who are capable of intimacy with God—not so that God can gain something but so that these created beings may live in joy." The strange thing here is that this language is so much more vague than that which we find in the *Romanzas,* where it is not mere intimacy with God but union with the *Person* of the Son and, through him, the Father and Spirit. Nor is the denial of benefit to God entirely accurate. John clearly *does* see the Son receiving something new through creation and consummation—a bride who will celebrate his beauty along with the Father. At the same time the Father also receives praise as the Son points back to the Father. Williams seems to have downplayed the inter-personal drama that is surely the most wonderful feature of John's work.

104. Williams, "Incarnation and the Renewal of Community," in *On Christian Theology,* 227.

105. Williams, "Beginning with the Incarnation," 89–90.

106. From a response to John Shelby Spong; Williams and Spong, "No Life, Here—No Joy, Terror or Tears," http://www.anglicantas.org.au/tasmaniananglican/200310-spong.html.

107. Williams, "Doctrinal Criticism: Some Questions," 251.

108. Williams, "No Life, Here—No Joy, Terror or Tears," n.p. In *Ponder These Things,* 36, Williams describes the idea of God abandoning his safety to become our God as a "metaphorical extravagance."

109. Williams, "What is Christianity?" Lecture delivered by the Archbishop of Canterbury at the Islamic University, Islamabad, http://www.anglicancommunion.org/acns/articles/

Can we really not do better than this? Of course we have to recognize that imaginings of divine conversations cannot be taken literally. Of course there is no point in pretending that we *really* know what it meant for the Son to take on flesh—historical theology has always been rightly wary of restricting or limiting the divine Word to the flesh of Jesus Christ. But does Williams need to retreat this far? And isn't this austerity and reticence itself problematic—giving the impression that if we remove a few mythological extravagances (continuity of consciousness, coming down from heaven, and so on) then we might be closer to the unadorned truth? Can we actually speak of "the eternal word and wisdom" "occupying" Jesus' "human mind" with any greater confidence than we speak of the Son "coming down to earth?"

In short, can't we enlarge our sense of the mystery of Christ? If we can say that it is *Jesus* who reveals the mystery of the ineffable God, can't we also say that he is *sent, comes into the world,* takes a *bride,* and dies *for her sins*? If these are the words God gives us along with his Son, then must not we, along with him, retain these *concepts* that tell us about him, albeit in the same apophatic manner—far less than univocal, yet far more than merely human poetry or art?[110] Don't these too belong to the hidden center?

40/75/acns4081.cfm. In "Trinity and Ontology," 156, Williams argues that *anhypostasia* has been misunderstood and means simply that Jesus' relationship to God fundamentally constitutes who he is. Williams is not alone in this austere interpretation, but does the New Testament—not to mention the *enhypostasia* clarification—not say something stronger? Not just that God is central to the man Jesus, but that *his person* is the person of the Son; that we see in him one member of the Trinity enfleshed. The problem with everything Williams says here is that it appears only *quantitatively* different from what might be said of any saint: "It is no longer I who live but Christ who lives in me" (Gal 2:20).

110. In fact they are better described as divine art: God creates his own analogies and offers his own verbal commentary—both artist and then critic. It scarcely needs to be added that this does not mean that the different images and concepts given to us ("speaking," "love," "becoming man," "marrying" etc.) do not necessarily relate to the reality of God in the same way, nor that *we*—because God has spoken—can therefore claim any final grasp of either his words or that to which they refer. Whatever any such a form of *analogia entis* and *fidei* is going to mean (a task far beyond us here, but for a start see Karl Barth, *Church Dogmatics* II/1 [London: T. & T. Clark, 2004] 81–82; and Trevor Hart, "How Do We Define the Nature of God's Love?" in *Nothing Greater, Nothing Better: Theological Essays on the Love of God*, ed. Kevin J. Vanhoozer [Grand Rapids: Eerdmans, 2001]), the sufficiency and appropriateness of the knowledge it promises is not going to make it less messy. Of course all we are arguing for is an enlargement of what we have already seen in his own cautious and apophatic depiction of analogical connections between God and human relationality/personhood.

3

Disruptive History:
Rowan Williams on Heresy and Orthodoxy

BENJAMIN MYERS

I

In spite of all the recent developments within the fields of cultural and intellectual history, much contemporary theology suffers from a rationalistic conception of doctrinal history. Few theologians today would be willing to speak of a linear "development" of doctrine; but the assumption that there is a relatively stable Christian tradition, moving through history with its own immanent doctrinal "grammar," remains entrenched in some of the most influential contemporary theologies.

The work of T. F. Torrance is a case in point. Torrance argues for a wholly realistic and anti-constructivist understanding of doctrine. In his view, doctrinal knowledge arises under the direct impact of God's own self-revelation, so that the church's thinking "take[s] its shape from the structure of the object."[1] The formulation of doctrine is thus never a construction,

---

1. Torrance, *God and Rationality* (London: Oxford University Press, 1971) 9.

but only a discovery of what is always already there, "latent in reality" itself.[2] Revelation has its own intrinsic structures, and the task of doctrinal formulation is simply to allow these objective structures to impose themselves on the human mind.[3] If there is any struggle in the history of doctrine, therefore, it is only the struggle to articulate explicitly the "deposit of faith" that is always tacitly present, waiting to be uncovered and formulated theoretically. It is clear that *history* in the proper sense has no place in this rationalistic conception of doctrine. The history of doctrine, for Torrance, is simply the story of the progressive unfolding of the immanent logic of Christian truth, with various false starts and deviations along the way.[4] In his account, there is no genuine newness within doctrinal history, since the only "new" event is the act of God in history that subsequently imprints its own immanent logical structures on the church's thinking. Similarly, in Torrance's conception the conflictual and agonistic character of doctrine disappears. Indeed, from his standpoint it is hard to imagine the possibility of *any* conflict within doctrinal history, since theological thinking is always either objectively determined by revelation (and therefore properly doctrinal) or a subjective deviation from revelation (and therefore an "unnecessary accretion"[5] that does not belong to doctrine as such). But without the dimensions of *newness* and *conflict*, it becomes impossible to make sense of the history of doctrine as we actually find it, or indeed to account for the irreducible contingency and untidiness of doctrinal formulations.

A similar cluster of problems emerges in George Lindbeck's theory of the nature of doctrine. Drawing on a Wittgensteinian account of language, Lindbeck considers each religion to be analogous to a language with its own grammatical rules;[6] and the grammar of religion is doctrine, understood as authoritative teachings that organize and regulate the practice of a given community. Although admittedly Lindbeck's aim is not to explain the historical formation of doctrine, and although his Wittgensteinian con-

---

2. Torrance, *The Christian Doctrine of God, One Being Three Persons* (Edinburgh: T. & T. Clark, 1996) 84.

3. Torrance, *Theological Science* (London: Oxford University Press, 1969) 341.

4. See for example Torrance's history of Nicene theology: *The Trinitarian Faith: The Evangelical Theology of the Ancient Catholic Church* (Edinburgh: T. & T. Clark, 1988).

5. Torrance, *Reality and Scientific Theology* (Edinburgh: Scottish Academic Press, 1985) 152–53.

6. Lindbeck, *The Nature of Doctrine: Religion and Theology in a Postliberal Age* (London: SPCK, 1984) 33.

strual rightly resists foundationalist assumptions about the universality of Christian experience, his entire account nevertheless presses toward a rationalistic conception of history. The internal logic of a particular community is already immanent within the practices of that community, and is only later codified explicitly. Thus Lindbeck distinguishes between a doctrine's essential, ahistorical *content* and its accidental, historically conditioned *form*. The form itself is merely one historical "instantiation" of those rules that are "unconditionally and permanently necessary" to Christian identity; doctrinal history contains nothing new, then, but only "descriptions and redescriptions" of an always-antecedent "content."[7] Even though Torrance's objectivist theory of doctrine differs sharply from Lindbeck's more sophisticated constructivist account, both thinkers nevertheless share a common vision of a set of grammatical rules or structures that is always there in the advance, waiting only to be articulated and codified in the formal language of doctrine. And just as Torrance's conception of doctrine tends to erase the possibility of real doctrinal conflict (since everything in doctrinal history is either an authentic development or a deviation), so too Lindbeck's account provides rather neat "criteria . . . for distinguishing between legitimate and illegitimate (or orthodox and heterodox) developments and adaptations,"[8] without accounting for the real complexities and ambiguities of doctrinal history. For Lindbeck, one either plays by the rules or one doesn't; there can be no fundamental dispute about what the rules are, or about the kind of game that is being played.

The fact that Lindbeck's theory is essentially rationalistic becomes clear when one considers that the notion of *decision* plays no role in his theory. Lindbeck imagines a community in which all persons, given the proper training, will be led ineluctably to agreement about the use of doctrinal rules. As Kathryn Tanner observes, this account suggests that "with training people should always come to the same conclusions without the need for deliberation," so that Lindbeck envisions the production of "automatic results."[9] Doctrinal formulations, then, are the product of a kind of immanent communal reason, rather than of conflict, negotiation, and decision; strictly speaking, there can be no real decision about doctrine,

---

7. Ibid., 92–96.

8. Ibid., 12.

9. Kathryn Tanner, *Theories of Culture: A New Agenda for Theology* (Minneapolis: Fortress, 1997) 141–42.

since the rules are merely waiting to be discovered by anyone who properly observes the game. The result is thus an ahistorical construal of doctrine, which provides no resources for comprehending the personal, political, agonistic dimensions of doctrinal formulation, nor the occurrence of moments of genuine newness within doctrinal history. To quote Tanner once more, Lindbeck's theory isolates a "pre-existing" tradition "from the messy course of history,"[10] just as Torrance isolates a purely "objective" event of divine self-disclosure from the conflicts and contingencies of history.

The problem with such accounts is not simply that they misconstrue the past, but that they undermine the very significance of any engagement with the past. For both Lindbeck and Torrance, the *history* of doctrine becomes redundant. There is no threat that anything new could emerge from history, no possibility that the study of the past could expose the present to a radical critique, nor any possibility that such historical study could drive the church toward surprising new decisions about the nature of doctrine or about the nature of its own identity. In short, when doctrinal formulations are isolated from the vicissitudes of history, the past itself is rendered safe and harmless.

In contrast, one could sum up all Rowan Williams' historical scholarship with the statement that Williams wants to make the past *dangerous*. A recurring theme throughout his work is the sheer unaccountable strangeness of the past, the capacity of the past to disrupt and unsettle our complacency, to bring us into contact with a reality that questions us and submits us to judgment. For Williams, good historical writing is writing "that constructs that sense of who we are by a real engagement with the strangeness of the past," so that our present identity is seen to be bound up with things that are no longer easy for us to grasp.[11] The purpose of historical study is thus to invite us into "a process of questioning and being questioned by the past," so that we come to see that the Christian past necessarily belongs to the Christian present.[12]

Williams himself has pursued such a process of "questioning," especially in his large body of scholarship on the emergence of heresy and orthodoxy in the first four centuries. It is to this scholarship that I want

---

10. Ibid., 131–32.
11. Williams, *Why Study the Past?* (Grand Rapids: Eerdmans, 2005) 23–24.
12. Ibid., 28.

to turn now. As well as drawing attention to the scope and creativity of Williams' historical work, I will argue that his approach provides resources for a critical and constructive new retrieval of the doctrinal past.

II

Williams' 1987 work, *Arius: Heresy and Tradition*,[13] is his single greatest contribution to the study of doctrinal history. The book has justly been described as his *magnum opus*, and indeed as a "wonderful" and "masterfully executed" work of historical analysis.[14] After two decades, it remains one of the most important and influential interpretations of the fourth-century Arian controversy, and it is a crucial text for understanding Williams' distinctive approach to doctrinal history.

According to Williams, the Arian controversy was fundamentally a series of debates about the nature of Christian continuity. How does the church in a new historical situation remain faithful to tradition? Should the church simply remain committed to the language and formulations of the past? Or is theological innovation necessary in order to secure a deeper continuity? Although Williams depicts Arius as an unconventional philosophical thinker, a central claim of his study is that Arius was "a traditionalist"[15] and "a committed theological conservative."[16] Indeed, Arius emerges not only as the "archetypal heretic," but also as an *archetypal conservative* who viewed himself as a guardian of Christian formulae, standing firm against the threatening encroachment of the Nicene innovators. Central to his thought, for example, was an uncompromising commitment to traditional formulations of divine freedom. He followed Christian tradi-

---

13. Williams, *Arius*. For an extended analysis of Williams' book in relation to other scholarship on the fourth century, see Richard Vaggione, "'Arius, Heresy and Tradition' by Rowan Williams: A Review Article," *Toronto Journal of Theology* 5 (1989) 63–87.

14. Adolf Martin Ritter, "Arius redivivus? Ein Jahrzwölft Arianismusforschung," *Theologische Rundschau* 55 (1990) 182–83.

15. Williams, *Arius*, 156.

16. Ibid., 175. See in contrast the wry observation of Jacques Berlinerblau in "Toward a Sociology of Heresy, Orthodoxy, and *Doxa*," *History of Religions* 40 (2001) 344: "the belief that the heretic is a progressive element, one who heroically . . . expands the parameters of a restricted conscience collective for future generations to benefit, constitutes a veritable axiom in recent heresy research."

tion in insisting that God alone is self-subsistent (*agennetos*) and without beginning (*anarchos*); that the Son is freely begotten before all ages; that the Son inherits all the Father's glory; and that together Father, Son, and Spirit form a triad of divine subsistents (*hypostaseis*). And Arius' commitment to traditional formulae was matched by his fierce hostility toward the innovative thinking that had produced concepts such as the *homoousios*, the Son's coexistence with the Father, and the Son's knowledge of his own *ousia*. Against all this, Arius presented himself both as a biblical exegete and as a defender of doctrinal tradition. In Williams' account, the Arian controversy is thus a series of debates about "how to be loyal to a tradition under strain"[17]—about how to remain faithful to the theology of the third century amidst the changed conditions of the fourth.

In contrast to Arius' staunch attachment to traditional language, it was Athanasius' genius to perceive that continuity with tradition can demand a sharp break in linguistic continuity. Against the Arians, Athanasius saw that "strict adherence to archaic and 'neutral' terms" can in fact be a betrayal of the tradition; the innovative introduction of the term *homoousios* was therefore "a necessary moment in the deeper understanding and securing of tradition." Indeed, Athanasius realized that there can be no question of a choice between conservation and innovation *tout court*. The question posed to the church, rather, was "what *kind* of innovation would best serve the integrity of the faith handed down," since the continuity of Christian belief involves much more than the mere conservation of dogmatic formulae.[18] In short, then, the Nicene prelates reluctantly adopted fresh terminology in order "to hold on intelligibly to a threatened belief"[19]—a belief that had been threatened precisely by the archaic repetition of church language.

Williams thus argues that the theology of Nicaea represents a crucial moment in doctrinal history—a moment in which the church perceived that critical theological reflection is not only legitimate but necessary:

> The loyal and uncritical repetition of formulae is seen to be inadequate as a means of securing continuity at anything more than a formal level; Scripture and tradition require to be read in a way that brings out their strangeness, their non-obvious and non-contem-

---

17. Williams, "Baptism and the Arian Controversy," in *Arianism after Arius*, ed. Michel R. Barnes and Daniel H. Williams (Edinburgh: T. & T. Clark, 1993) 177.

18. Williams, *Arius*, 235.

19. Williams, *Why Study the Past?* 50.

porary qualities, in order that they may be read both freshly and truthfully from one generation to another. They need to be made more *difficult* before we can accurately grasp their simplicities. . . . And this "making difficult," this confession that what the gospel says in Scripture and tradition does not instantly and effortlessly make sense, is perhaps one of the most fundamental tasks for theology.[20]

To elucidate this point, Williams turns to the German church struggle of the 1930s as a modern parallel to the fourth-century crisis. The Barmen Declaration of the Confessing Church represents not a confessional conservatism or a repetition of dogmatic formulae, but a profound struggle for new theological self-awareness, for a new encounter with the church's founding event, so that the gospel becomes at once more difficult and more immediate in its concrete judgment and demands. The lesson of Barmen, Williams suggests, is that "proclaiming *now* the same gospel as before is a great deal less easy than it sounds"[21]—it is a matter of intense struggle, of risk and decisive commitment. As at Barmen, so too at Nicaea, the question is that of the identity of the Christian community and the kinds of changes that are necessary in order to secure authentic continuity with the past. And this question cannot be resolved through a repetition of dogmatic language, but only through a critical and creative re-engagement with the past.

In contrast to all rationalistic conceptions of doctrine, therefore, Williams' account foregrounds the role of conflict in doctrinal history. The history of doctrine is a history of formative conflicts and struggles; there is no pure doctrinal "meaning" that can be abstracted from these conflictual contexts. As Williams puts it, "what the articulation of doctrinal truth concretely *is* can be traced only through the detailed reworking and re-imagining of its formative conflicts."[22]

It would be a mistake, however, to think of such conflict merely as the clash between truth and error, or between a pre-existing "orthodoxy" and a divergent "heresy." On the contrary, orthodoxy comes into being only through processes of struggle and conflict. It does not pre-exist the conflict with "heresy," but emerges from it. Williams points out, for example, that the Arian controversy "is very far from being a struggle by 'the Church'

---

20. Williams, *Arius*, 236.

21. Ibid., 237–38. See also the discussion of Barmen in Williams, "Beginning with the Incarnation," in *On Christian Theology* (Oxford: Blackwell, 2000) 86–89.

22. Williams, *Arius*, 25.

against a 'heresy' formulated and propagated by a single dominant teacher"; instead, it is "a debate about the kinds of continuity possible and necessary in the Church's language."[23] The Nicene formulation *became* "orthodox" precisely because it constructed a new way of securing continuity with the Christian past. There is genuine newness here; orthodoxy is never merely a given, but it is constructed as a radical new mode of faithful continuity. The Nicene prelates did not discover or preserve orthodoxy, but *created* it.

III

With this in mind, we can see why Williams is at pains to underscore the *unfinished* character of doctrinal orthodoxy. The production of authentic continuity—that is, the construction of orthodoxy—is always a new task and challenge. As the Arian controversy so vividly illustrates, there is no straightforward "deposit of faith" that needs only to be conserved and defended; rather, doctrinal orthodoxy must be experienced as "something still future,"[24] as a continuing "project" that is not yet finally settled or resolved.[25] The task of Christian theology, we might say, is to take up this project of "traditioning" the past, generating new forms of continuity so that the past is constituted not merely as history but as *tradition*, and thus as an authentic possibility of faithful practice in the present.

For Williams, then, orthodoxy is understood not so much as a defined or settled system of beliefs, but as a "tool," a set of self-reflective practices, "a tradition of discriminating, imaging and symbolizing." Orthodoxy is "a method for creation" in which the community generates new forms of continuity with the past. The project of orthodoxy is the production of the right kinds of questions, the right posture of faithful attentiveness, rather than the creation of any "system of final and satisfactory answers." At the source of the Christian community's life, Williams argues, is an unrepeatable event; and the community remains "orthodox" in so far as it remains attentive and answerable to this generative source. Orthodoxy, in other words, is not primarily a mode of remembering or reproducing the past,

---

23. Ibid., 234.
24. Ibid., 24.
25. Williams, "What Is Catholic Orthodoxy?" in *Essays Catholic and Radical*, ed. Williams and Kenneth Leech (London: Bowerdean, 1983) 14.

but it is the creative project of making room for the past to extend itself into the present.[26]

Indeed, Williams argues that only orthodoxy can free us for a properly critical stance toward the past. In the fourth century, the development of a new orthodoxy was precisely the struggle against an uncritical and complacent repetition; in this context, orthodoxy was the attempt to produce a real engagement with the past, to become critically self-aware of the limits and possibilities of the community's received language. As Williams puts it: "Only tradition makes thinking possible—an engagement, even a struggle, with what is given, rather than a passive and meaningless observation. Paradoxically, it is only 'orthodoxies' . . . that enable us to ask questions."[27] Far from placing rigid restrictions on the church's theological imagination, therefore, the function of orthodoxy is to activate and renew that imagination, to supply the resources for an alert and critical confrontation with the past.

Conversely, Williams understands "heresies" to be those options in doctrinal history that unduly limit the range of Christian language. Heresy is the impoverishment of the church's theological imagination. Williams' reading of the Arian controversy is of decisive importance here. Arius' problem was not simply that he was a reactionary figure, but that he combined a fundamental conservatism with a profound systematizing impulse. He took diverse traditional ideas and reorganized them, using philosophical tools to produce "a new and more systematic unity."[28] The ambiguity of traditional concepts was erased, the difficulties ironed out, and basic doctrinal conceptions (such as the divine freedom, transcendence, and ineffability) were pressed to their most extreme logical conclusions.[29] Arianism was not, therefore, a complete deviation from orthodoxy—its basic premises were rooted in Christian tradition—but it was a failure of theological imagination, a failure of nerve, an inability to accept the incompleteness and ambiguity of Christian belief. Its "heretical" impulse lay in what Williams describes as a "destructive longing for final clarity, totality of

---

26. Ibid., 12–14.
27. Ibid., 12.
28. Williams, *Arius*, 178.
29. Ibid., 233.

vision"—a totalizing impulse "which brings forth the monsters of religious and political idolatry."[30]

Orthodoxy, for its part, also seeks a kind of theological comprehensiveness; but instead of pursuing a totalizing vision in which all tensions and ambiguities are eliminated, orthodoxy aims to provide a context that has an expansive capacity to interpret the complexities of Christian belief and practice. Such comprehensiveness lies in a refusal of any easy reduction, in a resistance of all glib solutions, and in a commitment to preserving the irreducible untidiness of Christian language. Here Williams remains a good disciple of Wittgenstein: "what's ragged should be left ragged."[31] For Williams, theological integrity is possible only when discourse about God "declines the attempt to take God's point of view," or to assume a "total perspective" that removes every conceptual difficulty.[32] Indeed, as Williams argues in his work on Arius, the problem with heresy is that it makes things too *easy*, whereas the role of orthodoxy is to render Christian language both more faithful and "more *difficult*."[33]

Heresy, then, represents a real threat to the church's belief and practice. By simplifying Christian language and making it too easy, heresy drastically reduces that language's range of available meanings. While orthodoxy seeks coherence as a means of access to truth, heresy pursues coherence as a matter of conceptual precision for its own sake.[34] It offers "a tidy version" of the church's language, "in which the losses [are] adjusted to distort or to limit the range of reference of religious speech."[35] The comprehensiveness and coherence of orthodoxy lie not in such conceptual tidiness, but in a constantly expanding network of interpretive resources in which the "raggedness" of Christian language is retained. One might say that the continuity that orthodoxy secures is precisely a continuity of *critical openness*—a tradition of holding Christian speech open to the judgment of its originating source. As Williams says of the fourth-century controversy: "The rejection of Arianism may have made Christian language more complex; but . . .

---

30. Williams, "What is Catholic Orthodoxy?" 25.

31. Ludwig Wittgenstein, *Culture and Value* (Chicago: University of Chicago Press, 1980) 45.

32. Williams, "Theological Integrity," in *On Christian Theology*, 6.

33. Williams, *Arius*, 236.

34. Williams, "What is Catholic Orthodoxy?" 17.

35. Williams, "Prologue" to *On Christian Theology*, xii–xiii.

it has militated against an intellectual complacency in the face of the unsettling effects of the gospel."[36] To keep the church properly "unsettled": *that* is the difficult and often unwelcome task of doctrinal orthodoxy.

IV

But if orthodoxy and heresy are divergent attempts to produce certain kinds of coherence and comprehensiveness, then it also becomes clear that these are not absolute foes, but rather adversaries locked in a common struggle. Even if the outcome of this struggle necessarily entails the exclusion of one party (and therefore its designation as "heresy"), Williams nevertheless argues that heresy plays a vital role in the creation of Christian orthodoxy. Indeed, a central theme of Williams' scholarship on the Arian controversy is the constructive function of Arius' theology in the formation of fourth-century orthodoxy. Both the Arians and the "Catholics" were conducting a debate within a common language, "acknowledging the same kind of rules and authorities."[37] Both theologies were formulated as interpretations of Scripture; both attempted to preserve continuity with the Christian past; both were attempts to negotiate the challenges of articulating the gospel in a changed cultural and intellectual context; neither was wholly successful in its solutions and formulations. According to Williams, we can therefore properly understand heresy only by "understand[ing] how orthodoxy itself unavoidably negotiates the same dangers as its critics, with comparably uneven success."[38] There is, in other words, no clear line between the aims of Arius and the aims of the Nicene prelates—indeed, Arius' own agenda was incorporated into the very fabric of what would become "orthodoxy."

Williams thus ascribes considerable value to heresy itself, and especially to the creative and turbulent processes by which "orthodoxy" emerges from its struggle with "heresy." Heresy is not a mere deviation from some pre-existing norm, or from a doctrinal grammar that regulates the community's beliefs; on the contrary, heresy is a failed attempt to achieve the same thing for which orthodoxy struggles. It is a mistake, but a very fruitful and

---

36. Williams, "The Logic of Arianism," *Journal of Theological Studies* 34 (1983) 81.

37. Williams, *Arius*, 24.

38. Williams, "Defining Heresy," in *The Origins of Christendom in the West*, ed. Alan Kreider (Edinburgh: T. & T. Clark, 2001) 334.

productive one. Indeed, Williams can even describe the whole history of theology as "a history of . . . fertile and suggestive mistakes."[39] There could be no doctrinal orthodoxy without these mistakes. And for just that reason, "theology continues to need its Ariuses."[40]

Of course, many writers attribute positive significance to heresy, by viewing it perhaps as a foil for the development of doctrinal truth, or as a necessary error against which orthodoxy can then define itself. But such conceptions are a far cry from Williams' historicized understanding of heresy. For him, the value of heresy lies not in the contrast between the truth of orthodoxy and the error of heresy—as though the truth were merely waiting to be discovered in a moment of conflict—but in the fact that heresy and orthodoxy participate in the same struggle for Christian continuity. The doctrinal priorities of the community do not precede the conflict, but they must be forged and constructed through the messy, painful, and always politicized processes of theological struggle. The function of heresy is not merely a negative one, therefore, but there is a "productive *conflict* about goals and priorities between Christians"[41]—a conflict through which orthodoxy is painfully negotiated and constructed. While rationalistic models of doctrine tend to eliminate the possibility that conflict itself is constitutive of the nature of doctrine, Williams' view here remains close to that of Alasdair MacIntyre, who describes the identity-creating operation of conflict in historical institutions: "When an institution—a university, say, or a farm, or a hospital—is the bearer of a tradition of practice or practices, its common life will be partly, but in a centrally important way, constituted by a continuous argument as to what a university is and ought to be or what good farming is or what good medicine is. Traditions, when vital, embody continuities of conflict."[42] Significantly, the final sentence forms the epigraph to Williams' *Arius*; such "continuities of conflict" are, for Williams, constitutive of the identity of the Christian church. The role of heresy is not merely to expose illegitimate deviations from a normative center, but to generate productive debate over the nature of precisely such a "center." If the interpretive strategy

39. Williams, *Arius*, 267.

40. Williams, "The Logic of Arianism," 81.

41. Williams, "Does It Make Sense to Speak of Pre-Nicene Orthodoxy?" in *The Making of Orthodoxy: Essays in Honour of Henry Chadwick*, ed. Williams (Cambridge: Cambridge University Press, 1989) 2.

42. Alasdair MacIntyre, *After Virtue: A Study in Moral Theory*, 3rd ed. (Notre Dame: University of Notre Dame Press, 2007) 222.

of "orthodoxy" finally emerges as a normative authority, this is not because orthodoxy has articulated a timeless truth that preceded the conflict, but rather because it has decisively *constituted* the community's proper identity through a new form of creative fidelity to the past.

This is why Williams can also suggest that "we might not discover exactly what orthodoxy involves, short of a major crisis or threat"[43]—a crisis in which doctrinal continuity can no longer be complacently taken for granted, but must be forged anew in the furnace of conflict. But the fact that orthodoxy is produced in periods of crisis does not mean that we can, by studying the past, gain "simple and authoritative models for our vision of the Church now"; instead, the study of doctrinal history offers "a hint as to the kinds of circumstance that provoke most deeply this question of identity and some of the theological resources that could be deployed in response."[44] The project of orthodoxy is a radically contingent and untidy business. It is impossible to predict what this project might involve in the future. But by studying the formation of orthodoxies in moments of historical crisis—the Nicene Creed in the fourth century, or the Barmen Declaration in the twentieth—we can start to glimpse what is really at stake in the struggle for doctrinal continuity, and what it might mean to produce in our own time a faithful confession of Christian identity.

V

My reading of Williams so far has been underscoring the constructivist dimension of his historical work: doctrine is created through formative conflicts; the construction of doctrine is the production of a new continuity that "traditions" the past; there is no a-temporal doctrinal remainder that escapes the vicissitudes of history. But to acknowledge all this—as I think we must—is not to commit ourselves to a thoroughgoing relativism, or to evacuate doctrine of its claim to *truth*. Indeed, it would be a great mistake to suppose that Williams wishes to undermine the truthfulness of Christian tradition, or that he regards the question of truth as unimportant. On the contrary: the question of the truth of doctrine is really the *one* urgent question facing the community. Orthodoxy is always constructed, to be

43. Williams, *Why Study the Past?* 58.
44. Ibid., 70.

sure—but it is not a "constructed fiction."[45] In fact, Williams' entire conception of Christian history is driven by the belief that this particular historical tradition has been generated by a unique and unrepeatable event—an event whose capacity for meaning is infinite and inexhaustible, but not infinitely malleable. For Williams, it is this unique event that produces a Christian community in the first place, and that uniquely constitutes this community's history as a never-finished history of interpretive struggle.

The Christian tradition began with an event of rupture, with a shattering disturbance of all existing forms of meaning and social belonging. The resurrection of Jesus from the dead is "an event on the frontier of any possible language," since it both shatters our speech and breaks it open to new possibilities.[46] The founding Christian narratives are likewise subversive and disruptive; the diverse Easter stories are "disorienting" and "confusing" testaments to the sheer impossibility of articulating the Easter event itself.[47] The Christian tradition is generated by this event, and by these radically untidy and disruptive narratives. So too, the basic social patterns of early Christianity are marked by rupture and discontinuity. The church is, from the outset, "separatist, subversive and universalist."[48] Right from the start, it is aware that its own social existence has been generated by a rupture in existing systems of meaning, and that its language is fundamentally a *new* form of speech that has been generated by the radical disturbance and discontinuity of Jesus' resurrection from the dead. The church has thus always been faced with the task of negotiating problems of continuity and stability; in the second century, this is attested in the various "rules of faith" (*regulae fidei*), all of which insist on the unity of the Christian God with the God of the Old Testament, while also frequently asserting their own universality. The striking thing about these early doctrinal assertions is their extraordinary fragility, their precarious balance: a community generated by an event of rupture must try "to explain how it locates itself in a world decisively disrupted and contradicted by what has been revealed." Hence the struggle for a normative Christianity—an "orthodoxy"—belongs to the very essence of the Christian community. The community is always threatened by the

45. Williams, "What is Catholic Orthodoxy?" 19.
46. Williams, *Resurrection: Interpreting the Easter Gospel*, 2nd ed. (Cleveland: Pilgrim, 2002) 89.
47. Ibid., 112.
48. Williams, "Defining Heresy," 326.

possibility of sheer fragmentation and disorder, so that it is forced "to recompose a *world*," to construct for itself a coherent social environment.[49]

On the basis of this analysis of the church's origin in a moment of generative disturbance, Williams can thus argue that the problem of heresy is already tied up with the church's identity right from the outset. If the community must struggle to construct a sense of unity and coherence in a world that has been ruptured by its own founding event, then "heresy" comes to be defined as anything that breaks apart this delicate balance and coherence. The world remains fragile, held together by means of paradoxical and apophatic language; and heresy, with its too-rigorous systematizing impulse, threatens to dissolve this essential precariousness. As Williams puts it: "Christians are aware that, because of Jesus Christ, a familiar world has been broken apart and reassembled; so what becomes most frightening is anything that threatens to break up the universe again, driving wedges between what has been carefully stitched together by way of paradox and skilful redefinition."[50] In the early centuries of Christianity, therefore, heresy is simply "whatever pushes Christian speech over from its precarious balance into a rhetoric of cosmic fragmentation."[51]

Nevertheless, the fragile norm that orthodoxy constructs is not any "finally reconciled metaphysic" in which every wrinkle of discontinuity is ironed out, but it is rather "the continuing labor of engagement between the disruptive narrative and the conventions making for historical intelligibility."[52] Williams' point here is that the church must *proclaim* and *re-tell* its disruptive narrative, and that such proclamation requires, if not tidy schematization, at least a workable set of guidelines, and thus an orthodox interpretive norm. In principle, of course, there is no way to predict in advance what "heresy" will look like, or how it will differ from a future "orthodoxy." This question can never be settled: that is the whole point of Williams' construal of heresy and orthodoxy. There must be continual negotiation and dispute over the church's message and identity; as long as the church endures in history, there is no resolution, no final overcoming of

---

49. Ibid., 324–27.

50. Williams, *Why Study the Past?* 8.

51. Williams, "Defining Heresy," 334. For an extended analysis, see Williams, "Origen: Between Orthodoxy and Heresy," in *Origeniana Septima: Origenes in den Auseinandersetzungen des 4. Jahrhunderts*, ed. Wolfgang Bienert and Uwe Kühneweg (Leuven: Leuven University Press, 1999) 3–14.

52. Williams, "Defining Heresy," 335.

difficulty and ambiguity. At every stage of the church's journey, the gospel must become stranger and more difficult.

Indeed, in Williams' account, the Christian community can never avoid the risks posed by heresy, since one of the church's fundamental tasks is to challenge those norms of meaning and coherence that seem self-evident to the contemporary social context. The role of orthodoxy is not to navigate around the difficulties of rupture and discontinuity, but to guide the church's language into confrontation with its founding event. Again, Williams' construal makes it clear that orthodoxy continues to *need* heresy—"theology needs its Ariuses"—since heresy "perpetually nudges the agenda of 'orthodoxy' away from inflexible ideological settlements." Indeed, the tradition constructed and defended by orthodoxy is distorted whenever its apocalyptic and discontinuous moments are "domesticated," or whenever it fails to take seriously the questions that heresy poses to Christian language.[53] Paradoxically, then, orthodoxy always subverts its own finality; the comprehensiveness that its seeks is simply a holding-open of the community's language toward its source-event, a radical resistance of any easy closure or final systematization.

Such a conception of orthodoxy should make it clear that a thoroughgoing constructivist account of Christian doctrine need not entail a relativization of the unique truth-claims of doctrinal tradition. The strength and sophistication of Williams' approach here may be clarified through a contrast with Kathryn Tanner's theory of Christian continuity. Tanner advances an acute and often compelling response to the work of Lindbeck; her account takes with great seriousness the historical constructedness of all doctrinal formulations and the irreducibility of conflict in doctrinal history, and it rightly construes doctrinal history as a history of debate over the community's identity. But when it comes to answering the fundamental question of the nature of Christian continuity, Tanner can only suggest that such continuity is "more a matter of form than of substance," so that it lies not in any particular doctrinal account but only in a shared commitment to certain kinds of "investigation." What makes us Christians, then, is simply the fact that particular questions and cultural materials are important to us—irrespective of how we answer those questions or use those materials.[54]

---

53. Ibid.
54. Tanner, *Theories of Culture*, 124–25, 174–75.

But this construal fails both to account adequately for the formative role of *heresy* in the construction of Christian identity, and to take seriously Christian doctrine's own claim to provide a truthful account of the way things really are. In contrast, Williams is able to view the constructedness and contingency of doctrine as a necessary correlate of doctrine's concern with truth. Doctrine *has* to be constructed and reconstructed, since it is a response to the disruptive event that lies at the source of Christian tradition; and since this event can never be fully assimilated into a stable system, the tradition that it generates remains inherently unstable, with normative interpretive orthodoxies emerging only through conflict with competing interpretive accounts. Further, while Tanner views Christian history as devoid of any criteria by which some meanings and interpretations may legitimately be privileged over others, Williams' account suggests that there is indeed a fundamental criterion by which the faithfulness and legitimacy of doctrinal formulations can be measured: for Williams, this criterion is not some stable core or grammar that inheres in the community itself, but it is rather the *event* through which the community was created. This radical singularity, this shattering disruption that occurred in the resurrection of Jesus—*this* is the criterion that stands in judgment over all Christian speech. And since this is the *only* ultimate criterion, the church can never rest assured in its own possession of "orthodoxy": it must be unceasingly disturbed and unsettled and brought to judgment. The purpose of doctrine is to facilitate this process of judgment, to teach Christian speech the discipline of remaining open to the reality of its own strange past.

Indeed, following Williams we might say that the truth of doctrine *is* its openness to the past, its capacity to clear a space for ever-new confrontations between the specificity of a past event and the present life of the community. In Barthian language, we could say the truth of doctrine lies in its capacity to bear *witness*: to "point beyond itself and summon us to hear, not itself, but Him."[55] In order to function as such a witness, doctrinal orthodoxy must achieve some measure of coherence and intelligibility. But its task is always to subvert its own coherence by pointing away from itself to the rupture of God's advent. And to that extent, the aim of doctrine is to expose its own limitations, to formalize its own unfinishedness, to hold

---

55. Karl Barth, *Church Dogmatics* IV/3 (Edinburgh: T. & T. Clark, 1961) 419.

open a space for encounter with the shattering and uncontainable eventfulness of God's disruptive grace.

VI

I began this essay by observing that a good deal of contemporary theology remains underwritten by rationalistic and ahistorical assumptions about the nature and formation of Christian doctrine. If the history of doctrine is merely the story of the community's articulation of its own always already latent "grammar," then the study of the past is reduced to a mirroring of our own doctrinal assumptions, combined perhaps with an edifying documentation of heretical deviations from the doctrinal norm. In such approaches, the nature of "orthodoxy" is evident from observing our own belief and practice, while "heresy" is a mere lapse in judgment, a failure properly to grasp the rules of the game. Here, the significance of church history dissolves, and the doctrinal past offers up a fundamentally unthreatening confirmation of what we already knew in advance. The past is thus domesticated, stripped of its capacity to judge and disrupt. As I have tried to show, however, Rowan Williams' historical scholarship provides resources for a renewed critical retrieval of the church's doctrinal past—a retrieval in which the past becomes dangerous, unsettling, authentically *strange*.

In his work on the emergence of heresy and orthodoxy, Williams articulates the conflictual and agonistic structure of Christian doctrine. The identity of the Christian community is not stable or settled, but it is subject to ongoing debate, negotiation, and revision. Conflicts between heresy and orthodoxy are conflicts over the nature of this identity, and over the kinds of continuity possible for the community thus identified. This means that the church does not merely transmit its identity—or some "relatively fixed core"[56]—from one generation to the next, but it receives its identity *from* history. There can be no "neutral" formulation of this identity.[57] The community's normative identity is *constituted*—not once and for all, but repeatedly—in the conflict between heresy and orthodoxy, and through new encounters with the community's disruptive founding event. Continuity with the past is thus not something that can be taken for granted, but it

---

56. Lindbeck, *Nature of Doctrine*, 81.

57. See Hugh Nicholson, "The Political Nature of Doctrine: A Critique of Lindbeck in Light of Recent Scholarship," *Heythrop Journal* 48 (2007) 858–77.

must be achieved ever anew through critical engagement with the past. As Ernst Käsemann has also observed, continuity with the past is preserved at times only "by shattering the received terminology, the received imagery, the received theology."[58] Authentic continuity becomes possible through such revision, through an invention whose faithfulness to the past lies precisely in its surprising newness.

If we press Williams' account a little further, we can add that continuity with Christian tradition extends not only from the past to the present, but also from the present to the past: continuity is the creation here and now of a new coherence between past and present, a construction that "traditions" the past so that the community is identified—precisely in its difference—as the *same* community that extends backward into the past.

What I am trying to articulate here is the capacity of Christian tradition to generate moments of real *newness*. In the fourth century, for instance, we witness something new and unanticipated, a surprising improvisation that never could have been predicted from the possibilities of the past, but that nevertheless created a new harmony, a new coherence, between past and present. As John Milbank has aptly observed, such a doctrinal formulation is no mere "development," but it is at once "inventive" and "excessive": it exceeds the community's own founding narrative as an "ungrounded addition," but it nevertheless secures continuity with the tradition by "work[ing] *back* into the first-order level of mythical narrative and devotion."[59]

If doctrinal continuity can be accomplished only through an invention that exceeds tradition, it follows also that Christian theology is essentially a risky and precarious business. Theological thinking is not driven ineluctably by the necessity of reason, nor does it consist in the mere articulation of a pre-existing doctrinal grammar. What theology might require in the future can never be extrapolated from past trajectories, since the church's continuity consists not in any linear development, but in inventive improvisations that remain faithful to the past only by virtue of something unfounded and excessive. Theology, therefore, is always a risk and a venture; there is no legitimate way to ensure its safety in advance. The practice

---

58. Ernst Käsemann, "The Problem of the Historical Jesus," in *Essays on New Testament Themes*, trans. W. J. Montague, Studies in Biblical Theology 41 (London: SCM, 1964) 20–21.

59. John Milbank, *Theology and Social Theory: Beyond Secular Reason*, 2nd ed. (Oxford: Blackwell, 2006) 386–87.

of theology involves the irreducibility of *decision*—a decision that is not the necessary outcome of any rational process, and so cannot be rendered safe and assured. In its newness and its non-necessity, the decision refuses all guarantees—which is simply to say that theology is a venture of *faith*, and thus always "dangerous thought,"[60] thought balanced on the edge of a knife.

Williams' own theological and ecclesial career provides ample testimony to the essential riskiness of Christian thinking. One can see this capacity for risk and decision in his writings on spirituality, with their sharp accent on God's "anarchic mercy"[61] and on the psychological fragmentation and ambiguity of human life before God. One can see it in his ethical thought, where even a youth's desperate suicide can be dimly but shockingly recognized as a legitimate protest against the world's intolerable disorder, and so as "a converted act" that points to the hope of the gospel.[62] One can see it in his recent intervention in British jurisprudence over the question of *sharia* law—an intervention that caused immediate international disturbance and alarm.[63] Perhaps most strikingly of all, one can see it in his critique of the church's tendency to absolutize certain models of "the family,"[64] and in his attempts both to raise difficult questions about human sexuality and to rethink the nature of Christian identity itself in the context of sexual relationships.[65] Such instances of theological disruption and innovation—characterized as they are by risk, decision, interruption—illustrate vividly Williams' whole conception of orthodox Christian thinking, and of the kind of difficult venture that genuine continuity with tradition demands. Indeed, Williams himself has remarked that the best theology is like "the noise of someone falling over things in the dark"[66]—it is the noise of danger and disruption, of a venture without guarantees. Even if this venture is not

---

60. Williams, "'Adult Geometry': Dangerous Thoughts in R. S. Thomas," in *The Page's Drift: R. S. Thomas at Eighty*, ed. M. Wynn Thomas (Bridgend: Seren, 1993) 82–98.

61. Williams, *Wound of Knowledge*, rev. ed., 17.

62. Williams, *Resurrection*, 42.

63. Williams, "Civil and Religious Law in England: A Religious Perspective," February 7, 2008, http://www.archbishopofcanterbury.org/1575.

64. Williams, "Incarnation and the Renewal of Community," in *On Christian Theology*, 237.

65. Williams, "The Body's Grace," in *Theology and Sexuality: Classic and Contemporary Readings*, ed. Eugene F. Rogers (Oxford: Blackwell, 2002) 309–21.

66. Williams, "Telling the Christmas Story Like It Is."

always wholly successful—and how could it be?—its sole aim is to bear witness to the God who "fully enters into a world of confusion and ambiguity, and works in contradictions."⁶⁷ Through its precariousness, its fragility, its subversion of its own finality, doctrinal formulation bears witness to the God of disruptive grace; and in the moment of witness, the past breaks into the present and so becomes an active, living tradition.

There is therefore no contradiction between doctrine's inventiveness and its fidelity to tradition; on the contrary, it is precisely the excessive moment that generates tradition in the proper sense. Through creative improvisation, the past and present are brought into harmony. Indeed, such improvisation effects a kind of coinherence in which "time present and time past" are united in a single present,⁶⁸ forming one continuing—yet always fragile—tradition. It is thus only through the paradoxical risk of faithful newness that "past" is transposed into "tradition." The tradition finds its own identity retroactively; it is constituted by the creative excess of orthodoxy. Orthodoxy reaches backward. Its *raison d'être* is fidelity to tradition, but, unlike conservatism, it perceives that there is no place—or rather, no time—for tradition other than the present.

The theology of Rowan Williams may sound at times like a person falling over things in the dark; but if that is the case, it is only because Williams wants to exemplify the essential character of doctrinal orthodoxy. The formation of doctrine is never something on which we may calmly look back. It always lies ahead of us as an unfinished task, full of risk and promise.⁶⁹

---

67. Williams, *Wound of Knowledge*, 14.
68. T. S. Eliot, *Four Quartets*, "Burnt Norton."
69. I am grateful to Paul DeHart, Halden Doerge, Kim Fabricius, Michael Jensen, and Matheson Russell for their criticisms of an earlier version of this essay.

4

Krisis? Kritik?:
Judgment and Jesus in the Theology of Rowan Williams

MICHAEL JENSEN

I

In his contribution to the *Festschrift* for Maurice Wiles,[1] Rowan Williams sketches out, with a characteristic deftness of touch, some aspects of their shared commitment to a critical approach to the study of the truth and adequacy of doctrinal statements. Though the two theologians were colleagues at Oxford during the 1980s, what becomes readily apparent is that they were of different generations. Wiles, as Williams presents him, is to be thanked at least for asking the right questions about Christian doctrine—

---

1. Maurice Wiles (1923–2005) was Regius Professor of Divinity at Oxford University from 1970–1991. In *The Making of Christian Doctrine* he explored in critical fashion the validity or legitimacy of early doctrinal affirmations in their shifting intellectual context. Maurice Wiles, *The Making of Christian Doctrine: A Study in the Principles of Early Doctrinal Development* (London: Cambridge University Press, 1967). In 1977 he was prominent among the contributors to an essay collection whose authors challenged the traditional Christian doctrine of the Incarnation. John Hick, ed., *The Myth of God Incarnate* (London: SCM, 1977).

inquiring, for example, as to the production and rhetorical purpose of doctrinal statements.[2] Wiles was raising the pertinent problem of how traditional doctrinal statements, conceived as they were in particular historical and intellectual conditions that are nigh on unrecoverable from the contemporary standpoint, might now be received. For Wiles, the propositional truth of doctrinal formulae is only of secondary interest: he argues that the real focus ought now to be in the "experiential impulse" (Williams' phrase) that generated them. Doctrinal claims (such as the Incarnation) arose rather haphazardly in the patristic era out of an impulse to find an ontological ground for the dramatic experience of the transforming impact of Jesus. Whatever else, Wiles affirms that Jesus does make a difference. The challenge of doctrinal criticism (offered by Wiles, and which Williams accepts) is to "read" this difference, and, furthermore, to read properly the first and subsequent "readings" of him. The tools of this criticism are to be the fine surgical instruments of rational and historical inquiry assisted by the analysis of the role of metaphor in theological language, and the critical awareness of what interests are possibly at work in such doctrinal utterances as have been handed down to us.

Wiles' determination not to park Christian doctrine off the highways of historical criticism makes him an important conversation partner for Williams. Williams is not, however, happy with Wiles' take on the way in which the transforming impact of Jesus is to be described and applied. On Williams' account—and this is why I say rather cheekily that there is a *generational* dispute between the two—Wiles comes very close to the profession of a "very full-blooded abstract universalist rationalism."[3] While professing agnosticism about the veracity of Christian truth-claims, in reality his stance is positively skeptical. In other words, Wiles does in practice tend to favor the settling of issues of truth, whatever his protestations to the contrary. Like the more conservative Pannenberg, Wiles in practice assumes for his criticism the standpoint of a universal tribunal in a quasi-legal paradigm.

2. "Wiles has succeeded in placing on the map of Anglophone theology a set of issues of the first importance." Rowan Williams, "Doctrinal Criticism: Some Questions," in *The Making and Remaking of Christian Doctrine: Essays in Honour of Maurice Wiles*, ed. Sarah Coakley, David A. Pailin, and Maurice Wiles (Oxford: Clarendon, 1993) 240.

3. Williams, "Doctrinal Criticism: Some Questions," 260. Earlier, Williams says of Wiles that he is *not* a "positivist with a pious gloss, looking for simple universal proofs," ibid., 240–41. By the end of his essay, however, one suspects that for Williams, this charge might have some credence, in fact.

He resolves the questions of the veracity of doctrinal propositions—in the negative.[4] Williams reminds us of the Kantian origins of the idea of "criticism" in this mode, and of the post-Enlightenment turn against such "legal" universalism. Williams writes:

> To say that there is no universal tribunal, that pluralities of perception cannot be settled by "legal action," is not necessarily to doom ourselves to irrationalist relativism. It is, though, to acknowledge that what is sustainable, what can be asserted without arbitrariness ... has more to do with how particular perceptions cope with and absorb contesting claims and maintain elements of critical "listening" provisionality within their own frameworks than with meeting foreordained universal conditions of legality.[5]

For Williams it is axiomatic (he describes it as an epistemological "commonplace") that neutrality is not available in the assessment of traditional doctrinal statements.

The alternative is not, however, hopeless nihilism. Rather, it is the process of "coping with" and "absorbing" the various transitions along the line of Christian tradition that requires attention. That is, one can't posit beforehand the terms by which the validity of doctrinal statements ought to be judged, not least because these statements themselves exist in a dialectical relationship to the conventions of making sense, and involve, repeatedly over the course of history, the transformation and renewal of theological discourse. This is (for Williams) a Christological conviction, as we shall see; but it has a hermeneutical corollary. From Williams' perspective, there is no way in which Jesus can be merely *illustrative* of theological truths which are independent of him: he must rather be *constitutive* for Christian speaking about God. If this is so, doctrine will be "an attempt to do justice to the way in which the narrative and the continuing presence . . . of Jesus is held actively to shape present horizons, in judgement and in grace."[6]

---

4. Especially this is true of his work in the Incarnation. See Wiles, "Christianity without Incarnation?" in Hick, *The Myth of God Incarnate*, ed. John Hick (London SCM, 1977).

5. Williams, "Doctrinal Criticism: Some Questions," 259.

6. Ibid., 260. Commenting on this very essay in his author's introduction to *Wrestling with Angels*, Williams indicates just how central a thought this is for his whole theological outlook: "The conclusion presses on a Christological point echoed in several other essays directly or indirectly: is the person of Jesus an illustration of something we could know by other means? Or the phenomenon that ultimately demands and moulds a new language for itself? The latter is the presupposition of traditional doctrinal theology, and, as will appear, it is a presupposition that I share." Williams, *Wrestling with Angels: Conversations in Modern Theology*, ed. Mike Higton (London: SCM Press, 2007) xix.

The way in which Williams carefully distances himself from Wiles reveals a great deal about the tenor of his own theology. This piece in conversation with Wiles touches on themes that are given a more full-orbed expression in several other essays. Though definitely affirming the need for "doctrinal criticism," Williams wants to prevent criticism from overwhelming the potential of the theological talk to critique *us*. The objectivist stance of the modernist scholar, *a la* Wiles, will not do.[7] By not allowing the theologian to hold Jesus and the tradition of talking about him at arms length, Williams hopes to show how the "narrative and continuing presence" of Jesus functions as a judgment on the Christian, the church and the world, in such a way that new and surprising possibilities are brought to light. As Williams finally asks, "Wiles is far from insensitive to this priority of *krisis* over *Kritik*; but how can his model of doctrinal criticism allow it its proper weight?"[8]

By "*Kritik*" Williams is referring not just to that historical criticism which questioned the integrity and historical objectivity of the New Testament texts *qua* texts, but also to *Tendenzkritik*—that criticism, originating with F. C. Baur and the Tübingen School, which sought to uncover the *interests* at play in the text: "[I]n whose interest does this text work?" While *Tendenz-* or *Ideologiekritik* is usually a practice of biblical criticism, Williams suggests that it may validly be put to work on doctrinal formulations and theological language.[9] In other words, like the texts of Scripture, doctrinal statements are a site of, or a move in, a power struggle. If the scholar can reconstruct the struggle, she may then interpret the text or the doctrine in the light of the struggle. Latterly, postmodern and liberationist hermeneutics have taken up the project of *Tendenzkritik*, deploying Foucauldian, Derridean, Marxist, and feminist paradigms and theoretical

---

7. Is Williams then a "postmodernist"? I am not sure that this term has today the descriptive usefulness it once might have had. Certainly, Williams is determined to understand from within as much as possible, whereas Wiles finally determines to stand over and against. However, as he insists, Williams is not a radical skeptic, just critically wary of epistemological claims that are a little too sanguine. In another respect, Williams is quite "postmodern": throughout his work, he is acutely sensitive to the charge that theological language can be and has indeed been used in the service of power in a malevolent way; though as we shall see, this sensitivity came in with *Tendenzkritik* in the nineteenth century.

8. Williams, "Doctrinal Criticism: Some Questions," 261.

9. His particular complaint with Wiles is that not all styles of biblical criticism may be validly applied to doctrinal statements. Literary and historical criticism turn out to be a rather blunt instruments for deciding the validity of dogmas.

methods to the same ends. Williams hopes that this kind of criticism may be the start of a process of study that is finally quite constructive; *Tendenzkritik* ought to alert us to features of the text or doctrinal utterance which point to subversion of its own power claims, thereby alerting us to its potential to generate *our own* process of self-criticism and growth.

The "priority of *krisis* over *Kritik*" is a—perhaps *the*—salient feature of Williams' own theological landscape. Williams insists repeatedly that the narrative of Jesus in a unique and remarkable way brings us to a point of judgment from which new possibilities in human life may spring forth. This is after all what the foundational texts themselves show (on Williams' account): their testimony to the encounter with Jesus of Nazareth shows the process of reflection, development, and change, and the stumbling, barely articulate attempt to give expression to the experience of new life found in him. Thus the theologian must ask, what is it that is true of Jesus that makes some sense of the church's experience of transformative new life as human beings in relation to God?

In turn, *krisis* properly received actually propels *Kritik*: if we are exposed as we ought to be by encounter with the life of Jesus, a critical scrutiny of theological language is what ought to follow. Williams would argue that self-subversion is already a feature not only of the early history of Christian doctrine but also of the New Testament texts themselves. There is, inbuilt in Christian speech about God, a holding-back, a reservation, and an awareness of its own limitations, which "authorizes" a similarly self-critical approach to dogma. *Kritik,* as Williams conceives of it, is a practice that is faithful to the trajectory of Christian experience itself.

Williams thus offers what might be described as a "judgment Christology," a Christology that is offered as an ever critical and unsettling point against which human persons and cultures—and even the church itself—are to be measured, and by which they are to be opened up to the new. The person of Jesus is the eye of the storm, as it were. But is it enough? Has Williams escaped the bite of his own question to Wiles? Isn't Williams himself making Jesus secondary to a more general concept of judgment? This present essay, then, attempts to analyze and evaluate the presence of "judgment" (*krisis*) as a hinge in Williams' theology.

II

Williams speaks of "judgment" (with "conversion") as the basis of Christian dogma itself.[10] This is an essentially Christological claim—it is Jesus who is constitutive for Christian thought. As he writes in another piece: "the meaning of Jesus is not the container of all other meanings but their test, judgement and catalyst."[11] Williams is well aware that this is not an approach shared by all theologians, many of whom would offer something more akin to a dogmatic proposition or affirmation as a first principle—the Incarnation, for example.[12] So, how does William come to place "judgment" in such a significant position?

The answer, as Williams painstakingly works it out in a number of studies, is hermeneutical. Williams largely accepts that almost two centuries of historical-critical work on the text of the Bible have made reading Scripture as a seamless unity hopelessly naïve. However, this is not a cause for dismay, as far as Williams is concerned. Contrary to those older voices who would see the authority of Scripture as greatly diminished by historical criticism of the Bible, Williams actually sees the authority and significance of Scripture as found *in* the diverse, partially inchoate and evidently worked-on text. Scripture always incorporated within its boundaries a plurality of voices and indeed a plurality of perspectives. Its unity is an irreducible plurality. This plurality can be accepted as a unit, but only if it is seen as *responsive* to a generative event, a story of God's re-creative action. Because it is responsive to this event at its centre, it shows evidence of a *development* in thinking—the first steps in Christian theologizing, which in their turn reveal that the original encounter had the capacity to generate new possibilities. Historical criticism has only revealed what was in fact always the case: that the New Testament is the record of the first awed, stumbling responses to an encounter with Jesus of Nazareth. Conclusive access to the historical events behind the New Testament is not really possible; but then desiring it misses the point of the texts themselves. It is not as if there are layers of interpretative material that can be scraped away leaving a basic, factual core; rather, the New Testament is interpretation all the way down.

---

10. Williams, "Beginning with the Incarnation," 92.

11. Williams, "The Finality of Christ," 94.

12. See Williams' revision of R. C. Moberly in Williams, "Beginning with the Incarnation."

We should not expect consistency; in fact, we should be delighted *not* to find it, because the inarticulacy and disagreements of the first Christians give us hope that our meager efforts at talking about God are not ultimately futile, whatever their own inadequacy. The canon of Scripture itself serves to hold open the need for review, development, and self-criticism—this is what it means to be under the authority of Scripture.

Having rejected the older "liberal"-modernist paradigm of Wiles, it may have been expected of Williams that he identify himself with the postliberalism of Hans Frei and George Lindbeck.[13] Yet Williams also evinces unease with Lindbeck's construal of the theological task. He is certainly attracted by the possibilities offered by a revival of scriptural categories in theological thinking, as it is outlined in George Lindbeck's landmark book *The Nature of Doctrine*[14]—namely, "the project of inserting the human story into the world of Scripture." Yet Williams confesses to a disquiet at the "territorial" imagery that Lindbeck deploys. He proposes rather that there has been a misunderstanding of the alternatives: that the world of Scripture is a historical world in "which meanings are discovered in action and encounter."[15] Which is to say, Scripture has its own history of being read. It is not simply a matter of holding Scripture as an ahistorical entity into which we can "insert" ourselves; it too is encountered within history, and indeed has its own history.

This text has, of course, generated a huge variety of diverse and even inverse readings. For Williams, when the church comes to interpret the world through its foundational narratives, the very act of interpreting affects the narratives as well as the world.[16] This kind of reflection is *generative* in a further sense: namely, as we discover what the text may become and as we also discover the world afresh through that text. The church, as it absorbs scriptural exegesis even from its own margins and beyond, discovers what it itself has been saying all along. Thus, the church is exposed to a

---

13. Paul DeHart picks up Williams' disquiet with what has become known as "postliberalism." Paul J. DeHart, *The Trial of the Witnesses: The Rise and Decline of Postliberal Theology* (Malden, MA; Oxford: Blackwell, 2006) 178–9.

14. George A. Lindbeck, *The Nature of Doctrine: Religion and Theology in a Postliberal Age* (Louisville: Westminster John Knox, 1984).

15. Williams, "The Judgement of the World," 30.

16. It is, for example, not possible to read the Exodus story following its appropriation by the black slave culture of the Americas without being influenced, even subconsciously, by that appropriation.

judgment, even as it holds out a judgment: "[I]n judging the world, by its confrontation of the world with its own dramatic Scripture, the Church also judges itself."[17] This work of evangelization and self-evangelization requires an exploratory fluidity and provisionality—as it holds out the gospel, the church is always on the run, as it were, always under its own question: "[A]t any point in its history the Church needs both the confidence that it has a gospel to preach, and the ability to see that it cannot readily specify in advance how it will find words for preaching in particular new circumstances."[18] So, the church is constantly seeking a pathway marked by confidence that there is a message, but also characterized by an openness to discovering what form that gospel might take as history twists and turns. It cannot point to a technique or a method that will at once and with ease supply it with the articulation it requires; this will rather be discovered through silent, prayerful, and repentant discernment.

The church has after all an essentially missionary core, "seeking to transform the human world by communicating to it in word and act a truthfulness that exposes the deepest human fears and evasions and makes possible the kind of human existence that can pass beyond these fears to a new liberty."[19] Precisely what this is cannot be predicted ahead of time; but it involves a passing of judgment. But this is a difficult and ornery concept—as (by Williams' reading) John's gospel shows.[20] This "judgment" is a complex process of interaction and reflection rather than a simple matter of condemnation or affirmation. Jesus' words and actions require choice for and against; they have the ability to expose hidden motives and understandings, bringing in to the public sphere things that are ordinarily personal. Discipleship itself is constituted by the willingness of the disciple to come to judgment and be part of the community created and sustained by the love of God. What we receive or may receive in encounter with Jesus is a new identity, a change or conversion: "you may recognise your complicity in the rejection of Jesus and at the same time accept the possibility of a different role . . ."[21] The effect of meeting Jesus is to find oneself *both* under sentence of judgment *and* (hence) a recipient of grace.

17. Williams, "The Judgement of the World," 31.
18. Ibid.
19. Ibid.
20. Ibid., 32.
21. Ibid., 33.

The gospel of Jesus—the (re)telling of his story—enables this dual self-discovery in human beings. The Christian then is involved in seeking conversion, as he or she seeks to bring contemporary struggles to judgment and to appropriate some new dimension of the transforming summons of Christ in his or her own life. No totalizing account of this is really possible—which is why Williams finds it hard to be specific at this point. Or (better), this is why he is deliberately not specific at this point, because he would not wish to forestall what possibilities God has in store. What transformations may come or may be hoped for are in a way not the focus—the struggle for sense in the present is. Contrary to what Lindbeck wishes for, namely, to discern the times on the basis of Christian criteria, in a contemplative or noninterventionist way, "the Christian is involved in seeking conversion—the bringing to judgement of contemporary struggles, and the appropriation of some new dimension of the transforming summons of Christ in his or her own life."[22] That is, in preaching the gospel the Christian will inevitably be in the thick of it, not sitting on the sidelines observing.

It is not too much to say that Williams is reticent about any criteria other than judgment in and of itself. The bringing of the world—and the church—to judgment by means of the story of Christ *is* the decisive criterion. This is true even to the extent that what is bedded down as an axiom of Christianity in one generation may well itself require "judgment" in the next. Just what it is about Jesus that will provide that test of judgment, likewise, is not a frozen dogmatic formula, but rather something dynamic, even unforeseen. A dogmatic formula such as the Nicene Creed may both reflect and in turn provide just such a means of allowing Jesus to be our judge; but it certainly will not suffice if it is used as a way of bolstering very human forms of hegemony. Even the truth may become untruthful if it is used without the prior awareness that the encounter with the person of Jesus proclaimed in the gospel ought to bring us to repentance.

Williams is well aware that to speak of judgment in a culture which is so fragmented, and which doesn't accept the language of judgment or a shared set of points of reference, is more than a little problematic. Judgments always take for granted a public, a shared community of speaking and responding in which the judgments made are to be tested and discerned. So, the problem becomes one of how to speak the gospel in the world. What

---

22. Ibid.

is to be said? How to put it so that you yourself are not exempt from the judgment of such a word? The answer is not that the church becomes a kind of morals lobby group, or the keeper of society's "values": "[T]he Church misconceives its missionary task if it . . . echoes the individualistic and facile language of moral retrenchment that often accompanies a further intensification of administrative control and attrition of participatory politics."[23] The Christian message makes global claims, so it is never satisfied with liberal syncretism. (Though, there is a danger in theocratic totalitarianism too: a post-millennial triumphalism, not seeing history as the opportunity for repentance.)

The Christian claim is thus always evolving and being reconstrued along the line of history: "Christians in general and theologians in particular are thus going to be involved as best they can in those enterprises in their culture that seek to create or recover a sense of shared discourse and common purpose in human society."[24] This may mean collaboration with groups that share a common purpose.[25] What Williams advocates is that the church play a supportive role in the search for human unity in Christ. This is a search for what recognizably shares in the same project that the gospel defines. He pleads: "Can we so *rediscover* our own foundational story in the acts and hopes of others that we ourselves are reconverted and are also able to bring those acts and hopes in relation with Christ for their fulfilment by the re-creating grace of God?"[26]

This account of Christian mission involves contemplative attention to the unfamiliar, and a humble realization of the difficulty of speaking. The skills for this should be learnt from speaking, but also from those transformations of scriptural narrative that restore to us or open to us the depth of that with which the narrative deals. Here we are reminded of his account of *Tendenzkritik* in the Wiles piece. So, for instance, feminist exegesis (Williams' example) provides a reading of Scripture that disturbs and upsets our more comfortable readings and so makes possible the judgment—and with it the transformations—that is itself part and parcel of responding to

---

23. Ibid., 35.
24. Ibid., 37.
25. Williams characteristically envisages these groups as "left-leaning" in political terms: Marxists and feminists, for example. But this seems arbitrary. Why not conservatives also? Surely, *some* parts of a conservative agenda might mesh with a Christian one at some points?
26. Williams, "The Judgement of the World," 38.

the gospel of Jesus Christ. Such exegesis keeps character with Jesus' own disruption of the comfortable religious sensibilities of his own day.

III

One of the aspects of Maurice Wiles' thought that Williams especially appreciates is his emphasis on parable. For his part, Williams proposes the intriguing idea of "parabolic speech" as a catalyst for a new kind of life, for "conversion." The parables that Jesus told have the capacity to transform people's perceptions of themselves and their communities. And indeed, his own life is a larger parable of the gospel of challenge and transformation. Jesus' telling of parables and his teaching the disciples how to receive them prepares us for the pattern of loss and recovery of the self that we will see in his death and resurrection story. As Williams puts it:

> The transfiguring of the world in Christ can seem partial or marginal if we have not learned, by speaking and hearing parables, a willingness to lose the identities and perceptions we make for ourselves: all good stories change us if we hear them attentively; the most serious stories change us radically . . . And if we can accept a very general definition of parable as a narrative both dealing with and requiring "conversion," radical loss and radical novelty, it may not be too farfetched to say that the task of theology is the exploration of parable, and so of conversion.[27]

Here *in nuce* is an explanation of what parables do, as Williams sees them. They invite a certain kind of listening first of all: an attentiveness and receptiveness that requires patience and humility. The listener needs to divest himself or herself of attempts to construct personal identity and prepare to be read by the story as much as to read it. This is an ongoing and dynamic process of personal and societal change made possible by engagement with a very significant set of stories. The conversion process is never completed: there is no moment at which even the believer can see himself or herself as above the challenge of the parable. Doctrine alone will not protect us from becoming Pharisees; we must also be open to conversion.

In a telling passage, Williams describes the parables as "crystallizations of how people decide for or against self-destruction, for or against

27. Ibid., 42.

newness of life, acceptance, relatedness."[28] Jesus presents his mini-narratives in the midst of situations and encounters in which the kingdom of God is sought after, or described. Christians do not of course read the parables in isolation, but rather as they have been embedded in the life of the one who spoke them. They are parables which are identified by their association with the life of their author. They are "part of a life."[29] The parables are suggestive of a transformation in human affairs. They teach first the pattern of challenge and change, of loss and recovery, which then makes sense of the Easter events. This has its sense by contributing to the large parable of Jesus' life, death, and resurrection, events which show how the new thing of which the parables speak becomes "concretely possible."[30] In particular, the new thing that arises out of Jesus' life is the new community, the church.[31]

Part of the power of the parables lies, for Williams, in their "secularity." As he says in one of his sermons: "Jesus, in his acts and parables, is a strikingly secular figure, unconcerned to ask questions about the status or purity of those who come to him."[32] Taking his lead from Bonhoeffer's famous appeals for a non-religious language with which to proclaim the gospel, Williams describes Jesus' own language as "non-religious," and so a model of speaking the word of God to be followed. By "non-religious" Williams means that "it is not primarily concerned with securing a space within the world for a particular specialist discourse . . . whether or not it uses the word 'God,' it effects faith, conversion, hope."[33] There is the characteristic Williams emphasis here on what the scriptural words do, as opposed to what they say. Their right function is not imperial, as certainly is the case with some religious talk. So,

> what is mysterious in Christian beginnings is not the experience of hearing the Christian kerygma but the record and image of Jesus himself. His is conceived as a parabolic story, yet it is remembered in diverse and less than wholly coherent narrative forms, whose

---

28. Ibid., 41.
29. Ibid.
30. Ibid.
31. In another place he calls this "dramatic" reading of the text, a notion for which he is indebted to Nicholas Lash. Williams, "The Discipline of Scripture," 50.
32. Williams, *Open to Judgement: Sermons and Addresses* (London: Darton, Longman & Todd, 1994) 54.
33. Williams, "The Judgement of the World," 41.

> historical foundation is uncertain. To be introduced into relation with such a figure is to encounter what is not exhaustible in word or system—or so Christians have concluded: it is to step into faith (rather than definitive enlightenment). In so far as certain features of the development of canon and orthodoxy paradoxically worked against the absorption of Jesus into a thematized religious subjectivity and a system of ideas, they preserved the possibility of preaching Jesus as a questioning and converting presence in ever more diverse cultures and periods, and the possibility of intelligible debate and self-criticism within Christianity.[34]

While this is an intriguing observation regarding the missionary genius of Christianity, I sense here the tendency to some universalized conception of what "religious" means. Jesus did not encounter in the religious rulers of his day merely "religious" rulers but Jewish ones. His specific critique is not of them as religious *qua* religious, but as those who were entrusted with the covenant and its laws and ceremonies. It is not religiosity that is critiqued in and of itself. To posit Jesus as a critic of religion itself risks making him into a Marcionite—or, perhaps less alarmingly, makes him too much of a Harnack, preaching faith to the exclusion of law. Yet the Jesus who taught the parables seems very Jewish: he is radical in the very sense that he calls Israel back to its roots, as well as preparing her for an entirely new act of God. The parables themselves, we ought to remember, make use of profoundly Jewish symbolism: they do not appear as "secular" in the sense that vineyards, sowers, sheep, and seeds were symbols already deeply embedded in the religious self-identity of Israel. They turn the religious life of Israel back to its central meaning and purpose, learnt from the great events of its history. Certainly, the parables are part of the story of a particular man; but, in turn, his story is part of the history of a particular people.

It is worth noting, by way of a genealogy of Williams' thought, that he appears very much indebted to Paul Ricoeur's work on hermeneutics, and especially his work on the parables. In particular, Ricoeur's emphasis on the rhetorical effects of the text—what the text *does*, rather than what it "means," or what its author intends—comes through in Williams' descrip-

---

34. Williams, "Does It Make Sense to Speak of a Pre-Nicene Orthodoxy?" in *The Making of Orthodoxy: Essays in Honour of Henry Chadwick*, ed. Rowan Williams (Cambridge: Cambridge University Press, 2002) 17.

tion of how the parables serve to bring readers to judgment.[35] It is important to emphasize that Ricoeur is no Derridean deconstructor of texts. Ricoeur is not engaged in some power-critique of textuality in itself, but rather is interested in texts as phenomena and in what they do (and have done). Of the parables he writes: "the kingdom of God is not what the parables tell about, but what happens in parables."[36] The parables themselves bring about the kingdom: they explain it by establishing it; they also establish it by explaining it. In another piece we read a point we have previously encountered in Williams:

> we have learned from Joachim Jeremias' marvelous work on the parables that Jesus does something in telling the parables, but the parables in their turn are productive of meaning at the level of the narrative of the life of Jesus. We must understand therefore . . . not just how this personage produces something with this narrative, but how this narrative produces something in the story of this personage.[37]

The necessity of a reading of the parable embedded in the narrative of Jesus' life is paramount if one is to be true to what the parables do.[38]

With this Ricoeurian reading of the parables to hand, Williams gives his account of what theology is and how it relates to its sources. The narrative of the life of Jesus is the point beyond which the theologian's critique must not pass without some awareness of the demand made on him or her. That is to say: theological work cannot keep Jesus at arm's length if it is to be true to its "object." Above all, it is the parables of Jesus themselves that

---

35. For a thoroughly Ricoeurian piece of hermeneutics, see Williams' Larkin Stewart lecture: "The Bible Today: Reading & Hearing," 2007. In this lecture Williams makes what I take to be a characteristic comment: "[T]he Bible itself gives us a cardinal example of 'texts'—oral recitations in this case—clearly intended to effect change: the parables of Jesus. And the sort of change they envisage is the result of being forced to identify yourself within the world of the narrative, to recognise who you are or might be, how your situation is included in what the parable narrates."

36. Ricoeur, *Figuring the Sacred: Religion, Narrative, and Imagination*, trans. David Pellauer (Minneapolis: Fortress, 1995) 165.

37. Ibid., 150.

38. It is not clear whether "the narrative of Jesus' life" means "as reconstructed by scholars" or "as the evangelists depict it." However, both Ricoeur and Williams do give space to the theological voices of the gospel writers (in contrast to the more skeptical approach of a John Dominic Crossan, for example).

draw attention to the world-shattering impact of the gospel; and, indeed, bring *krisis* to pass.

IV

This is of course a truncated and piecemeal account. I have tried to trace but a single theme in Williams' broad and somewhat unsystematic theological canvas in order to point to its continuities and connections, its origins and possibilities. Having said that, the presence of the theme of judgment in Williams' writings is one of the most attractive and fertile things about them. His attempt to break with the rationalism of Wiles is as admirable as his refusal to be corralled into a postliberal ecclesiological foundationalism. The theologian, on Williams' account, must not only be a master of his subject, but be mastered by it. He in turn must be judged and converted by his encounter with the risen Lord, even as he offers his judgments. In this way, Williams accounts for the (by any account) remarkable presence of Jesus as an ongoing, dynamic force in the actual lives of people.[39] What is more, he shows how Christian theology might be—and indeed must be—alert to its own tendency to use both Scripture itself and doctrinal formulae for self-serving ends.

It only remains to ask once again: has Williams himself evaded the problems that he identifies in Wiles? Like Wiles, Williams has a sense that patristic, creedal dogma is secondary to an experience of God. It is in accounting for that experience, and for what elements of that experience can be articulated in an ongoing way, that they differ. But has Williams managed to burrow into the world of the text such that *krisis*—that moment of decision when we are confronted, and even judged by what we meet in the text—is allowed its prominence (in a way that he feels it isn't with Wiles)? Williams attempts to see from within, but has he smuggled in an objectivism—the kind of objectivism he repudiates—somewhere along the line? *Tendenzkritik*, that form of criticism most concerned with uncovering in the text the interests of various individuals and communities, *per definition* tends to be hypersuspicious of "interests." It holds as its moral

---

39. One way to sum up Williams' theological project might be to say that it is attempting to answer the question, "How is it that the church exists?"—a question both of historical and contemporary interest.

starting point the critique of "interest" itself. Is it not the case, however, that Williams' version of *krisis*—his teaching on the judgment of Christ—resembles the values of *Tendenzkritik*?

That is to say: Williams seems to operate with a definite set of moral presuppositions. For example, he is tentative in his claims about language because of the tendency of individuals and groups to use language—and perhaps religious language more than any other kind—for their own interests. This is what the life and death of Jesus of Nazareth exposes to us, on his account. Williams argues that *Kritik* is the right kind of intellectual work prompted by an encounter with Jesus: it takes his judgment and applies it self-critically to the practice of Christian speaking and thinking about God. This is modeled for us in the foundational documents themselves, especially in the parables. Yet is it not surely the case that this reading of Jesus, and this application of Jesus' teaching, is itself generated by the application of critical methods to the New Testament (and to Christian doctrine)? It goes without saying that the history of New Testament scholarship is dominated by the triumphant revelation by each generation of the prejudices and preferences of the previous one.[40] It is as value-laden and interest-serving as it claims the New Testament is. Indeed, liberationist and feminist theologies are explicitly cross-referenced to ideologies that are not generated from the narrative of Jesus. If *Tendenzkritik* reveals that Jesus was also a *Tendenzkritiker,* ought we not be a little suspicious as to whether *krisis* really has the priority?

Williams in reply would insist that it is genuinely possible to do theology in a way that is responsive to God and generated by the impact of Christ's life and death, and resurrection. His idea of "judgment" is not, he claims, simply equivalent to Wiles' objectivist rationality. Even if it makes use of tools that arise from outside theological discourse, the tools selected are complementary to it. What is more, Williams remains confident that attention to the difficult questions raised by *Tendenzkritik* will reveal that there is a good deal of the Christian message which is subversive of its own claims to absolutist and self-assertive speech—that is, we will find the New Testament and the developing stream of theology happily aware of the ambiguities and limitations of their own claims.

However much we might like to grant this point—discovering, for example, that the disciples clearly cast themselves in an unheroic role as

---

40. See Stephen Neill and N. T. Wright, *The Interpretation of the New Testament, 1861–1986,* 2nd ed. (Oxford: Oxford University Press, 1988).

they retold the gospel story—it still remains the case that the version of Christian theology produced by *Tendenzkritik* is subject to criteria that appear to come from elsewhere. And it could very well be argued that what they see in Jesus and his story is very much that which you would expect them to see. My first charge then is that Williams' exposition of *krisis* is a product itself of *Kritik*, rather than the other way around.

A second difficulty emerges from the first: once *Tendenzkritik* is in the tank, it tends to devour all the other fish. Where then does *Kritik* end and *krisis* begin for Williams? Can we so readily shift from one to the other? Is it a moral possibility to describe a text which, we are told, is so beset with interest-laden and inadequate human talk, as "Scripture"—namely, as an authoritative text in matters of the divine? It is difficult to see how, on Williams' account, we can read the New Testament and believe Christian doctrines with any confidence that we will be able to apply the right filtration to the texts and so be judged *by* them in exactly the right way. Can we really be both radically suspicious and humbly naïve about the text, and about Christian doctrine, at one and the same time? Can we begin as the judge and end as the judged? Are we not then, as suspicious readers on the one hand, and Christian believers on the other, involved in a kind of double life?

Perhaps Williams might say that this is precisely the tension Christian theologians *ought* to experience if they are to be driven to faith, not in their own critical work, but in Jesus. Above all, Williams is a theologian who seeks to mend the rift that has opened up between Christian spirituality and Christian thought. This is in the end what attention to "judgment" is meant to achieve in his writing. Even if we are uncertain as to whether Williams has built a bridge over which traffic may pass in either direction, there is still ample reason to applaud the identification of the chasm and the desire to build over it.

5

Dispossession and Negotiation:
Rowan Williams on Hegel and Political Theology

MATHESON RUSSELL

Rowan Williams' political writings are littered with *agonistic* language. Peace, unity, harmony, and reconciliation—these are, for Williams, nothing if not the fruits of *struggle, conflict*, and *confrontation*; they are the fruits, more specifically, of *difficult and risky "negotiations."* We may indulge in fantasies of peace as a state of passivity or pre-political innocence, but such fantasies betray a desire to be free of the responsibility of action, to be emancipated from the ambiguities of history, and to be liberated from dependence on others and their dependence on us.

On one hand, this emphasis derives from Williams' interpretation of the gospel as *krisis*. The gospel unsettles our illusions of peace and shows us that the path to peace—the true event of divine grace—is found not in sublime detachment but in the struggle of discipleship, the work of conversion. The gospel enables us and calls us to face the truth of ourselves and our world in sober judgment and with the resources of repentance and forgiveness.

On the other hand, the stress upon the necessity of "difficult negotiations" in Williams' social criticism is grounded in a sophisticated social theory and political theology that he develops through a confrontation with the philosophy of Georg Wilhelm Friedrich Hegel. What the gospel of Christ means for contemporary society, for Williams, is cashed out in this social theory and political theology.

The present chapter focuses on this social and political theory, and seeks to provide a critical assessment of it. It does so primarily through an analysis of Williams' three major essays on Hegel.[1]

The chapter begins, in section I, with a consideration of Williams' defense of Hegel's dialectical conception of the relation between self and other. Section II then analyses his *theological* interpretation of this dialectical movement in terms of "dispossession." Hegel's dialectics (now understood as a "thinking in dispossession") is cashed out by Williams in his theory of "negotiation," and this theory is explicated in section III. Section IV then attempts to draw out the normative implications of the theory of "negotiation"—in particular, its relation to the demands of justice. In section V, we turn from Williams' critical social theory to his political theology. Here it is argued that, for Williams, the mission of the church is to incarnate the ideal of "dispossessing" or "kenotic" communicative action. Section VI then offers some critical reflections, especially focusing on the resulting conception of the relation between the church and secular society.

I

There is a certain postmodern orthodoxy according to which Hegel epitomizes all that is most objectionable about Enlightenment rationalism. Hegel's philosophy, it is said, thinks of thinking as an ever-expanding conceptual comprehension by mind (or "spirit") of the pre-conceptual world (or "nature"), culminating ostensibly in a god-like standpoint of Absolute

---

1. Williams, "Hegel and the Gods of Postmodernity," in *Shadow of Spirit: Postmodernism and Religion*, ed. Philippa Berry and Andrew Wernick (London: Routledge, 1992) 72–80; "Between Politics and Metaphysics: Reflections in the Wake of Gillian Rose," *Modern Theology* 11 (1995) 3–22; and "Logic and Spirit in Hegel," in *Post-Secular Philosophy: Between Philosophy and Theology*, ed. Phillip Blond (London: Routledge, 1998) 116–30. Since work on this essay began, all three essays have conveniently been gathered together and reprinted in Williams, *Wrestling with Angels: Conversations in Modern Theology*, ed. Mike Higton (London: SCM, 2007). In what follows, I shall simply refer to the pagination of this edition.

Knowing. On Hegel's understanding, according to this reading, all that is external to the subject ("the other") is to be the possession of the rational self ("the same") and is desired as an instrument to serve the "rational" ends of the willing subject. What Hegel calls "reason," therefore, is essentially the *subjugation* of all that is, in all its manifold contingency and difference, to the univocal, monological, and exploitative reign of the knowing subject. Such, it is claimed, is the ultimate significance of the much-ventilated Hegelian "dialectic." But the colonizing pretensions of the knowing subject must be opposed; the otherness of the other must be preserved and defended; rationality must be made to recognize its limits, its finitude. The proximate goal of much "philosophy of difference" is thus the overcoming of Hegel. Different strategies are employed to achieve this end. But common to many is the tactic of using the spanner of otherness and difference—*absolute* otherness, *absolute* difference—a heteronomy that is irreducible, unspeakable, and sacred, to jam the cogs of exchange, system, and totality.

For Williams, however, this anti-Hegelian brand of postmodernism delivers us over to "a depoliticised—even anti-political—aesthetic"[2] and a "fundamentally tragic and ironic" a/theology[3] that paradoxically comes close to essentializing "a violent denial or repudiation of the other as beyond understanding."[4] In short, it leads to bad politics, bad theology, and bad philosophy.[5] The "overcoming" of Hegel thus brings with it its own set of characteristic aporias. What's more, Williams' view is that all of this rests on a fundamental *misreading* of Hegel. Properly understood, Hegel's dialectics is not guilty of the crimes of which it is accused, and on the contrary offers the very means by which justice can be done to the other.[6] Let us see how Williams fleshes out these arguments.

---

2. Williams, "Hegel and the Gods of Postmodernity," in *Wrestling with Angels*, 31.

3. Ibid., 27. Paraphrasing approvingly the analysis of Peter Crafts Hodgson, *God in History: Shapes of Freedom* (Nashville: Abingdon, 1989) 88.

4. Williams, "Between Politics and Metaphysics: Reflections in the Wake of Gillian Rose," in *Wrestling with Angels*, 70.

5. Limitations of space prevent a full discussion of Williams' critique of postmodernism. See especially Williams, "Hegel and the Gods of Postmodernity" and "Balthasar and Difference," in *Wrestling with Angels*, 77–79.

6. As Williams freely admits, this argument is deeply influenced by the work of Gillian Rose. See especially Gillian Rose, *Hegel Contra Sociology* (Cambridge: Cambridge University Press, 1981); idem, *The Broken Middle: Out of Our Ancient Society* (Oxford: Blackwell, 1992); and idem, *Judaism and Modernity: Philosophical Essays* (Oxford: Blackwell, 1993).

To begin with, he argues, we need to realize that Hegel's dialectic is not at all a "return to the same" or an "effacement of difference." The labor of reflection seeks, through novel and unforeseen conceptual transformations, a *mediated* relation to the other that is more satisfactory, more attentive—perhaps even more responsive and responsible—than the mere "abstract" opposition that determines the other as "not the self." And yet the mediated relation remains a relation to the other *qua* other. Through the labor of thinking, difference is not denied but rather, to use the Hegelian term, "sublated" (*aufgehoben*): it is both *preserved* and *overcome*. The reflective movement does not leave the other untouched, to be sure; a certain "violence" is necessarily visited upon the other as its illusion of absolute independence is shattered, just as it is concomitantly visited upon my own illusions of solipsistic or hedonistic isolation.[7] Neither party, neither standpoint is left unaltered by the encounter. Nonetheless, this is far from a suppression of otherness in the "return to the same"; it can be described as such, Williams writes, only "by a violent abstraction from the fact that this otherness is constituted substantially by the passage of (irreversible) time."[8] Hegelian dialectics, then, properly understood, does not reduce plurality or efface difference but precisely recognizes it as such by learning how to be alongside the other, how to make sense of the other *qua* other.

Reflecting on this more sympathetic reconstruction of Hegel's philosophy, Williams writes: "We are pressing towards a metaphysic in which difference is *neither* (at any moment) final, a matter of mutual exclusion, *nor* simply reducible, a matter of misperception to be resolved by either a return to the same or a cancellation of one term before the Other."[9]

From this point of view, the intelligibility of the other need not be denied in principle in order for justice to be done to the otherness of the other—*pace* the strategy of the anti-Hegelians, who attempt to preserve the other in its otherness by sacralizing the other as beyond understanding. On the contrary, for Williams, the *only* means by which justice can be done *to the other* in the actuality of a historical context is through "the painful job of discovering my moral substance *in relation* [*to the other*] and so honouring

---

7. The description of dialectical negotiation as "violent" is carefully taken up by Williams following Rose. See Williams, "Between Politics and Metaphysics," 60ff.

8. Williams, "Hegel and the Gods of Postmodernity," 28.

9. Williams, "Between Politics and Metaphysics," 71.

the other's moral substance in the process of uncovering and understanding my own."[10]

Williams thus defends Hegelian dialectical logic. But the argument is given force by a further claim: that the dialectical logic articulated by Hegel, the logic by which thinking self-critically thinks itself and relates itself to that which is other in ever more concrete terms, is not an abstract intellectual movement[11] but represents in fact nothing less than a comprehensive *social theory*. For, dialectics belongs precisely to the historical sphere of actual position-taking, and position-taking is evident in social relations just as much as it is in assertions or thoughts. Anything that embodies a stance with respect to self and world is the taking of a position and is, in principle, able to be taken up as a moment within the self-critical logic of thinking. The thinking of thinking is therefore necessarily a social theory since "thinking" occurs in the reflective self-corrections of the system of concrete social relations that constitutes "spirit." The goal of thinking is not a merely intellectual "product," but the movement "towards an actuality in which the dualisms of self and world, thought and deed, [are] sublated."[12] For this reason, according to Williams, "a social theory that is not ultimately a thinking of thinking is still stuck at a pre-speculative and so (strictly) pre-political stage."[13]

Below we shall see how this social dialectic is inherently related to the quest for justice. But already the direction of the argument is clearly anticipated: the anti-Hegelian stance discussed above equates the dialectics of reason with the sphere of unfreedom. But, for Williams (following Hegel), discourse, narrative, exchange, negotiation, history—these are not the problem but the very medium through which emancipation occurs. The social labor of thinking is the only path to social transformation. "If it is *not* to continue, then, in Hegelian terms, there is no liberation from that partial or pre-reflective or fetishistic practice that turns violently on spirit itself . . ."[14]

---

10. Ibid., 70, emphasis added.

11. Karl Marx was perhaps the first to erroneously charge Hegel with this kind of intellectualism, which Williams glosses as "the 'Fichtean' reading that reverts to a mythology of spirit diffusing itself in nature and fails to break through the opposition between thinking and the given, between the active Inside and the passive Outside," ibid., 69.

12. Williams, "Hegel and the Gods of Postmodernity," 30–31.

13. Williams, "Between Politics and Metaphysics," 69.

14. Williams, "Hegel and the Gods of Postmodernity," 32–33.

The work of social meaning—this, he says, is where we must locate the "authentically critical philosophy."[15]

II

What does the dialectical movement of thinking or reflection amount to? It is interpreted by Williams under the category of "dispossession," by which he means both "the constant rediscovery and critique of the myth of the *self as owner* of its perceptions and positions" and the unsettling of all claims to "the final resolution of how we define and speak of *our interest*."[16] The concept is fleshed out in the following passage:

> at each stage of reflection, we are made aware, if we do not run away from the contradictions and difficulties, of the impossibility of *thinking* reality in terms of individuals "owning" selves, ideas, property in a fixed and uncontended way. We are always redistributing, never timelessly sure of our "interest." Thought unsettles any definition of my interest or our (specific group) interest, and it does so largely through the tracing of the changes of consciousness in history. This does not seek to provide a teleological or evolutionary story in a simple sense; but it does or should lay bare to us the character of thought as sensing its own misrecognitions and non-communications, as dissatisfied with its self-positioning even though it never avoids self-positioning.[17]

A number of important ideas are introduced here. Subjectivity, selfhood or position-taking is not a static structure. Reflection "dispossesses" us of our idea of ourselves; and insofar as this means relinquishing an entire existential mode of being-in-the-world, it signifies the loss of our very selves. When we undergo "experiences" (*Erfahrungen*) so profound that they bring us to a critical self-awareness that our fundamental interpretation of self and world is inadequate, we experience a conversion (of sorts) and we, like a snake shuffling out of its old skin, transpose ourselves into a new mode of subjectivity, a new fundamental interpretation of self and world. In Williams' estimation, a *constant* is named here: "truth requires loss." That is to say: "existence as a subject is recognised or re-learned all the time as a

---

15. Ibid., 32.
16. Williams, "Between Politics and Metaphysics," 70, emphasis added.
17. Ibid., 68.

process of self-displacement, a never-ending 'adjustment' in search of the situation where there is real mutual recognition and thus effective common action..."[18]

At this juncture, it is important to note that the term "dispossession" is, for Williams, meant to evoke—or even translate—the theological term *kenosis*.[19] In the theological context, *kenosis* or "emptying" refers to the career of Christ, i.e. his incarnation, suffering, and crucifixion (especially as narrated in Phil 2:6–8). In the Christian tradition this act comes to define the very essence of love. There is, for Williams, then, a deep connection between the "dispossession" of properly dialectical thinking and self-sacrificial love of the other.

This nexus between dialectics and the theology of the cross is, of course, by no means extrinsic to Hegel's own intellectual horizons.[20] As Williams explains, "Hegel's question ... is how, historically, we come to think of thinking in the framework of dispossession; and his answer is, of course, that this requires a history that can be told as the narrative of the absolute's self-loss and self-recovery. Hegel's genius is to read the Judeao-Christian narrative as precisely this."[21]

If we come to think about thinking as a dialectical movement of dispossession, this is "because of the presence of certain narratives about God and God's people, narratives that insist on speaking of divine displacement in one sense or another."[22] The Christian story is the historical *conditio sine qua non* of our understanding thinking as dispossession.

Put briefly, the Christian story centers around the narrative of the absolute's self-alienation into its other, into history, creatureliness, finitude. God is entirely self-sufficient, non-dependent upon the world; but God's aseity is unthinkable apart from self-differentiation into what is other and

18. Ibid., 70.
19. Ibid., 72.
20. Williams' insistence on giving full weight to the theology underlying Hegel's philosophical system mirrors a general trend in recent Hegel scholarship, driven largely by the impressive studies of Peter C. Hodgson. See Hodgson, *God in History: Shapes of Freedom*; and idem, *Hegel and Christian Theology: A Reading of the Lectures on the Philosophy of Religion* (Oxford: Oxford University Press, 2005). See also Robert M. Wallace, *Hegel's Philosophy of Reality, Freedom, and God* (Cambridge: Cambridge University Press, 2005); and Andrew Shanks, *Hegel's Political Theology* (Cambridge: Cambridge University Press, 1991).
21. Williams, "Between Politics and Metaphysics," 71.
22. Ibid., 73.

self-recovery *as* a non-dependent existence.[23] The Christian story says that God "surrender[s] the no-place of an abstract absolute being, enacting the indiscriminate love or inclusive compassion that eventuates from divine life in a historical process (Israel, Jesus, the Church)."[24] And this *act* of God's being—in theological terms, the begetting of the Son by the Father—is what constitutes God as "Spirit" or, what amounts to the same thing, as "eternal love."[25] This is the theo-logic underwriting the creation of the world and the incarnation of Christ; in Hegelian terms, God is "the living process of positing His Other, the world, which, comprehended in its divine form is His Son."[26]

The Christian narrative concerning God, the self-subsisting absolute who nonetheless gratuitously *empties* himself into his other as self-differentiation and self-recovery, represents the indispensable ontological ground for the Hegelian conception of reason and politics (since the two are one). The "grammar" of orthodox Trinitarian theology is the "grammar" of thought.[27] Or, to put the same point differently and somewhat provocatively, for Hegel the dialectical logic of thinking is the dialectical logic of love:

> Not enough is normally granted to Hegel's (admittedly tentative and undeveloped) assimilation of the process of thinking to love, understood as the self's being-in-the-other . . . It is precisely the model of thinking as a form of love that secures the real *otherness* of what is thought and thus the real voiding or negating of the self-identical subject and the final vision of thought as communal, its identity established only in the mediation of a shared language and in the recognition by each of the identity of the mental process in all . . .[28]

23. Cf. Williams, "Logic and Spirit in Hegel," in *Wrestling with Angels*, 47.

24. Williams, "Between Politics and Metaphysics," 72.

25. Hegel, *Lectures on the Philosophy of Religion: One-Volume Edition, the Lectures of 1827*, ed. Peter C. Hodgson (Berkeley: University of California Press, 1988) 418.

26. Quoted by Williams, "Logic and Spirit in Hegel," 41, from the second *Zusatz* of the Introduction to Hegel's *Philosophy of Nature* in *Hegel: The Essential Writings* (New York: Harper & Row, 1974) 209.

27. "[I]t is precisely the grammar (including the paradoxes) of classical pre-Cartesian theology that shapes the actual structure of thinking about thinking. To think about thinking must, for Hegel, bring us finally to the point to which theology directs us, to a reality that is determined solely as self-relatedness: the grammar of the God of Augustine, Anselm and Aquinas is the grammar of thought, and without the former the scope of the later could not be apprehended," ibid., 38.

28. Ibid., 48–49.

Furthermore, the grammar of Hegel's theology is, in Luther's terms, the "speculative" grammar of a *theologia crucis* (as opposed to a *theologia gloriae*).[29] For Hegel, "the humanity of God incarnate is not a 'picture' of the divine power, but the enacting of divine resource in the *poverty*, *pain* and *negativity* of a life and death which could not by any stretch of the imagination be held up as natural symbols of divine identity."[30] Because this or that historical actuality is *not* the absolute, *not* divine, the appearance of the divine in history can only have the character of *negation*. Thus, as Williams says, the most "divine" moment in human history is the one in which "the sheer historical vulnerability of the human is most starkly shown, where unfinishedness, tension, the rejection of meaning and community are displayed."[31] And this, of course, refers in the first instance to the cross of Christ. The destitution of Christ on the cross is the most profound revelation of God's grace *because* it is the most profound disclosure of the godlessness of humanity: "To understand the (historical) cross as God's is to understand the negative 'speculatively'—the negative not as absence or mystery but as the denial of human spirituality in oppression, suffering and death."[32]

How can this dark night of the soul be a moment of grace? Only because its stark judgment upon humanity is the condition for the possibility of conversion, repentance, and reconciliation with God, for (historical) movement towards the divine (future). The negation, the diremption, the scattering, the judgment, is itself the moment of grace insofar as it evokes a response of thoughtful re-formation, the re-creation of life in novel forms (the "spiritual community"); "Because [the negative] is the negation of the human itself, it demands to be *thought* if the project of communication is to continue."[33] And thus, after the speculative Good Friday comes the new life of Easter Sunday.

In good Hegelian fashion, Williams draws from this whole analysis the following threefold conclusion:

---

29. On what follows, see also ibid., 44–45.
30. Williams, "Hegel and the Gods of Postmodernity," 32, emphasis added.
31. Ibid.
32. Ibid.
33. Ibid.

(i) that the *future* of God and the *future* of the reasoning subject do not stand in contradiction but rather are confluent and compatible ("the sacred is our fruition not our annihilation");

(ii) that the *history* of God and the *history* of humanity are nonetheless at each point discordant and non-coincident, since only under such conditions is there history at all;

(iii) that, by implication, (as stated above) the most "divine" moment in human history, the moment of grace, is the one in which "the sheer historical vulnerability of the human is most starkly shown, where unfinishedness, tension, the rejection of meaning and community are displayed."[34]

Hegel thus gives us a new way to understand the idea of "negative theology." It is "negative" not because it faces an absolute limit or prohibition (Kant, Levinas), but because it is structured by the *dialectical* labor of diremption and reconciliation, dispossession and recreation, or, if you will, judgment and redemption.[35] Negativity remains, like the event of "grace" as conceived by the anti-Hegelian postmodernists, an event of interruption, even de-construction. However, the Hegelian conception of negativity also makes it possible to see the re-constructive labor of exchange, negotiation or reflection as a participation in the gracious activity of God. And this, Williams remarks, places us back squarely within "a religious tradition committed to both divine liberty and divine 'commitment' to a historical life and a social practice, whose mark of godliness is self-critical vigilance (what used to be called repentance, I think)."[36]

In the following two sections, I show how Williams concretizes this Hegelian understanding of "thinking in dispossession"[37] in terms of a practice of "negotiation."

---

34. Ibid.

35. This reading of Hegel evidently brings the discussion into close proximity to Karl Barth's "dialectical" conception of theology. An explicit nod in this direction is given in Williams, "Beginning with the Incarnation," 91. It is worth comparing in this connection the analysis of the relation between Barth and Hegel in Williams, "Barth on the Triune God," in *Wrestling with Angels*. However, it must be borne in mind that Williams' own understanding of Hegel has undergone significant development since writing that piece in 1979.

36. Williams, "Hegel and the Gods of Postmodernity," 33.

37. Williams, "Between Politics and Metaphysics," 73.

III

In Williams' essays on Hegel, it is not always easy to discern where the German Idealist ends and the Welsh Anglican begins. By now it should be clear that Hegel is a major source of inspiration for Williams' philosophical attitudes. On the other hand, Williams is by no means an unreconstructed Hegelian; and, even where Hegel's influence is present, Williams' work tends not to be governed exclusively by the horizon of Hegelian ideas and vocabulary. His standpoint is manifestly the product of an engagement with wider philosophical horizons; it testifies to an independent philosophical imagination. This becomes clear, for example, when Williams translates Hegel's social theory into the language of "negotiation."

"Negotiation," as Williams uses the term, designates all those forms of social interaction "from plain conversation to political activity" through which we seek to disclose the truth concerning our situation and to organize our collective existence. And "exchange" is his umbrella term for "the whole range of *negotiated* human activity," encompassing

> all those contexts in which resistance and misunderstanding have to be overcome, concealed interests and agenda drawn out and confronted, the implicit or explicit refusal of a voice of an interlocutor overturned, and a concluding position, not simply determined by one speaker, arrived at . . .[38]

As we have already seen, Williams is committed (for theological reasons)[39] to the development of a social and political theory that explicitly includes a *theory* of—not merely a *critique* of—exchange. So how does Williams develop his account of "negotiated" human activity?

Negotiations are necessitated by practical issues that arise in common life, by the fact that "desire can be and is frustrated by the access of others to goods."[40] "To find our way around in such an environment is

---

38. Williams, "Hegel and the Gods of Postmodernity," 28.

39. In summary, we might locate these theological reasons in Williams' commitment to the so-called incarnational principle. On the basis of the doctrine of the Incarnation, which signifies that the temporal sphere *can be*—and in fact *is*—a theater of divine grace, this principle represents a fundamental affirmation of the temporal sphere *as such*—the sphere of language and communication, social interaction and political activity. The "negative," "speculative" or "prophetic" character of Williams' *interpretation* of this principle, however, signals a deliberate departure from the Anglican "incarnationalist consensus." See Williams, "Incarnation and the Renewal of Community," in *On Christian Theology*.

40. Williams, "Between Politics and Metaphysics," 55.

inevitably to be brought up against exchange and labour in respect of the desire of others; so that an account of speech which ignores scarcity and the consequent problem of mutual limitation is one that has no purchase on material agency."[41] We negotiate because of the tensions between desires, available goods, and the social norms and institutions that more or less adequately mediate the two.

These pragmatic conditions framing the process of negotiation in turn give rise to implicit normative demands upon the speakers and actors who participate in that process, in particular the demand that their interactions with each other *contribute* to the project of negotiation, and hence that each act of communication be discursively justifiable (at least in principle) in terms of that project. These implicit normative demands are satisfied to the extent that the speech act or behavior in question "*sustains intelligibility* in the exchanges and negotiations that constitute our actuality."[42] If, for example, someone proposes that tax relief be given to a certain class of individuals in a society, interlocutors are entitled to seek clarification as to how this intervention would sublate existing social-material tensions and restructure the society in an intelligible and sustainable fashion. Where such justifications cannot be given, these interlocutors would have reason to suspect that the proposal may actually render the society less intelligible (or, if you like, more meaningless—here we have in view, at least obliquely, the problem of nihilism). The proposal therefore will not count as a legitimate contribution to the social project of negotiation.

Notice that what gives coherence to the process of negotiation is the struggle for "recognition."[43] What matters at each step is whether the community at large is able to recognize the speech acts or behavior of another as "analogous to their own" and hence as intelligible within the horizon of the project of exchange and negotiation.[44] An act only serves to further the

41. Ibid.

42. Ibid., 54, emphasis added. These normative demands are evidently implied *both* when speech or behavior is conventional and follows established patterns *and* when novel speech or behavior is introduced, since in either case the acts constitute an episode in the ongoing negotiations (whether they are intended to or not).

43. Williams speaks of "the question of recognition and thus of internal critique," ibid. As will become clear, however, we are referring here to a different phenomenon than that named by Axel Honneth as the "struggle for recognition." Cf. Axel Honneth, *The Struggle for Recognition: The Moral Grammar of Social Conflicts*, trans. Joel Anderson, 1st MIT Press ed. (Cambridge, MA: MIT Press, 1996).

44. Williams, "Between Politics and Metaphysics," 57.

project of negotiation when others are able to make sense of the act as a legitimate "move" in the ongoing negotiation and either dismiss it or adopt it for themselves as a provisionally settled position. If it fails to receive intersubjective recognition, an act—irrespective of the actor's intention—has no significance in the evolution of the social system; it does not affect the common self-understanding of the society. Others must be able to "see" the act as something that is able to be "followed" in order for it to be a *communicative* action, in order for it to *count*; this means, at the same time, that others must be able to "see" the initial act itself as following a rule.[45] Of course, an act may be "seen" as following a *socially deleterious* rule (e.g. smashing every car window in the street, proposing the abolition of all taxes), in which case the act is intelligible but illegitimate as a contribution to the project of negotiation because it is incompatible with sustaining broader social meanings. In any case, the "intelligibility" demanded by the pragmatics of negotiation is an intersubjective intelligibility, a publicly recognized intelligibility; "the sense I make is not under my control."[46]

But why should agents consider themselves bound by intersubjective evaluations? The framework of intersubjective normativity only binds an individual or group to the extent that the individual or group endeavors to "determine and maintain a position from which to communicate."[47] In other words, as individuals or groups we bind ourselves in principle to the normative structures governing acts of communication, insofar as we aspire to the role of participants in the community. Or, to be more precise, we are in fact bound to these normative structures *ab initio* since we always already find ourselves as inheritors of a language and a framework of intelligibility of which we were not the authors, embedded in a community and inhabiting a set of negotiated standpoints and roles within that community. The

---

45. This discussion invokes the work of Wittgenstein on rule following. See Wittgenstein, *Philosophical Investigations*, trans. G. E. M. Anscombe (New York: Macmillan, 1953) §§185–242.

46. Williams, "Between Politics and Metaphysics," 57. Or, more fully: "To 'produce' or to engage in work that issues in the changing of the environment, material or conceptual or imaginative, is to accept conventions or standards, communicative and evaluative conventions, outside the power of the producing agent, if what is produced is to 'count' as a recognisable production, an entity capable of being described and discussed with reference to more than the producer's will in itself." Ibid., 58.

47. Ibid., 54.

task of negotiation, therefore, is one into which we are "thrown" (Heidegger) and not one we opt into.[48]

Some proposals, interventions or acts in the public sphere will fail to contribute to the project of negotiation because they are simply naïve, misdirected or incoherent. However, according to Williams, there are other more insidious "distortions or evasions" that can in effect sabotage the process of negotiation. Of particular importance are those cases where the common project of reaching mutual understanding is short-circuited by sectional or local interests being "absolutized against possible criticism."[49] Such postures, motivated by fear, anxiety, and defensiveness,[50] simply aim to ensure that the interests, perspectives or beliefs held *in advance* by certain parties are made to prevail, that partisan or local interests are imposed without being subjected to intersubjective validation and hence without having been evaluated and critically assimilated. Interventions of this kind are insidious because they seek to stall the very process of negotiation, thereby actually *undermining* the intelligibility of the social system—they are in a strong sense *irrational*. A related but more subtle distortion occurs when "each phase of dialectic, each act of negotiating, systematically ignore[s] its location in a history of exchange, believ[ing] its positions to have no past, no process of construction."[51] Where an ahistorical conception of subjectivity and knowledge is assumed, negotiation appears at best to be an irrelevance and at worst a devilish temptation to compromise what one knows *in advance* to be true. Whereas, in fact, "such a prior commitment to ahistorical

---

48. This is not a *direct* criticism of social contract theory, since few if any social contract theorists think that we do *in fact* opt into civil society. Nonetheless, the "original position" heuristic utilized in one form or another by all social contract theories fundamentally distorts the analysis of our *normative* position vis-à-vis the civil community since it fails to consider the implications of the fact that our communicative involvement in the public sphere is conditioned by inherited positions, arguments, and language, all of which position us from the very outset in a complex set of obligations (as speakers and actors) *by means of which* concrete political thought and action is possible.

49. Williams, "Hegel and the Gods of Postmodernity," 28. It is the absolutizing of one's understanding of one's interests and goals, Williams claims, which leads inevitably to the *domination* or *annihilation* of one party by another, i.e. slavery or war. Cf. Williams, "Between Politics and Metaphysics," 55.

50. See Williams, *The Truce of God: Peacemaking in Troubled Times* (Norwich: Canterbury, 2005) chapters 1 and 6. The logic of fear and defensiveness is nicely discussed in Byron Smith's essay in this volume.

51. Williams, "Hegel and the Gods of Postmodernity," 28.

truth would be precisely one of those claims to power that dialectic's business is to dismantle, or at least put to the test."[52]

IV

Now, when we come to see that it is inadequate for public debate to be merely a "battleground of competing bids for the use of goods," we face the question of how access to goods *ought* to be mediated. For Williams, the inherent character of reflective thinking or "negotiation," as described above, dictates that this question can only be answered through "the project of continually challenging localised and incommunicable discourses about human interest."[53] The demand for intelligibility or communicability underwrites an inexorable movement from the local to the universal. And when we begin to look for ways to speak about "an interest that is more than local," we have entered into the "metaphysical" discourse that belongs properly to politics, the discourse concerning *justice*.[54]

Notice, however, that because justice is a task of thinking, and thinking properly understood is "dispossession," justice demands individual transformation or, if you will, conversion. More concretely, it demands "the laborious process of evolving a practice in which my desire, my project, redefines or rethinks itself in symbiosis with others."[55] Negotiation involves the communication of our interests and goals, but once they are communicated, these positions will not be immune from reinterpretation and critique. Indeed, these positions are the very material on which negotiation labors. Negotiation can therefore be glossed as "the work by which human beings constantly *query what they have assumed is their interest* as individual or definite groups."[56]

To clarify, what Williams calls "negotiation" does *not* involve the giving up of the desire for x in exchange for the right of access to y, i.e., a compromise in the face of limited resources based on, say, the principles of fair distribution. The more radical view Williams takes is that the process

---

52. Ibid., 28–29.
53. Williams, "Between Politics and Metaphysics," 68.
54. Ibid., 56.
55. Ibid., 55.
56. Ibid.

of negotiation is able to reveal to us how the pursuit of certain interests and goals *need not be a zero-sum game*, that it can reveal to us how, even in a context of scarcity, the fulfillment of my desire need not curtail or compromise the fulfillment of your desire and vice versa, provided I am willing to see that the fulfillment of my desire is or can be socially mediated. That is, through the intersubjective labor of negotiation—through communication and the development of common social projects—it is often possible to discover ways for my access to goods and yours to be *mutually enhanced* through the coordination of action and labor:

> The environment is one of scarcity in the sense that goods and their use have to be the object of *thought*, of planning; but it is one of potential abundance insofar as it is possible for goods in an environment to be "underwritten" by the intelligence of others—insofar as the work of others can secure my or our interest as the object of their thought and labour (and vice versa).[57]

The institution of farming practices is one emblematic historical example of what Williams is referring to. But a moment's reflection will no doubt bring to mind countless other examples. In contemporary societies almost every aspect of our desiring existence is socially mediated. When I want milk, I don't find a cow and milk it; I buy it from the corner store. When I want to sleep, I don't find a cave and curl up in it; I hop on a bed. These possibilities are the fruit of countless iterations of communicative labor, through which practices and activities have evolved to serve collective interests.[58]

In this way, Williams argues, negotiation tends towards the overcoming of the "illusion of rivalry." It leads to a deepening realization of the interconnectedness of our interests and facilitates the evolution of social practices and structures through which labor can be reconceived, redeployed, and coordinated to serve those interconnected interests. More particularly, the practice of negotiation tends to dispel two "illusions" concerning our social

---

57. Ibid.

58. It could be argued that Williams here fails to distinguish the communicative and instrumental rationality involved in labor, i.e., the way labor intersects "system" and "lifeworld" (Habermas). This may well be a major weakness in his account. On the other hand, as we have seen, Williams does rigorously distinguish between communicative and strategic action in the sphere of interpersonal negotiation; he is clearly well aware of the critiques of instrumental reason. Charitably, then, we might take him to hold the view that, in the sphere of labor, instrumental and communicative modes of rationality are more intimately intertwined than is usually assumed.

Dispossession and Negotiation • Russell

situation: (i) "the illusion that any specific (individual or group) subject has unlimited access to the use of the goods of an environment," and (ii) "the illusion that any (individual or group) subject can intelligibly define its good as the possession of such use in exclusion of all others."[59]

Justice, therefore, cannot be understood simply in terms of fair distribution. This misunderstands the nature of socially mediated relations to the environment, and it underestimates the potential inherent in a social system in which the use of goods is "'underwritten' by the intelligence of others." Our very idea of justice must be refracted through the newly-gained standpoint of reason, which has overcome the illusions of natural consciousness. In fact, what we find in Williams is an ideal of justice as the universalization of freedom and autonomy through participation in a community of spirit; or, put negatively, as the overcoming of inequalities and privatized interests in the discernment of a common interest.[60] He accepts Hegel's insight that freedom and autonomy are the *consequence* of well-ordered social relations and not inherent characteristics of human subjects from out of which we negotiate our social relations.[61]

Once we have made this "Hegelian turn" with respect to our idea of freedom and autonomy, the challenge before us—indeed, the challenge each of us has always already accepted as a participant in the social project of negotiation—is to discover "what it might be to exercise a *historical* freedom" from *within* this "environment."[62] Williams admits that negotiation is "not a process that can necessarily of itself deliver a social ideal, a programme for concrete improvement."[63] Nonetheless:

> Insofar as this is always critical thinking about particular historical varieties of unfreedom or inequality, it is in fact always suggesting specific kinds of historical liberation, directions in which we can look for change, even if the speculative alone doesn't and could

59. Williams, "Between Politics and Metaphysics," 55, emphasis added.
60. Cf. Ibid., 68.
61. The *locus classicus* for Hegel's insight is Hegel, *Elements of the Philosophy of Right*, ed. Allen W. Wood, trans. Hugh Barr Nisbet (Cambridge; New York: Cambridge University Press, 1991) §149, where it is argued that submission to the universal (rational) will in its objective forms as law and custom is the condition for the possibility of a genuinely free existence, i.e. "positive," "concrete" or "actual" freedom. Apart from participation in the ethical community, the individual only possesses an "abstract" freedom, the absence of constraint on their arbitrary will, which is no freedom at all.
62. Williams, "Between Politics and Metaphysics," 54.
63. Ibid., 60.

never deliver a "programme" for political action, since this (*ex hypothesi*) could emerge only through the particular negotiations that are necessary and possible in a particular setting; to think otherwise would be to surrender to the temptation to apocalyptic resolutions, ends of history, final solutions.[64]

This explains why, for Williams, negotiation is not only difficult but also *risky*. It involves what Gillian Rose calls "authorship": the irrevocable intervention in social actuality, taking a stand, challenging prevailing models of thought and practice—and, above all, risking being wrong and having a negative impact on actual lives as well as the social whole. "The underlying *riskiness* of strategy cannot be circumvented: all strategy is 'agonistic,' involved in a struggle of the will against the resistance of an environment, and it becomes impossible to disentangle this from some account of violence."[65] To take flight and to retreat into the apparent security of inaction, however, is merely to acquiesce to whatever are the prevailing social conditions, in which violence is always already being done to existing human subjects ("Subjects are always already unequal").[66] What cannot be sanctioned, then, is "the withdrawal into the private cultivation of a 'beautiful soul'" as a substitute for the "properly *political* task . . . [i.e.] the labour of public construction."[67] Such a retreat simply gives over the public sphere to be made the instrument of economic powers and hegemonic interests. There is no path to justice that does not step outside the security of the given ethical order.[68] "[M]y action, by *inevitably* in some measure misrecognising the nature of the interest of others, establishes a new imbalance of power and justice. Yet there is no way of being actively and historically within the ethical without such risk, since the ethical without risk is powerless . . ."[69] Justice is always necessarily an unfinished project. Every act of justice necessarily fails to achieve an ultimate state of righteousness; but, conversely, within the limitations of creaturely finitude it still genuinely participates in a movement *of* justice.

64. Ibid., 70.
65. Ibid., 62. Cf. Rose, *The Broken Middle*, 150–51.
66. Williams, "Between Politics and Metaphysics," 62.
67. Ibid.
68. This is an allusion to the idea of "the suspension of the ethical" in Kierkegaard's *Fear and Trembling* (1843), which Williams interprets following the analysis of Rose, *The Broken Middle*, 148ff., in "Between Politics and Metaphysics," 64.
69. Williams, "Between Politics and Metaphysics," 64.

V

We are finally in a position to see how the Hegel-inspired concepts of "dispossession" and "negotiation" provide the resources for a political theology in the strict sense—that is, a theological conception of the political identity and vocation of the church vis-à-vis secular society.

Williams writes about the political identity and vocation of the people of God in this way:

> The supreme disinterestedness of the divine, which, by definition, has no "positional" corner to defend, articulates itself in the interest of a human community—a profoundly dangerous moment, since the interest of the community can then easily be elevated into a pseudo-independence of history. But the paradoxical reality of a community believing itself to stand for the "interest" of a God without interest or favouritism is somewhere near the centre of how reflective Judaism and reflective Christianity have tried to imagine themselves . . . In the language of both traditions, though in dramatically different ways, the people of God are a specific and vulnerable human group whose perception of their interest is as flawed and liable to violence as any other's, but who understand their fundamental task as embodying the "non-interest" of God, the universal saving generosity of divine action . . . As Gillian Rose sees so clearly, the temptation is for both [Judaism and Christianity] to lose the paradox—and so to lose the *political* vocation implicit in the paradox, the task of realising a corporate life whose critical practice constantly challenges sectional interest and proprietorial models of power or knowledge.[70]

The "paradox" of the people of God is that they represent in the *interests* of a particular community the *non-interest* of God. This implies that the people of God must understand themselves as that local or "sectional" community who refuse to "negotiate" from the standpoint of a sectional interest but instead embody in negotiation the very essence of "dispossession," the readiness to empty oneself—even acting against one's immediate and perceived self-interest—for the sake of the other. The sphere of exchange, understood as the domain of negotiated activity, is then the sphere in which the kenotic love of God is to be recapitulated by the church. And this is to characterize not only communicative action within the Christian community but also communicative action by the Christian community in broader

70. Ibid., 72.

societal negotiations, i.e., in relation to secular society. As such, the kenotic communicative action of the church is at the same time a *witness* to the truth of being, i.e., the truth of the Triune God as love or *ekstasis* (being-outside-itself-in-the-other) and the truth of created being as finding its life and its identity outside of itself in the other—in humanity as such, in the created order as such, and ultimately in God.

For Williams, then, the church is and ought to be a martyr community—that is, a community whose position-taking in the public sphere risks judgment and actual loss *for the sake of justice*, namely the promotion of ever more universal forms of concrete freedom in historical societies. The calling of the church is to sacrifice itself in this sense. But the logic of sacrifice is here understood in a very specific fashion as *self-gift*. The act of gift or grace transcends whatever is the existing horizon of the ethical and answers to a higher law: the law of God, *the law of love*. It fulfills this law to the extent that it gives itself *for the other* in an act of dispossession, not standing upon its own rights over against the other. And this it does in faith that after this "speculative good Friday" it will be raised up again in "the power of the spirit" to see more fully realized the freedom of the community of the spirit of life. In this, as it testifies and acts in love, the martyr community *is* the agency of God in the realization of a universal social freedom or the "kingdom of God,"[71] it is the proverbial yeast that leavens the whole batch of dough. Humanity as a whole is thus in principle included—through the mission of the church—in the divine life.

But the church only facilitates this universal renewal insofar as it remains faithful to its vocation and does not collapse into the actuality of the world. The church must remain a moment of negativity within the contemporary world, just as Christ was a negativity within the world of first-century Palestine: "God-with-us can only be thought first as the negation of all external, politico-legal forms as they are historically constituted . . . The kingdom, in other words, can only appear initially as that which has no place in the "normally" constituted world: it is first interiority, then death, death without any sanctioning glow of heroism or any consoling sense of

---

71. "Jesus is active in the corporate life of the Church; what he gives to human beings, he gives in significant part through the mediation of the common life, which is itself his 'body,' his material presence in the world, though it does not exhaust his identity or activity." Williams, "Between the Cherubim: The Empty Tomb and the Empty Throne," in *On Christian Theology*, 189.

resignation to natural mortality."[72] The history of humanity as the history of God would collapse without this divine discord between the church and secular society. But when the church is faithfully being what it is called to be, it points to the concrete possibility of a universal society or "community of spirit," a life of concrete freedom made possible through divine love, through the dispossession or giving of oneself in difficult and risky negotiation.[73]

In this sense, the world *needs* the church—the actual, concrete community of the church—in its midst; for the church represents, as a concrete moment within the social whole, the normative demands of reason to think the "shared territory of social acts," it represents (without fully actualizing it) the possibility of a *universal, reconciled social whole* in which there is a coincidence of intelligibility and being.[74] In Williams' words, the "form" adumbrated by the church is just "the optimal form of reflective human sociality."[75] In this sense, the church embodies in a particular community within society a social vision that is truly *universal*. That is, it is a vision that does not merely relate to the ethical substance of the church; on the contrary, it consists precisely in a refusal to see humanity mired in the false universals of national, racial, and religious identity.[76]

Williams admits that the expressly "internationalist" thrust of his interpretation is somewhat at odds with Hegel's own views on the limits of international moral community in the *Elements of the Philosophy of Right*. According to Hegel, international relations can *only* take the form of treaties between individual states as "particular wills" and not the substantial

72. Williams, "Logic and Spirit in Hegel," 45.

73. See also the discussion in Williams, "Incarnation and the Renewal of Community," 232–38.

74. Williams, "Logic and Spirit in Hegel," 46.

75. Ibid., 49.

76. Needless to say, Williams is not naïve enough to think that the church has always lived up to its calling. On the contrary, few are as keenly aware of the frailty and failures of the historical Christian church. The ideal form of "reflective human sociality" is "adumbrated *but not realised* by the Church" (ibid., emphasis added). Nonetheless, the foregoing theology holds out hope that even weak, compromised, and imperfect acts of grace, caught in what Rose calls "the broken middle," can realize the purposes of God. In a kenotic theology of this kind, "thy kingdom come" is not contingent upon a purism of heart or act. "After Calvary, ... the human knowledge of humanity as vulnerable and finite, becomes inseparable from awareness of God ... we can understand that this weakness is a moment in the life of God." Ibid., 45. And so *even the church* can be the instrument of God's saving power—indeed, *especially the church*, insofar as it recognizes itself as the powerless one whose only "interest" is *for humanity as such*.

form of a universal will, a universal ethical life.[77] But this, Williams argues, merely exposes a tension in Hegel's own thought, as it were, between the *Lectures on the Philosophy of Religion* and the *Philosophy of Right*. Williams resolves this tension by prioritizing the former over the latter: "what is said [in the *Lectures on the Philosophy of Religion*] has to do with the life of *humanity* as such, and it is wholly unclear how, in the light of this, local loyalties (to this state as opposed to that state, instead of loyalty to *the* state as social form) could be said to be intelligible."[78] If there are limits to internationalism, these must be regarded as "external contingencies"; they do not mitigate the "ought" of international reconciliation.[79]

Now, even if one does not object to this reading on philological grounds, there remains a fundamental *theoretical* issue here that is not so easily disposed of, an issue to which we will have to return. In the meantime, Williams is right that "we are left with an uneasy tension ... insofar as *neither* [Church nor state] realises what it portends or promises as possible."[80] What are we to make of this tension? Williams himself insists upon it, as though the impossibility of the church ever passing over into a genuinely universal society of love, and the inverse impossibility of the state passing over into a genuinely universal society of love, were together *constitutive of absolute spirit* understood as the process of participating in the divine life in history.

The insistence upon this "uneasy tension" has the virtue of exposing "illusions of peace," e.g., the illusion that peace is found in disengagement and passivity.[81] It also has the virtue of overcoming the negative "messianisms" of postmodern philosophy (Benjamin, Adorno, Derrida) to the extent

---

77. Hegel, *Elements of the Philosophy of Right*, §§330–40. Hegel, Williams notes, does recognize a "*universal* right which ought to have international validity in and for itself" (§333). But it has a very narrow content: the obligation or duty to observe treaties. For Hegel, the air of normativity becomes thinner the higher one goes. By this point we have left the thicker ethical substance (the family, civil society, the state) far down below and are left with a rarefied, formalistic (quasi-Kantian) moral law.

78. Williams, "Logic and Spirit in Hegel," 49.

79. Ibid. It should be noted that Williams' hopes for internationalism are nonetheless reasonably modest. He aspires to a "degree of mutual accountability" and "critical scrutiny" or "interchange" between nations, and sees useful "global moral community" already existing in such unassuming forms as international NGOs and professional organizations, not to mention the Christian church. Like many, however, he is critical of the United Nations and advocates a more robust formulation of international law. See Williams, *The Truce of God*, 118–21.

80. Williams, "Logic and Spirit in Hegel," 49.

81. See Williams' incisive discussion in *The Truce of God*, chapter 3.

that these identify the "divine" with that which is *essentially* absent, beyond history, language, and the sphere of human interaction. Yet Williams reinstates the sphere of history, linguistic exchange, and human self-overcoming as the sphere of divine grace in such a fashion that the divine life *pro nobis* is entirely equated with *self-transcending movement*, the movement of dialectics or conversion. Williams is satisfied with the tension between church and state because it is the condition for the possibility of movement, and movement is *life*—and *kenotic* movement is *divine life*.[82] In other words, no tension, no transformation; no transformation, no grace. But, on this view, it becomes unintelligible to speak of an *eschatological rest*. What then of the Christian hope? What then of there being no more death, no more mourning, crying or pain, "for the first things have passed away"?[83] For fear of emptying the gospel of its transformative power, Williams essentializes the moment of negativity, pain, and death, replacing the finality of the cross with an endless reiteration of its procedure.[84] There is no "it is finished," no "death no longer has dominion over him," but only the somber declaration that "you shall never enter my rest." To be sure, this gospel offers concrete hope for social improvement; it is not an eternal recurrence of the same. But it does not proclaim an end to violence, injustice, and death. These are strictly ruled out as false hopes and seductions, threatening to obscure the divine calling to the difficult work of historical emancipation.

Suspicion towards the ideological uses of the gospel of peace is entirely legitimate; we must theologize with a hammer, to misquote Nietzsche. What's more, the intention here is not to reject Williams' social theory out

82. In an extraordinary passage, Williams *equates* the power that is "the irresistibility of the motion of thought" with "God's power": "Dialectic is what theology means by the power of *God*, just as *Verstand* is what theology means by the goodness of God." Williams, "Logic and Spirit in Hegel," 37. This is a remarkably bold theological assertion. Whether or not it is orthodox—and it is by no means clear that it is—there is no denying that this articulates a *radically* Christocentric doctrine of creation: the very form of the created sphere's temporal being is viewed theologically through the lens of the Easter story.

83. Rev 21:3-4 (NRSV).

84. Whatever reservations one may have with respect to the rest of his reading of Paul, on this point Alain Badiou's "anti-dialectical" interpretation is no doubt correct: "For Paul, death cannot be the operation of salvation . . . It was, properly speaking, *invented* by Adam, the first man . . . What constitutes an event in Christ is exclusively the Resurrection, that *anastasis nekron* that should be translated as the raising up of the dead, their uprising, which is the uprising of life. . . [The resurrection] eradicates negativity, and if, as we have already said, death is required for the construction of its site, it remains an affirmative operation that is irreducible to death itself." Alain Badiou, *Saint Paul: The Foundation of Universalism*, trans. Ray Brassier (Stanford: Stanford University Press, 2003) 68, 73.

of hand as insufficiently scriptural. Neither is it to deny the cruciform pattern of Christian discipleship, since discipleship is indeed a matter of ongoing transformative repentance and conversion. Nor is my desire to reassert a static, neo-Platonic eschatology.[85] Rather, the intention is to discern how Williams' remarkably sophisticated work nonetheless leads us into areas requiring further theological deliberation. And, in this spirit, I want to return first to the *theoretical* aporia mentioned above. This, in turn, will reveal some ways in which we might need to rethink the political theology described above.

VI

The theoretical aporia is this (I give you Hegel's version): each individual state has the character of an absolute sovereign power since it represents "the spirit in its substantial rationality and immediate actuality."[86] For this reason, every existing political community has *universality* as the form of its law and as the presumption of its ethical life. And hence, as Williams rightly points out, the labor of negotiation cannot be separated from the demand for universal validity any more than the labor of science can be separated from the idea of objectivity. This is why individual states represent themselves internally as absolute and why international conflict is in part always a struggle between conceptions of what is (universally) right, good, and true. These arguments point to the plurality of states being a provisional or contingent state of affairs, a state of affairs in principle needing to be transcended.

On the other hand, even "absolute" sovereign states are in a limited sense dependent upon there being a plurality of states; namely, insofar as the self-knowledge that it is an *individuum* is contingent upon being recognized as a state by other states. What's more, since "negation is an essential component of individuality," each individual state "must generate

---

85. Far from it. Any Christian eschatology must anticipate a God-given mode of *life*, which will necessarily be *temporal* and *dynamic*. Life, even as "rest," cannot be conceived as "passive repose"; it must be a "sharing in God's activity" (cf. Williams, *The Truce of God*, 60–61). There is no disagreement on this fundamental point.

86. Hegel, *Elements of the Philosophy of Right*, §331. As such, each state is not constituted through the recognition of other states but on the contrary "has a primary and absolute entitlement to be a sovereign and independent power *in the eyes of others*, i.e. *to be recognized by them*," ibid.

opposition and create an enemy."[87] A world government or federation of states (after Kant's proposal), then, could at best be forged in a momentary and contingent agreement between the several "absolutely sovereign" states; any state would be within their rights to suspend involvement at any time.[88] So much for internationalism through federation. Could a universal society be achieved instead by war and conquest? This too leads to aporias, since there is a fundamental dis-analogy between states and individual persons as they confront one another: the latter are able to discern the truth of their being in a form of mediated interdependence (spirit) whereas the former discern the truth of their being when they recognize each other's ontological independence *as* "spirit in its substantial rationality and immediate actuality." It is impossible at an international level, therefore, to progress beyond the master-slave relation to the emergence of an "I" that is "we" and "we" that is "I," i.e., to the emergence of spirit,[89] since each "I" is itself already spirit. As such, a struggle for recognition can never produce a higher and more stable configuration that decisively transcends "the state of nature" in which nations find themselves with regard to each other.[90] An international body, whether a federation or an empire, then, could never be a "spiritual" actuality in and for itself, a universal *society*. These arguments suggest an irreducible plurality of states.

Another author has put the paradox rather more succinctly: "Truth does not permit contradiction; but society does not permit unity."[91]

The introduction of the work of Oliver O'Donovan at this point is not accidental. His account provides an alternative and, in my view, more satisfactory interpretation of how the gospel of Christ relates to the paradox in question. With Hegel, O'Donovan affirms that the *plurality* of social identities *as such* is not a problem to be overcome; but, with Williams, he also affirms that the conflict of national identities cannot mark a final

87. Ibid., §324, *Zusatz*.

88. Cf. ibid., §322.

89. Cf. Hegel, *Phenomenology of Spirit*, trans. Arnold V. Miller (Oxford: Oxford University Press, 1979) §177.

90. ". . . since the sovereignty of states is the principle governing their mutual relations, they exist to that extent in a state of nature in relation to one another . . . Consequently, if no agreement can be reached between particular wills, conflicts between states can be settled only by war." Hegel, *Elements of the Philosophy of Right*, §§333–34.

91. Oliver O'Donovan, *Common Objects of Love: Moral Reflection and the Shaping of Community*, The 2001 Stob Lectures (Grand Rapids: Eerdmans, 2002) 37.

horizon, that "the desire of the nations" is precisely for a unity of truth and social actuality, and hence for universality. What needs to be resolved, then, is not plurality into unity, but the antinomy at the heart of each society; the antinomy between the desire for a universal knowledge of the world and self (including knowledge of how we ought to live), and the implicit awareness that *our* ethical life is but *one* way among many of representing the world and the self. The question then is how the gospel speaks of the redemption of society in the face of this antinomy.

The answer is found in the content of the Christian proclamation itself, the proclamation of the advent of the kingdom of God, and in the way this proclamation relativizes the status of nation-states and other contingent identities.

The positive content of the gospel in its political aspect, according to O'Donovan, is "the disclosure of a universal society, a Kingdom of Heaven, a new identity capable of weaning us from dependence upon our varied identities."[92] "Jesus Christ, very God and very man, is the double representation around whom such a community has come into being."[93] In the ascended Christ, the church knows a genuinely absolute sovereign who represents the universal (divine) law, and a figure in whom each and every human being can legitimately see themselves as represented since he is one of us, the *true* human being. The rule of *this one* resolves *in concreto* the paradox of social universality: it welcomes under its banner all people, people from every tribe, nation, and tongue, while also preserving and redeeming them in their particularity. It is not that each individual or social group is assured that their particular form of life is the truth, but instead that each is gifted with a new and more fundamental socio-political identity within which their form of life is laid open to judgment (to use Williams' phrase). Their reassurance is not that they possess the truth, but that the truth possesses them—that their history, culture, beliefs, and practices have been brought decisively within the sway of God's loving, redeeming, and sanctifying action, and hence that it is possible to re-imagine their very own form of life under the sign of the cross.

This is the self-consciousness of those who have become members of the historical Christian church. As O'Donovan goes on to emphasize: "the

---

92. Ibid., 44.
93. Ibid.

mere imagination of a universal society, as an ideal or a project, will not suffice . . . for it can provide no real social identity, but only entangle us in a contested cause. We must become actual members of a real community constituted by the real and present image of God as uniquely lord, and the real and present image of mankind as subject uniquely to God."[94]

If the Christian church knows itself to be the beginning or forerunner of a universal society, in which there is genuine multiplicity and difference and yet neither Jew nor Greek, slave nor free, male nor female, this is not merely an *ideal* it bears within itself, nor is it merely a project with which it busies itself. It is a reality in which the church already participates insofar as it is a diverse body of people constituted as one society under the government of a representative authority. To be sure, its head, the one in whom its unity is represented, is absent. In his absence, the church depicts Christ as the crucified and risen Lord of all, and recognizes him as such through its sacraments, its gathering together, its acts of worship, and so forth. Moreover, it refuses to install a visible unifying representative at its head, for this would be to close the circle and pretend that the church were already the universal society in its fullness. The circle remains open—the universal society in its consummated actuality is still to come—and this is why the church must retain its posture of groaning expectation and continue to wait for God's Son from heaven.

The presence of the church in the world, in the meantime, is a sign of the advent of the truly universal society, the kingdom of God. Negatively, the sheer fact of the church thus brings into question the idolatrous pretensions of historically existing communities, whether they be racially, religiously or nationally constituted. Positively, it says to the various existing communities that they are relieved of the burden of representing themselves as absolute, of representing themselves in divine terms; and that, in fact, for them to do so would be to assume the posture of the anti-Christ—it would be to refuse to recognize, for example, that *this* state's rule is *not* the rule of God. Here we arrive at the heart of what constitutes the Christian conception of the "secular state." The "secular state" is the state whose self-knowledge is formed in recognition of the divine rule of God in Christ. Fundamentally, to recognize the latter is to acknowledge that the sovereignty of the state is

94. Ibid.

not, after all, absolute, and thus to curtail the idolatrous pretensions of one's own cultural and political self-representations.

Neither the gospel nor the church provides material or conceptual means to bypass or surmount the aporia of internationalism within the conditions of "the present age" as such. The aporia of internationalism is *only* surmounted *in* the future kingdom of God itself as the true polis established under the rule of Christ. Nonetheless, what the gospel does provide is the good news that members of particular societies may *also* belong to the universal society—in advance, as it were—through baptism into Christ, and that the societies themselves, at the level of their self-representations, may step back from the universalizing pretensions that lead to conflict and war *without compromising their desire*. The desire of the nations is fulfilled in the coming kingdom of God, whereas the future of the nations and their rulers themselves is to cast down their crowns before the throne of heaven.

On this interpretation, the church and the state do not stand in dialectical tension. Their vis-à-vis does not constitute the means by which existing non-universal communities are able to negotiate their way towards the actualization of the kingdom of God, toward universality. Quite the reverse. The "witness" of the church is to train non-universal communities to receive their particularity as a gift and *not* to project themselves with universalizing pretension.

This is not to reject the desire for justice and truth in their properly universal form; nor is it to embrace provincialism and irrationalism, and to relinquish the quest for international fellowship, understanding and universal knowledge. On the contrary, it merely lays out the conditions under which "negotiation" of the kind envisaged by Williams is *necessary*, whether in the sphere of politics, science, philosophy or theology—as an interim measure, as a task for the present age, in which we know in part and prophesy in part.

VII

Williams' theory of dispossession and negotiation is an impressive and original contribution to contemporary debates over the character of social or communicative reason. He makes a convincing case that "negotiation" does indeed promote a mode of mutual relation that is to a greater or lesser degree analogous to the divine life, i.e., a mutuality of love understood as being-with-oneself-in-the-other. Williams' work shows how it is possible to see the creative love of God at work through the church as it recapitulates the love of Christ in self-sacrificial advocacy for the other. And it is surely true that "kenotic" communicative action should be seen as a core part of the Christian vocation in all domains of social interaction.[95]

What's more, there is no dispute that the gospel discloses the hidden centre "between politics and metaphysics."[96] If a point of disagreement has emerged, it is over exactly *where* this hidden centre is located. For Williams, it is located in the dialectical power of the cross, whose transformative potentiality is unleashed in some measure in all acts of communicative self-giving. I have argued, by contrast, that the hidden centre is Christ himself, around whom God is gathering a people and thus creating a new humanity, a universal society of which the church is a prolepsis and sign. Insofar as it faithfully recapitulates the love of God, the church will be a divine agent of transformation in existing societies. But the Christian hope is not grounded upon the church's faltering efforts. It is grounded upon the faithfulness of God, who has declared that the present age is passing away, and has presented us in Christ with a preview of the resurrection, justice, and life of the age to come.

Our hopes and dreams for this age, therefore, ought to be both bold and sober: "bold" because aware of the grace of God, and "sober" because under no illusions about the weakness of the flesh or the promise of history. It is in "things unseen"—the lordship of Christ and the future of the kingdom of God—that we are to place our unqualified confidence. It is in

---

95. Williams' recent comments on *sharia* law in the UK give a taste of what this might entail. As Archbishop of Canterbury, Williams takes it to be within his sphere of responsibility not merely to be a spokesperson for the views and interests of the Anglican community in Britain, but also—and perhaps especially—to aid in the effective communication between various segments of British society, including in this case between the Islamic community and the legal community. His gentle suggestion that British society consider recognizing some form of "supplementary jurisdiction" for *sharia* law is expressly grounded in "a non-negotiable assumption that each agent (with his or her historical and social affiliations) could be expected to have a voice in the shaping of some common project for the well-being and order of a human group" (Williams, "Civil and Religious Law in England: A Religious Perspective," 7 February, 2008, http://www.archbishopofcanterbury.org/1575). Here we see the universalist stance that Williams understands himself to be required to inhabit as a *Christian* leader, irrespective of the fact that it appears to undermine the cultural hegemony of his own religious tradition.

96. Williams, "Between Politics and Metaphysics," 73.

the knowledge that it is not for us to build the kingdom of God that we are liberated to lose ourselves in the service of God; it is in the faith that we will be raised up at the last day that we find courage to seek the good of our neighbor and to disregard the cost.[97]

---

97. I would like to thank Michael Jensen, Ben Myers, and Byron Smith for their feedback on an earlier draft of this essay.

6

The Humanity of Godliness:
Spirituality and Creatureliness in Rowan Williams

BYRON SMITH

> [O]ur holiness is not the denial but the acceptance of being creatures—made possible in that great central mystery of the creator himself becoming a creature, uncreated love working through the created humanity that is Jesus of Nazareth so that created mortal life is touched and glorified.[1]

Spirituality

"Spirituality" has often been associated with an almost superhuman and heroic exertion of the will that seeks to gain a new plane of inner experience through denying oneself what is worldly, bodily, sensual, or socio-political. Alternatively, spirituality may be associated with finding one's own way in

---

1. Williams, "Creation, Creativity and Creatureliness: the Wisdom of Finite Existence. Study Day organised by the St Theosevia Centre for Christian Spirituality, Oxford," Archbishop of Canterbury Web site, http://www.archbishopofcanterbury.org/997 (n.p.).

the religious marketplace, fashioning a unique blend of practices and ideas to suit one's tastes in the epitome of consumerist freedom. Either way, such notions of spirituality reflect the individualist assumptions of contemporary society.

Into this context Archbishop Rowan Williams has written a number of pieces—some academic and some for general audiences—that directly challenge such popular understandings of "spirituality." He argues that in the light of Christ, such everyday experiences as community, gift-giving, memory or failure are opened to a new world of sometimes unexpected meanings. In particular, he claims that we find our most authentic spirituality in coming to understand ourselves as dependent creatures of a self-giving God. We most faithfully open ourselves to the truth when we abandon our quest to be gods and accept the limitations and frailties of being human. This path, ironically, leads to a properly creaturely imitation of God. Humans are most godly when, like Jesus, we accept the role of servant, stop trying to grasp after divinity (as we misconceive it) and so discover the freedom found in simply being ourselves. Thus, our highest godliness consists of living most truly as creatures.

In contrast to both the common conceptions of the "spiritual" as essentially a series of private, "inner" decisions, Williams presents a compelling picture of spirituality as a way of life that is to be shared, since it is based on God's generosity. Moreover, this way of life can only be received as a gift, not bought or fashioned. This, for Williams, is at the heart of what it is to be a creature. It therefore makes sense to begin by considering his views on creation.

Creation *ex nihilo*

Williams grounds his understanding of spirituality in the traditional doctrine of God as Creator. All that is finds its source in God and yet is distinct from God. God's creation of a realm not identical to God is achieved without external compulsion. Created realities are dependent upon God's gift of continued existence but this relation is strictly asymmetrical. This has traditionally been expressed in the affirmation of the act of creation being *ex nihilo*, out of nothing. The universe does not condition the fact of its own existence. God is not merely the manipulator of matter, he calls it into and holds it in existence.

Furthermore, God is not obliged by nature or craving to create. Creation is not in order to scratch a divine itch, fulfill a divine need or complete a divine lack. God has no hidden agenda in which external realities serve an instrumental function.

Thus, creation is thoroughly *unnecessary*; it is gratuitous, an act of unconstrained freedom, purely from grace. This has at least two implications: one for God, one for us. First, creation *ex nihilo* is the act of a God entirely content and yet supremely generous, so filled with plenitude that there is plenty to share. This, according to Williams, is "one reflective path towards understanding God as trinity," that is, as "*intrinsic* self-love and self-gift [. . .] the divine being as being-for-another."[2] Thus, a traditional doctrine of creation serves to underscore the *trustworthiness* of a gracious and non-manipulative God. Second, it means our very existence as creatures is a gift: unmerited, unsought, unnecessary. Our lives are contingent. Our primary orientation is receiving and at its heart all sin is a resentment towards pure gift.

Although this traditional doctrine has been criticized by some feminist theologians as perpetuating a dualist partiality towards a distant, disembodied, and disconnected masculinity, Williams defends a careful understanding of creation *ex nihilo* as crucial to the very theological and political concerns driving such critique.[3] Only a God who is not dependent upon or conditioned by creation is able to sustain the dignity and value of the entirety of that creation. Only a God who is contentedly *other* and unthreatened by difference will set us free to be truly and distinctively human. By supplanting pure gift with reciprocity, contingency becomes necessity and gratuity is replaced by functionality. The sheer givenness of existence as creatures turns into obligation or instrumentality in a project imposed upon us. From here, it is not far to the treatment of some segment of humanity (or the creation) as merely functional in the limited interests of the few. This, claims Williams, is folly and blasphemy.

Therefore, instead of a "simple, undialectical affirmation of God's identity with the cosmic continuum (an uncritical maternal image to replace an uncritical patriarchal image?),"[4] our moral imagination needs to

---

2. Rowan Williams, "On Being Creatures," in *On Christian Theology* (Oxford: Blackwell, 2000), 74.

3. Ibid., 63–78.

4. Ibid., 78.

be fed by the grace of our Lord Jesus Christ, the love of God, and the fellowship of the Holy Spirit—by the reassurance that God's stance of generosity towards us is unmitigated by our failure, need, limit or difference.[5] Williams' articulation and defense of creation *ex nihilo* is an articulation and defense of the primacy of God's grace, love, and fellowship over whatever humans might be and do to staunch, control or pollute it.

Yet, while finding fault with revisionist accounts that undermine the spiritual riches of belief in creation, Williams also rejects naive literalistic perceptions of the doctrine too. Williams follows Aquinas in understanding creation not so much as a claim about a *process*—an event that occurred at some point in the primordial past—as a claim about a *relationship*: "[The doctrine of creation] simply tells you that the entire situation of the universe, at any given moment, exists as a real situation because of God's reality being, as it were, turned away from God to generate what is not God."[6] The doctrine of creation does not therefore speak of a before and after which might be compared and contrasted, but of an always actual direction of gift and receipt: from God to everything.

This places all of us in a relation to God before we have done or thought anything: the relation of being a creature. Every one of us continually receives our existence and life from an extrinsic origin. God is first and foremost a generous giver of life and breath, rather than a controlling monarch making demands.

For Williams, this relationship is the primary horizon within which any genuine account of Christianity spirituality must find its bearings. To be a creature is the fundamental reality of being human. In contrast to many popular conceptions of spirituality, Williams takes this not as a problem to be overcome, but as an obscured reality to be uncovered and embraced. The state of creatureliness is not the background against which the deeper spiritual truths stand in contrast, but the irreplaceable foundation of true

---

5. "With God alone, I am dealing with what does not need to construct or negotiate an identity, what is free to be itself without the process of struggle. Properly understood, this is the most liberating affirmation we could ever hear. God does not and cannot lay claim upon me so as to 'become' God; what I am cannot be made functional for God's being; I can never be defined by the job of meeting God's needs," ibid., 72–73.

6. Ibid., 68. Cf. Williams, *Tokens of Trust* (Louisville: Westminster John Knox, 2007) 35: "It should be a rather exhilarating thought that the moment of creation is now—that if, by some unthinkable accident, God's attention slipped, we wouldn't be here. It means that within every circumstance, every object, every person, God's action is going on, a sort of white heat at the centre of everything."

Christian living and experience. To advance this contention, let us consider in more detail the implications of being creatures.

Creation and *Kenosis*

In saying above that God has no external or internal compulsion to create, this is not to affirm that creation is an arbitrary exercise of divine volition. Instead, importantly for Williams, creating is "the sort of thing that God does."[7] That is, God's eternal being is found in self-sharing as Father, Son, and Spirit. The movement of simultaneous gift and differentiation that is creation, while being unnecessary, is not "out of character," since this is God's own characteristic movement: "God *is* a reality moving away from a centre of self-possession towards being-in-another."[8] "God is eternally one who generates what is other, who eternally makes different his own life in the outpouring and exchange of the life of Father, Son and Holy Spirit—that tells us that in the heart of God there is what you might call the energy of difference, an outpouring of life into otherness."[9] There is, as the creed affirms, a distinction between the begetting of the Son and the making of the world, yet these activities are not unrelated. Creation is a translation "into time and limit and history the eternal fact of God."[10]

And this similarity extends beyond the generosity of overflowing abundance; it also includes a *kenosis*, a self-emptying, in each case.[11] The Father empties himself, making room for the Son to be the Son. As well as the mutual indwelling of being-in one another is a kenotic being-with that allows difference. Or, to put it a different way, intra-Trinitarian self-giving is not an unwelcome imposition or a grasping that seeks to devour the other, but a letting be. In a similar way, the very contingency of creation is assured by God's refusal to foist divine identity directly upon the cosmos. God makes space for what is not God. The primary category here is *grace*, not authority.

---

7. Williams, "Creation, Creativity and Creatureliness," n.p.
8. Williams, *Teresa of Avila* (London: Continuum, 1991) 209.
9. Williams, "Creation, Creativity and Creatureliness," n.p.
10. Ibid.
11. Ibid.

This kenotic wisdom unthreatened by difference and found in God's own life is also the mode of divine creating. The result is a creation with such wisdom as its hidden centre.[12]

In highlighting this theme so prominently, Williams could be misunderstood to be endorsing a very "English" aloofness, a non-intervention. Yet he is clear that the divine Trinitarian gift (both immanent and economic) is not the polite distance of a neighbor who has the good manners not to intrude, but an engaged desire for communion, a genuine sharing. He is simply making the point that genuine sharing requires a simultaneous respect for difference lest the communion become mere union, an annexation or merging in which the identity of one or both parties is submerged.

Where this really starts to carry weight for William's account of Christian spirituality is that such self-giving in which difference is preserved is essential not only for God's own being, but for authentic human being as a creature of this God:

> Creation then is to be understood as that which is other than God and yet in being other than God is exactly what God desires, because God desires to give and realise his love in what is other. That eternal pattern of the Father, the Son and the Spirit is translated, to use Bulgakov's terms, into the relation of God and creation. And because that creative act is essentially an act of self-forgetting, self-giving, self-sharing, creation becomes itself when it lives into the reality of self-giving, self-sharing.[13]

Being Creatures

At this point, one might be forgiven for conflating creatureliness and divinity. If it is most true to our being as creatures generated by God's kenotic self-giving to reflect (or "translate") God's self-giving, then are we not rightly attracted to the serpent's offer of being "like God"?

---

12. Ibid.: "Before the Word of God empties himself to take on human flesh, the trinity is involved in a self-emptying act in shaping the world. That the world should be is for God (so to speak) to withdraw but not to be absent. It is for God to let be a world with its own freedom, its own integrity. The God who creates a world of freedom, a world that is itself, is a kenotic God, a self-giving, a self-emptying God whose being is for the other. And as we understand this in the eternal life of the Father, the Son and the Spirit, we understand how it is in creation."

13. Ibid.

No, the imitation of God, the human calling to be "godly" has its limits; or rather, it's proper context. We are properly both like and unlike God, and Williams is careful to delineate an appropriately *creaturely* godliness.

So although in one sense true spirituality means imitating and expressing God's eternally generous wisdom, crucially, we do so *as creatures*. In order for a human to be faithfully godly, she must also know that she is *not* God. Humans, like all creatures, are finite and dependent. God's resourcefulness knows no bounds, whereas we discover, sometimes painfully, that there are limits to our attention, empathy, potency, memory, stamina, self-consciousness, and even our lifespan. We are unable to secure the conditions of our continued existence. And so we are dependent upon the actions and inactions of others, perpetually vulnerable to their attacks, in need of companions with whom to co-operate. More fundamentally, we are dependent upon God for our being and life. The possibility of imitating divine generosity is something we first receive; our very ability to give at all is dependent upon a prior gift to us. We must be beloved before we can be a lover.[14] Our attempts to echo God's benevolence involve more difference than similarity because our giving is always partial, conditioned, and a "re-gifting."

And so Williams' account denies *imitatio Dei* as the foundational model of ethics and spirituality. We are *not* God, and to attempt to be "like God" is fraught with danger. If we set ourselves up as arbiters of meaning, as "full" and without needs, we thus cast ourselves *out* of the world of interdependence in which we live and move and have our being. To follow God, we must become more truthfully *creatures*, more aware of our need and interdependence, more consciously recipients from God's hand of all that we are and have. As recipients, rather than demanders, we must learn to accept our limits, even our death. To be mature as a Christian is to live in light of the knowledge that we are *not* God, and never can be.

This is true for every aspect of our existence. There is not some part of us that is more god-like, whether soul or intellect or will. These are "as much creaturely as the body and the passions."[15] We are finite and dependent creatures through and through. Our existence needs no spark of divinity to provide justification for God's creative act. "There is no substantial conti-

---

14. Williams, *Teresa of Avila*, 108.
15. Williams, *Wound of Knowledge*, rev. ed., 68. Williams is here exegeting Gregory of Nyssa, but he is sympathetic to this point.

nuity between soul and God,"[16] and this need not threaten the created goodness of our lives since God's gift subsists in such differentiation.

Nonetheless, not all dependence is healthy. There is an infantile undifferentiated dependence, often associated with "the effort to please (and thus 'harness') a parental authority."[17] So our wholesome dependence must be carefully understood in the light of God's characteristic "letting be" lest it be misunderstood as limitless dependence. God creates true agents with the capacity for action and who are genuinely other. God is not the direct cause or explanation for every event; he does not want to be everything.[18] Hence the continual dependence of creatures in every aspect of their being does not imply their utter constraint or maximal passivity.

So life as a limited creature in which everything is ultimately received from God nonetheless has the space for transactions whose meanings are not exhausted by reference to God. As creatures, not only are we free from being made functional to God's being (God doesn't need us in order to be God since Father, Son, and Spirit are eternally sufficient for one another), God is also released from having to provide our complete principle of intelligibility. This allows us to focus on created realities as they actually are without having to fear that we dishonor our creator if God is not the world's immediate totality of meaning. In this way, the difference between God and creation also opens the possibility of genuine difference within creation.

Consequently, as creatures we are not required to "resign from nature by treating 'God' as a successful rival for our attention or devotion over against the things and persons of the world."[19] Instead, it is possible (indeed *usual*) for God to be honored through our being-in-the-world. Not that God therefore becomes superfluous. On the contrary, although God is not

---

16. Ibid., 87.

17. Williams, *Resurrection: Interpreting the Easter Gospel* (London: Darton, Longman & Todd, 1980) 80.

18. "[T]o treat God as 'Everything,' as the immediate totality of meaning for each and every subject in the world, is to misunderstand the nature of our unconditional dependence on God. God establishes the worth, the legitimacy, the right to be there, of what is in the world, and in that sense gives meaning; but precisely what God does *not* do is to intrude onto the integrity of this or that aspect of being in the world as a justification or explanation for specific events. If the explanation of every event, every determination of being, every phenomenon or decision were simply and directly God, then the life of creation would not be genuinely other than God. God grounds the reality and, in the theological sense, the goodness of the world's life, but does not answer specific 'Why?' questions." Williams, "On Being Creatures," 75.

19. Ibid., 73.

a competitor against his world for our attention, belief in God as unique creator nonetheless functions to deny the possibility of any other ultimate source of authority or identity, anything else that can comprehensively and definitively name reality. Consequently, belief in God also unmasks any creaturely attempt at such definitive naming as flight from a genuine being-in-the-world in which our ability to specify reality is partial.

Flight from Creatureliness

If dependence and limit are fundamental features of created human life, then the most basic paths of flight from the conditions of creaturely existence will be the attempt to become invulnerable and the attempt to act with decisive finality. In these ways, we attempt to become "like God" in self-sufficiency and plenitude: "Human beings are perennially vulnerable to the temptation of arrogating divinity to themselves. It is a temptation manifest in the refusal to accept finitude, creatureliness and dependence—what Ernest Becker has called the '*causa sui* project,' the delusion that the world is *my* world, a world controllable by my will and judgement."[20] This delusion is self-destructive. Living as though one's bank account is infinite is a recipe for bankruptcy. Thinking we can fly, our attempts to live without support may feel exhilarating at first, but are headed for a messy end. We have a "deeply rooted aversion to our own creatureliness"[21] and so "it is not natural for us to be natural."[22] Trying to become greater, we are diminished; attempting to become gods, we thwart even our good creatureliness.

This problem is more complex and stubborn than the failings of any one person; it subsists in a network of faulty and self-perpetuating relationships. The illusion of my self-sufficiency prevents the reception of gifts from another and so undermines her generosity. Her consequent miserliness reinforces my feeling of independence. In a similar dysfunctional relational pattern, the illusion of my control requires the threat or use of violence to be maintained and her subsequent experience of violation reduces her capacity for accepting her vulnerability. Finding it accordingly

---

20. Williams, *Resurrection*, 17.
21. Williams, "On Being Creatures," 77.
22. Williams, *Teresa of Avila*, 180.

more difficult to entrust herself to others, she begins instead to crave her own form of control.

Our misplaced desire to be more than creatures thus becomes self-defeating. To pursue this desire, in the long run, often renders its goal even less attainable. This is why Williams can argue that in this cycle of failure "[s]elf-dependence is revealed as a mechanism of self-destruction; to cling to it in the face of God's invitation to trust is a thinly veiled self-hatred."[23]

Ironically, this predicament is exacerbated and propagated by the very vulnerability and dependence we seek to transcend:

> We are born into a world where there is *already* a history of oppression and victimization: our moral and spiritual growth does not occur in a vacuum. And so, before we can be conscious of it, the system of oppressor-victim relations absorbs us. It is this "already" which theology (sometimes rather unhelpfully) refers to as original sin—the sense of a primordial "diminution" from which we all suffer before ever we are capable of understanding or choice.[24]

This image of sin as a diminution or privation for which we compensate through depriving others is an important one for Williams. It combines an implied affront to the creator's ability to provide with a sense of injury to the self that is evident in and propagated through all our relationships.[25]

We are each less than we feel we ought to be and disastrously respond by a further denial of our creatureliness. Our perception of lack leads to the avoidance of anything limited and so we seek refuge from the apparent deficiency of the particular and local in the abstract and general. Williams' analysis therefore helps to explain the enduring popularity of various versions of Gnosticism, in which the contingent and fleshly are placed squarely outside the purposes of God.[26]

The desire for extra-creaturely invulnerability is not the unique preoccupation of a defiant pride but can also be expressed in a timorous shrinking from responsibility. Yet even the flight to the relative safety of passivity is a refusal of the creaturely responsibility to act and nurture others.

---

23. Williams, *Wound of Knowledge*, 17.

24. Williams, *Resurrection*, 18.

25. In this way he avoids an account of sin that is voluntarist and one-dimensional: whether with reference to God (as the transgression of divine will), self (as self-contradiction) or neighbor (as constraint of freedom).

26. Williams, *Wound of Knowledge*, 34.

The insecurity of a finite self may also result in another self-defensive (but ultimately self-destructive) move: the fantasy of securing impregnability through irrefutable acts. Refusing our creaturely limitations, we may have a desire to wrap things up, to impose neatness and cohesion, indulging in "the apocalyptic delusion, the belief that we can stop, reverse or cancel history, that we can assume the 'divine' prerogative of acting with decisive finality in the affairs of the world, that we can 'make an end.'"[27] This misdirected protest against our own finitude is not only futile, it is also destructive. The echoes of finding a "final solution" to our problems ought to make us shudder. As creatures, our projects remain provisional and ambiguous; they are open to correction, misunderstanding, clarification, reinterpretation, confusion, and opposition. The attempt to leave an indelible and irrefutable stamp upon history is an inhumane megalomania. Williams thus sounds a warning against all utopian dreams.

Our common susceptibility to death feeds this desire for finality by enabling fantasies of destruction, obliteration, erasure. The past and its problems can be swept aside by playing god. But God doesn't work like this. He is the creator of new things through the resurrection and transformation of the old. The "end of the world" of which Jesus' resurrection is a sneak preview is not really an end, but a new beginning in which all things are made fresh. There is no un-making, simply re-making: "Grace will remake but not undo. There is all the difference in the world between Christ uncrucified and Christ risen: they speak of two different hopes for humanity, one unrealizable, the other barely imaginable but at least truthful."[28] His resurrection does not cancel his crucifixion; his appearances included scars and so disallowed any easy triumphalism.

This hints at another irony exposed by Williams. Our sinful flight from limitation and dependence involves the temptation to be "like God." Yet the gods whose outlines we mimic in our disgust at being mere creatures turn out to be nightmarish distortions of the God revealed in Jesus. We dream of being untouched and untouchable, safe from the vicissitudes of human society, but the only God we find in Jesus is one "whose being is directed towards the world"[29] and who therefore sends us back into engagement with it. If Christian spirituality is to take Christ seriously, then

27. Williams, *Resurrection*, 17.
28. Ibid., 81.
29. Williams, *Teresa of Avila*, 206.

there is no promise of escape from a messy world: "[T]he Word is flesh and is communicated in flesh—in historical tradition, in personal human encounter, in material sacrament. The Word re-forms the possibilities of human existence and calls us to the creation of new humanity in the public, the social, and historical world—to the transformation of behaviour and relationship, knowing God in acting and making."[30]

However, if there is no authentic Christian spirituality that is fundamentally world-denying, Williams is equally scathing of a shallow and bland world-affirmation that fails to realize that this Word-in-flesh is rejected and crucified by the world. Following an *incarnate* Savior means Christian spirituality must embrace the created order of finitude, contingency, and dependence; following a *crucified* Messiah means this order cannot be uncritically embraced as it is.

Furthermore, if the gospel narratives will not prescribe for us a univocal attitude towards the world, neither do they allow a comfortable appropriation of God to our cause. Emmanuel, God with us, nonetheless also stands over against us as a stranger and an other. Williams frequently underscores not only Jesus' identification with the Christian community as his body, but his refusal to be absorbed into it.[31] He is never simply the pattern to imitate, but a lover and judge with a dynamic relationship to the community that finds its life in him.

Therefore, if thankful recognition of God's gracious creation is the foundation for Williams' subversive account of spirituality, its heart is found in an acceptance of the task of becoming truly human in the shape and community of Jesus. His sharing of our humanity reversed and transfigured Adam's resentment at not being God into a free acceptance of that reality. Jesus "restores the glory of creatureliness" through his loving dependence upon the self-giving of God.[32] Jesus reveals that "fleshly life is not a burden to be borne, nor a prison to be escaped from, but a task to be perfected in grace."[33] And that task is to share Jesus' own humility in not grasping after equality with God, and thus to share the divine life in a properly human

---

30. Williams, *Wound of Knowledge*, 189–90.

31. Williams, *Resurrection*, 76, 84, 95; idem, *Teresa of Avila*, 116; and idem, "Between the Cherubim: The Empty Tomb and the Empty Throne," in *On Christian Theology*, 192–93.

32. Williams, "Creation, Creativity and Creatureliness," n.p.

33. Williams, *Wound of Knowledge*, 30. Williams is here approvingly summarizing Ignatius of Antioch.

way. In so doing, we are "deified." Williams is not averse to this language, as long as it is understood as "enjoying the divine relationship of Son to Father," not "sharing the divine 'substance.'"[34] Our true godliness consists in truly embracing the fact that we are creatures: "Salvation, then, is in no sense a flight to God from what is human, but the realizing of God's 'likeness,' and so the sharing of his life, in what is human."[35]

The Healing of Desire and Memory

This is no easy calling. Coming as we do into a system of relationships already stuck in patterns of diminution, our desires are compromised by delusions of false grandeur (and false worthlessness). To do what comes "naturally" will not suffice since our created nature has been obscured by our resentment towards it. The re-forming and healing of the self requires the denial of self-sufficiency even in knowing what is needed. To adequately recognize our poverty, we must also acknowledge "an inability to prescribe exactly what will supply that lack."[36] We must stay ever open to the further purification of our desires in the light of the truth manifest in Christ.

For instance, the recognition of sin and self-destructive tendencies may be associated with a desire for a clean slate and a fresh start, unhindered by the present struggles. Yet Williams claims that such a desire is itself unhealthy. How so? Are not our old selves crucified with Christ, according to Paul (Gal 2:19–20)? Is there not a new creation if anyone is in Christ (2 Cor 5:17)? Yes, but remember that grace does not un-make, only re-make. Even the crucifixion of the self with Christ pictured by Paul does not leave a *tabula rasa*. Our past is not obliterated. Instead, it is from these very patterns of brokenness and failure that the first signs of true humanity arise; we abandon the fantasy in which we simply shed our history and memory and instead accept that we are to be re-made where we are. The start of this new creation may well be a right remembering of the very patterns that have not miraculously disappeared. To remember rightly includes awareness of our failures *and* that in Christ we are unconditionally accepted and forgiven by God. Unless I own my history as *my* history, there is no hope that forgiveness

---

34. Ibid., 59; cf. *Resurrection*, 87.
35. Williams, *Wound of Knowledge*, 39.
36. Williams, *Resurrection*, 77.

will function not only backwards in absolution but also forwards in transformation. To recognize both my poverty and God's grace is to receive an invitation, a summons, into a richer life of what relations with God and others can and should be: "Forgiven-ness is precisely the deep and abiding sense of what relation—with God or with other human beings—can and should be; and so it is itself a stimulus, an irritant, necessarily provoking protest at impoverished versions of social and personal relations."[37]

Forgiveness is not just a liberation from, it is also a liberation to a new way of living. However, in this quotation Williams perhaps overstates his case by *identifying* forgiveness with this new awareness. Unless forgiveness is first a liberation from fear and guilt over past failures, then it opens no new horizons. The picture of a better future becomes an intolerable burden if release from the past is conditional upon its realization rather than its enabling presupposition.

Nonetheless, Williams helpfully sees that a central goal of Christian spiritual disciplines is facing the truth about myself in all my messiness rather than hiding in a comfortable amnesia regarding the specifics of my past. In order to discover my true identity—hidden under surface desires, anxious chatter, and other semi-conscious stratagems of self-defense from the truth—I must not forget that these very distractions are both no disqualification from God's loving acceptance and are the "raw material" on which Jesus lays his healing hands.

At the same time, this new identity baptized in Christ demands a disciplined forgetting. It is quite possible to become so preoccupied and fascinated by the very self I am learning to become that I continue the fantasy of seeing the world revolve around myself. In his careful reading of Teresa of Avila, Williams agrees with her on this point: "Proper self-awareness is, for Teresa, the opposite of self-consciousness, not fascination with oneself but familiarity with oneself, candour about strengths and weaknesses, alertness to dangers."[38] Wholesome self-knowledge is therefore primarily a tacit, or prereflective, knowledge of oneself as creature, with a history and limitations: "a practised familiarity with certain constraining facts, so that we reflectively adjust our behaviour in accordance with them."[39] The point of this awareness is to avoid a consuming preoccupation with interiority as an

37. Ibid., 45.
38. Williams, *Teresa of Avila*, 130.
39. Ibid., 149.

end in itself, even if this is in the pursuit of personal holiness. We need to know ourselves well enough to know when and how we might get trapped in thinking about only ourselves.

Sin, Self-deceit, and Suffering

The temptation to an enthralling interiority lies in forever amassing more details about our inner life. Yet to do so is once again to succumb to the lure of ignoring our creaturely context, to pretend that we are the only or the central player in our lives. Our created selves are always dependent upon others, vulnerable to their actions and reactions. At the most basic nutritional level, we are dependent upon the "other" of our planet's ecology. There is no route to a location in which we are "safe" from others. Our identity is never secure and given. Even new life in Christ is not a "possession" that may be taken as a given and kept ready to hand when danger threatens: "the new life is not simply infused in all-conquering fullness in a single moment."[40] Instead, it is "a new world of possibilities, a new future that is to be constructed day by day."[41]

Within this new world, this very absence of such "safety" is a defining feature. The Christian life is to be lived unsheltered from the realities with which it necessarily intersects; it is to be the opposite of an escapist fantasy. Quite apart from a careful attention towards all the facets of creaturely existence as a human amidst a world of difference and nuance, there are two realities in particular which Williams repeatedly emphasizes as primary orientations for an authentic Christian being-in-the-world: "We belong to a community doubly vulnerable: to self-deceit, and to the unremitting leavening of the truth proclaimed in word and sacrament."[42] An uninterrupted double vulnerability—to sin and to grace—defines the tacit self-awareness that Williams seeks.

> Forget you have a self to be shielded, reinforced, consoled and lied to: hear the bitter truth that the cross enunciates, and accept the pain and disorientation of that enlightenment, in the trust that you are not hated or abandoned; and come up from the flood with a new

---

40. Williams, *Wound of Knowledge*, 18.
41. Ibid., 19.
42. Williams, *Resurrection*, 59.

person "alive to God," living with your eyes set firmly on the ground and goal of hope which is Jesus.[43]

We are to thus "forget" to protect ourselves (an impossible and self-defeating dream) and face squarely both the pervasiveness of sin and temptation at every level of human existence and the unconditional acceptance of God that opens new possibilities for our creaturely way of life. Sin does not disqualify us from being a vehicle of God's action, nor does grace magically and immediately render us immune to the patterns of deceit and hurt ingrained in our communities and consciousness. Even the pursuit of Christian spirituality can itself be an escape from Christ if the path does not lead into the darkness of the cross in which both sin and grace find their apogee.[44]

In his focus on the all-embracing infection of sin, Williams walks in the footsteps of Augustine, Luther, and Barth. He suffers from no cheap optimism about an innate human potential for perfectibility. Like them, far from seeing this doctrine as an impetus to misanthropic moroseness, it is seen as the flip side of the freedom of divine grace. Like creation *ex nihilo*, this gracious love of the unlovely is unconditioned by any factor outside God's own bounty and delight in self-giving.

God's gracious love draws the creature not away from but further into the actual conditions of its existence, stripping away the fantasies that keep it from being itself, even if this means a greater exposure to the pain of these realities. Growth in maturity will be likely to involve an *increase* in pain as the false shelters of self-justification and delusional hopes are removed; I am more injured than I feared, more guilty than I realized. Jesus' crucifixion is not simply my cross, a symbol of the ways I too am an innocent victim. Williams argues that it is first and foremost the cross of an other, who refuses to be co-opted as a martyr endorsing my cause and instead uncovers the ways I too might be oppressor, not simply victim: "To see the cross as another's is to learn that pain and violence is something I am capable of causing. [. . .] I must meet the crucified Jesus again as a risen stranger, who will not allow me to define the world in terms of undifferentiated and

---

43. Ibid., 54.
44. Williams, *Wound of Knowledge*, 189.

unalterable pain, but insists that suffering is produced by the complex interrelations of persons, by the impulse to reject self and others."[45]

A self who begins to observe these complex interrelations might well ache with sorrow and sympathy. Openness to this ache is a sign of health, of a self becoming "more capable both of pain and of love."[46] Being open to this pain is not a passive acceptance of harm but a hope-filled groaning in tune with God's own Spirit, yearning for God's future homecoming. This very groaning is a sign that we are being included in the life of the crucified, in his relationship to the Father, and so can cry with him, "Abba!" The point at which we are most aware of our adoption is in our own Gethsemane, when "Abba!" is a groan of desperate need. Thus, the experience of suffering under the intolerable contradictions of human life is a hope-producing confirmation of our increasing conformation to the likeness of Christ, our increasing transformation into true humanity, into those able to trust God from within our creaturely existence.

Thus, a spirituality in harmony with God's Spirit will be characterized by a *dissatisfaction* with the present. Having "tasted the reality of new life, God's life, already, the life of self-gift and self-forgetting," it is impossible not to protest against the continuing lostness of humanity and creation and against one's own shortcomings. Just as salvation is not a secure identity but a new path, so there is a "*daily* refusal to accept that lost, 'deprived' humanity can simply be lived with or shrugged off."[47]

Community as Context and Goal

The double vulnerability—to sin and to grace—of an authentic Christian spirituality is not merely the experience of individuals, but a communal reality. A community that knows itself as liable to both these influences is both the most effective *context* of the self's recreation and the *goal* of it. "Relationship with others is the form that our growth in virtue takes; it is more than merely the occasion."[48] The rediscovery of a trusting creatureliness is necessarily a journey out of individualism; a liberation from

---

45. Williams, *Resurrection*, 72, 74.
46. Williams, *Wound of Knowledge*, 21. Williams is here quoting Dorothy Sölle.
47. Williams, *Resurrection*, 41.
48. Williams, *Wound of Knowledge*, 114. Williams is here quoting Fergus Kerr.

the delusion of setting my own purpose, defining my own identity, and from my "strange preference for the heavy burden of self-justification, self-creation."[49] Christianity can never be a private religion.

The existence of "a historical human community characterized by certain kinds of relation" is a key medium through which grace is made concrete and the self is healed.[50] If, as already discussed, I am unable to entirely trust my self-evaluation, it may be that others have insights into myself that I lack. Perpetually vulnerable to sin, there is no guarantee that what I know of myself will be superior to what others know of me (nor vice versa).[51] I therefore need my neighbor to know myself. Similarly, the community itself, not simply its members, must wake up from any triumphalist dream; for it "has no option but to live in penitence, in critical self-awareness and acknowledgement of failure. It must recognize constantly its failing *as* a community to *be* the community of gift and mutuality, and warn itself of the possibility of failure."[52] Simultaneously, the community remains open to grace and so must also refrain from imagining that any failure can bring a decisive end to the community of gift. In fact, the "success" of the community in shaping people in the way of truth and life is almost impossible to measure because it is largely invisible except as struggle and weakness.[53]

True spirituality is necessarily communal because "the barriers of egotistic fantasy are broken by the sheer brute presence of other persons. The will 'co-operates' precisely because it is limited and constrained, attracted or repelled, irritated and tantalized by the boundaries set by others around it."[54] My vulnerability to self-deception makes private discipleship an oxymoron. Yet at the same time, the community needs the critical reflections of its members, since self-deception can be suffered collectively.

Moreover, community is not merely instrumental to our becoming more whole as creatures, but is itself also the fruit of wholeness. If sin divides and isolates then salvation is tasted in an experience of communion with others in which difference is respected and creaturely interdependence

---

49. Williams, *Where God Happens*, 68.
50. Williams, *Resurrection*, 93.
51. Williams, *Teresa of Avila*, 31.
52. Williams, *Resurrection*, 48–49.
53. Williams, *Where God Happens*, 25.
54. Williams, *Wound of Knowledge*, 115.

affirmed.⁵⁵ My project as a human creature in the image of God is essentially bound up with my neighbor's relation to God, because to grow is to become more in tune with a creation that is made by and for self-giving community. For creatures in a world generated by divine kenotic generosity, there is no such thing as solitary growth. Therefore, the deepening of my spirituality is found through helping to put my neighbor in touch with God in Christ, and so in touch with the whole community of his creation.⁵⁶ In this way, as a member of Christ's body, I participate in the mediation of his gracious healing, and am myself made more whole. ⁵⁷

As a result, "the church [is] the place where creation is itself [. . .] the church is the future of creation, the church is what humanity is about, the church is the promise of fulfilment" because this is where "matter is transformed into divine gift," where persons are there for each other.⁵⁸ The comprehension of such exalted claims requires one to remember two points already mentioned: the divine kenotic wisdom in creating, which places being-for-another at the heart of the universe; and the creaturely frailty and fallenness that make any present ecclesial experience of this wisdom partial, filled with contradiction and weakness.

Contemplative Prayer

No account of Williams' writings on spirituality would be complete without some consideration of his comments on contemplation. We are dependent creatures, whose lives and spirituality are inextricably woven together with others in communities of mutual need and giving. Yet if we come to a point where this means an absolutizing of a frenetic activism, even of mutual service, then we might well lose sight of the fundamental character of creatureliness as reception of a gift. It is very difficult to maintain a balance

---

55. It is worth noting that in his treatment of community as the proper context of creaturely dependence, Williams bucks a contemporary theological trend to draw more direct links between the sociality of the Trinity and human community.

56. Williams, *Where God Happens*, 15.

57. Of course, more needs to be said here about the foundational role of the Scriptures in the mediation of Christ to his church. This is a theme less frequently expounded by Williams.

58. Williams, "Creation, Creativity and Creatureliness," n.p.

between being "actively in the world and at the same time wholly exposed to the reality of God."[59]

Therefore, the spiritual discipline of contemplation serves to focus attention away from the self, and away even (at least for a period) from the neighbor, in order to discover in silence the joy of existence as pure gift. Such awareness cannot be grasped or produced, lest this very attempt undermine the experience of *reception*. When Williams follows Teresa of Avila's own reflections upon and defenses of this practice in some detail, he summarizes contemplation as "essentially a matter of the sustained awareness of living within the movement of God's love into creation through the life and death of Jesus Christ."[60] It is a matter of being open to God, not through a technique, but through prayer that is fully conscious of what it is, an approach to the throne of grace. When we confront a taste of God's reality as the sheer gift that is the source of our own creatureliness, our seductive illusions of control and sufficiency are mortally threatened. Thus, contemplation is not the denial of our creaturely limitations in seeking to be absorbed into a mystical union with God's being: "The union that matters is union with the divine will, not an experience of absorption."[61] And so contemplative prayer is "the struggle to become the kind of person who can without fear be open to the divine activity,"[62] that is, to be open to God's gracious self-giving in which we become truly ourselves. As discussed above, when God gives in creating he does so unconditionally and so establishes difference. Therefore, neither God nor the creature need be threatened that each is not the other. The practices of contemplation are an attempt to learn to not be threatened by this difference and so to become satisfied being a mere creature.

However, he is very clear, both in his book-length reading of Teresa and his series of reflections published as *Where God Happens*, that the goal of contemplation is not any particular psychological phenomenon during mental prayer, but the reception of God's kenotic wisdom into the self and the community: "If the 'mystical' ultimately means the reception of a particular *pattern* of divine action (creative love, self-emptying incarnation), its test will be the presence or absence of something like that pattern in a human life seen as a whole, not the presence or absence of this or that

59. Williams, *Teresa of Avila*, 208.
60. Ibid., 13.
61. Ibid., 204.
62. Williams, "On Being Creatures," 75.

phenomenon in the consciousness."⁶³ "What is to be learned in the desert [i.e., in contemplation] is clearly not some individual technique for communing with the divine but the business of becoming a means of reconciliation and healing for the neighbour."⁶⁴ The goal of both service and contemplation is to become self-forgetfully engaged in love for the other, which is the perfection of both creaturely and divine life.

In his various reflections upon contemplative or mental prayer, Williams aims to render intelligible such disciplines as appropriate and even necessary contributions to the historic and contemporary life of the Christian church. His consideration of contemplative disciplines is less a movement from theology to practice as it is a theological reflection upon practices that have proved fruitful in the experience and memory of the community. Hence, he does not deduce from first principles why these disciplines are a necessary part of Christian spirituality so much as seek in them the same eternal wisdom of divine generosity in which the universe coheres.

Appreciation

Williams' positive contributions to reflection upon the nature of Christian spirituality are numerous. Let us briefly consider a few of the more significant ones.

This account emphasizes commitment to the actual. Truth matters far more than sincerity and humanity is called to risk exposure to reality. The danger in losing our protective mechanisms and escapist fantasies is that we might learn who we really are.

A commitment to what is real extends beyond opposition to untruth to include a dedication to the here and now context in which we live. I must learn to be a creature not in the abstract, but in the particular difficulties and weaknesses of my skin and my environment. I am espoused to my body, my history, my limits, and possibilities: "there is no goodness that is not bodily and realistic and local."⁶⁵

63. Williams, *Teresa of Avila*, 187.
64. Williams, *Where God Happens*, 33.
65. Ibid., 107. Cf. 119: "Here we are daily, not necessarily attractive and saintly people, along with other not very attractive and saintly people, managing the plan prose of our everyday service, deciding daily to recognize the prose of ourselves and each other as material for something unimaginably greater—the Kingdom of God, the glory of the saints, reconciliation and wonder."

Such creaturely fidelity to local actuality includes a deliberate recognition and acceptance of limits, and as an important corollary, the embrace of vulnerability. This stands in stark contrast to a culture obsessed with security—personal, financial, social, military—and in which risk is minimized, calculated, and insured. Without an acceptance of thresholds to our abilities, we endlessly pursue mastery over our selves, our neighbors, and our environment—ironically, making ourselves less safe as a result. Instead, "the gospel tells us you never on earth get to a place where you are safe; but you will get to a place where you are blissful and united with your Father in heaven."[66] So wisdom lies in discarding the belief that we can secure our existence and instead joyfully embracing our creatureliness in its fragility and fallibility.

This embrace entails the acceptance of the full range of our human existence: emotional, social, material, artistic, economic, bodily, political, and so on. Nothing that is truly human is outside or opposed to Christian spirituality. Nor is anything truly human to be ultimately excluded from God's future. Accordingly, the present taste of that future in Christian community will include signs of proleptic transformation across the gamut of human reality. For instance, in the Eucharist we "recognize the possibility of the world's transfiguration, in the name and power of Jesus, into a world of justice and peace; not to allow this possibility to be realized, not to act in such a way that our belief in transformed relations is made evident, is to be convicted of unbelief."[67]

Thus here is found a far richer account of sin than the common perception of more or less arbitrary peccadilloes, isolated transgressions of an inscrutable divine will. Instead, sin can be understood as the denial of our most basic creaturehood, a self-destructive assumption of a counterfeit divinity.

Consequently, the illusory pursuit of impregnability is an attempt to foreclose the possibility of new life and of the surprising transformation of human existence into new permutations. In contrast, a spirituality rooted in

---

66. Williams, "Creation, Creativity and Creatureliness," n.p.

67. Williams, *Resurrection*, 106. Cf. Williams, *Where God Happens*, 115–16: "Only the body saves the soul. It sounds rather shocking put like that, but the point is that the soul left to itself, the inner life or whatever you want to call it, is not capable of transforming itself. It needs the gifts that only the external life can deliver: the actual events of God's action in history, heard by physical ears; the actual material fact of the meeting of believers where bread and wine are shared; the actual wonderful, disagreeable, impossible, unpredictable human beings we encounter daily, in and out of the church. Only in this setting do we become holy, and holy in a way unique to each one of us."

creaturely difference need not feel threatened by diversity but can pay sensitive attention to the unique and strange in a person, experience or culture, confident that the God who allows us to be other is not thereby dishonored. The Christian community thus has room for "distinctive vocations to be discovered in such a way that they are a source of mutual enrichment and delight, not threat. It is a place where real human difference is nourished."[68] Indeed, there is room for the exploration my own unique vocation without succumbing to a crude individualism based on self-assertion and mastery.

Finally, Williams' account gives a definite place, within the generative wisdom of God, to the non-human creation as also genuinely different to humanity. Liberated from seeing it merely as resources to be exploited in our projects, it retains its own specific creaturely dignity. "When we can imagine what is materially around us as existing in relation to something other than our own purposes, we are free to be surprised, educated and enlarged by it."[69]

Critical Questions

The scope and creativity of Williams' thought (not to mention the breadth of his published output) gives ample opportunity for critical questioning but makes comprehensive evaluation difficult. Therefore, I will confine myself to concluding with three lines of queries.

Firstly, how legitimate is it to pursue a fully kenotic reading of the Trinity? Is the Son's *kenosis* in incarnation transferable to our understanding of Father and Spirit? Barth, for instance, argued that the proper personhood of the Son is expressed in his obedience;[70] Bruce McCormack has recently extended this to claim that *kenosis* is the peculiar and definitive characteristic of the Son.[71] So when Williams wants to find parallels to the

---

68. Williams, *Where God Happens*, 66.

69. Rowan Williams, "Lecture: Ecology and Economy—University of Kent, Canterbury," Archbishop of Canterbury Web site, http://www.archbishopofcanterbury.org/1165 (accessed February 22, 2008), n.p.

70. Karl Barth, *Church Dogmatics* IV/1 §59.1 (Edinburgh: T. & T. Clark, 1956) 157–210.

71. Bruce McCormack, "The Humility of the Eternal Son: A Reformed Version of Kenotic Christology," T. F. Torrance lectures presented at St. Andrews University, Scotland, December 4–7, 2007, publication forthcoming from CUP.

Incarnation in the Father's eternal kenotic generation of the Son, and God's kenotic creation of the world, might this be to confuse the persons?

Yet, even if it is the case that we ought not to conceive of the Father's love as kenotic in a similar manner to the Son's, Williams' spirituality of creatureliness would not be seriously compromised since the Son's self-giving is still the wisdom through which the world was made. Therefore, for us to live as creatures in light of that divine self-giving wisdom remains an appropriate human vocation.

Secondly, as part of avoiding God's totalizing of all meaning, Williams denies the image of God as monarch, at least in some of its versions.[72] Indeed, perhaps this is related to the reciprocity of self-giving between Father and Son in Williams' thought; if the Son is not uniquely kenotic, the Father is not uniquely monarchic. As is often the case with Trinitarian theology, political implications are not too far away.

Yet might it not be the case that just as Williams re-invigorated a traditional doctrine of creation *ex nihilo* through a careful Trinitarian reading, so also the thoroughly scriptural notion of divine rule might be made intelligible through a Trinitarian reading, as good news through the reign (and obedience) of Jesus in the power of the Spirit? Certainly this will involve an unmasking of notions of universal divine "control"—of God the ubiquitous manipulator. But might it not also generate a *positive* conception of creative authority, an authority which gives life and liberates? Admittedly, in any proposal to revive the concept of authority there lurks the risk of sanctioning hubristic and authoritarian rule. That is why it is crucial to insist, with Williams, on the careful distinction between creaturely and divine resourcefulness, a distinction which warns against any direct attempts to derive a conception of monarchic human authority on the basis of the image of God as king. Thus, any naïve or insidious direct parallels between human and divine authority are disqualified. But this does not require the elimination of a conception of God the monarch. Quite the reverse, since the latter, when understood in the light of the Servant King, can function as a corrective to human abuses of power.

Thirdly, Williams repeatedly claims that the embracing of our creaturely existence includes the acceptance of death.[73] He thus helpfully rules

---

72. Williams, "On Being Creatures," 78.

73. Williams, "Creation, Creativity and Creatureliness," n.p; "On Being Creatures," 76, 78; "Politics and the Soul: A Reading of *The City of God*," *Milltown Studies* 19/20 (1987) 69.

out a naïve self-delusion in which we blind ourselves to the inevitability of our own mortality. Perhaps it also rules out certain kinds of longing for post-mortem existence that exemplify a failure to grasp our being as creatures. For instance, belief in the unconditional immortality of the soul may express a yearning for life outside of the need for openness, which can be secure in the knowledge of its untouchability. Instead, we must realize that all life, even resurrection life, is a gift from the author of life. There is no unconditional immortality for creatures; creaturely receptivity to God's gift is always apt. To put this in s criptural images: the tree of life upon which humanity depends is found in both Genesis and Revelation. Creaturely hope therefore does not require the circumventing of death, or for it to be downplayed through claims that we will survive; "We don't hope for survival but for re-creation."[74]

However, in asking us to accept our death, Williams seems to obscure the scriptural depiction of death as the final enemy of God and humanity (1 Cor 15:20–28), as an alien intruder and consequence of sin, not simply of creaturely finitude (Rom 5:12–21). Angels, however else we understand them, depict the possibility of a creaturely existence not subject to death. And in the light of Christ's resurrection, Christian hope includes a yearning for the death of death, for new life no longer ruled by death. This is not necessarily the hasty and bland response to Easter that Williams cautions against, the response that celebrates a shallow triumphalism—as though the cross has been cancelled or made obsolete.[75] Williams rightly claims that true spirituality includes liberation from the deadening fear of death, and that this must be through God's victory over death, not simply its reinterpretation into something less fearful.

Might it be not be necessary, therefore, for us only to "accept" our death in the same strictly circumscribed sense in which we "accept" the ongoing possibility and actuality of sin? That is, not embracing either as a good part of creaturely finitude, but neither disregarding them in willful ignorance? Does not resurrection hope make us perennially dissatisfied with both sin and death?

Williams' discussion is very fruitful insofar as he invites us to acknowledge our own death as a creaturely possibility, and not to avoid or

---

74. Williams, "Easter Day Sermon," Archbishop of Canterbury Web site, http://www.archbishopofcanterbury.org/1634 (accessed March 25, 2008), n.p.

75. Williams, *Resurrection*, 78.

minimize its significance. Yet where recognition becomes welcome, his language of "accepting death" may dilute the Easter hope for the end of death.

Spirituality is not something we fashion or select for ourselves. It is the experience of being authentically a creature before a generous God. It is the healing of our fearful and self-deceptive human condition and our being turned inside out, toward God, and one another. It is a creative project of sharing the very gifts we have received. "Freely you have received; freely give." In this, the risen Christ is not simply our model, but the author of our faith.

7

Desire and Grace:
Williams and the Search for Bodily Wholeness

ANDREW CAMERON

In his 1989 address to the UK's Lesbian and Gay Christian Movement, Rowan Williams outlines how sexual expression needs to be understood as an experience of "the body's grace," and as a discovery of that grace.[1] This evocative turn of phrase is meant to connote two distinctive Christian themes.

First, sexual expression is an act of grace at its core. It is only in mutual self-giving, rather than in individualistic sexual fantasy or pleasure- or power-seeking, that we discover sex at its most human and most

---

1. Williams, *The Body's Grace* (London: Lesbian and Gay Christian Movement, 2002). Reprinted in Charles C. Hefling, ed., *Our Selves, Our Souls, and Bodies: Sexuality and the Household of God* (Cambridge, MA: Cowley, 1996) 58–68, and in Eugene F. Rogers, ed. *Theology and Sexuality: Classic and Contemporary Readings* (Oxford: Blackwell, 2002) 309–21. Page references in the main text are to Williams' essay and will follow the Rogers edition.

The Rogers and Hefling versions are identical. The Lesbian and Gay Christian Movement (LGCM) version is identical to an online version (http://www.igreens.org.uk/bodys_grace.htm, accessed February 4, 2008). But the LGCM/online text differs from the Rogers/Hefling text. In view of the accessibility of the LGCM/online version, I will note where these differences seem significant.

meaningful. The grace consists in the way we may allow ourselves to be seen as desirable in the eyes of another. When we give ourselves to that desire, we in turn rediscover ourselves as desirable. This "recreation" (p. 314) of ourselves through the eyes of another "parallels," we might say, the central experience of the Christian gospel: that we have been desired by God, whatever else we may think of ourselves. ("Parallels" is too weak a way to summarize what Williams thinks happens. The best sex instantiates, recalls, and reflects divine grace, and although the term "sacrament" is never bought into play, the concept may hover in the periphery.)

Second, this grace is embodied. It is not an idea, a mental construct or a future state. It is in the melding together of self-giving, desire, and bodily awareness that we "come to ourselves" (to paraphrase Sarah Layton's experience, p. 311), finding both our creation and redemption enacted in the present.

Not all sex is like this, to be sure—far from it. In offering us a theological appraisal of sex, Williams also offers a diagnostic for sex at its worst. He is quick to point out the many ways in which sex falls terribly or drearily short of the bodily expression of grace. Not least of these are moments in or versions of marriage, which is not in its own right a guarantee of embodied grace. On Williams' account, sex is risky and precarious, for there is no legal or conventional or normed way to ensure the experience of grace.

If the best sex is constituted in bodily grace, a surprising outcome follows. Homosexual sex, which cannot be justified as instrumental to the population of the world, may instantiate embodied grace most clearly. Same-sex love "brings us up against the possibility . . . of non-functional joy; or, to put it less starkly, joy whose material 'production' is an embodied person aware of grace" (p. 318). In turn we discover the possibility of a Creator whose exuberance creates us for joy.

In such reflections, Williams is seeking to discern the "inner logic and process of the sexual relation itself" (p. 318). That is, he is seeking to discern the existential meaning of sexual expression—how we are to construe such experiences as humans and as subjects. By contrast, conservative appeals to nature, gender complementarity or the authority of Scripture do not necessarily explore the "inner logic" of sex, and so fail to render their own sexual ethic subjectively intelligible. (Proponents of these views could equally argue that a full account of sexuality's subjective inner logic is inaccessible to us; but generally they do not.) As a result, these appeals can seem facile, unable to explain how and why even married heterosexual sex fails to live up to its promise, and why so many married couples find themselves in situations where sexuality figures centrally in their reports of confusion and pain.

It is hard not to long for Williams' vision of the possibilities of sexual experience. The central advantage of his approach is not even that he interprets and articulates these possibilities in an existentially satisfying way. It is that he comprehends our sexual aspect in reference to the gracious love of the Godhead as revealed in Christ.

At the same time, he outlines what makes our sexual desire and its expression risky, leaving us vulnerable and opening us to embarrassment and disappointment. In doing so he suggests that much conventional sexual ethics is an attempt to control and minimize this risk, effectively banishing from our presence a means for discovering the nature of grace.

In this response, I want to join with Williams to discover whatever is discoverable about the inner logic of sexual relations. I will mainly confine my attention to *The Body's Grace*, even though Williams has recently distanced himself a little from it.[2] In his subsequent role as Archbishop of Canterbury, he has made other statements about marriage and sexuality. But the conceptual terrain laid out in 1989 deserves attention on its own terms. I take the liberty of this close engagement on the grounds that Archbishop Williams has not formally resiled from Professor Williams' arguments; and even if he had, they retain some force.

I make no attempt to hide my theological and social conservatism, and so will engage with the essay on that basis. But I will not recount what conservatives do and say at their best. Rather, I hope to outline what conservatives aspire to do, and to concede where Williams' account corrects us at our worst. In turn I hope he will receive some suggestions about what may be defects in his account. I will argue as follows:

---

2. "Twenty years ago I wrote an essay in which I advocated a different direction. That was when I was still a professor, to stimulate debate. It did not generate much support and a lot of criticism—quite fairly on a number of points." He does not enumerate the points on which he believes he was fairly criticized. Wim Houtman, "'The Church is not inclusive': an interview with Archbishop Rowan Williams," *Nederlands Dagblad*, August 19, 2006, http://www.nd.nl/htm/dossier/seksualiteit/artikelen/060819eb.htm.

1. A Christian sexual ethic fails badly when it ignores Williams' central insight that the gracious recognition and reception of embodied desire is necessary to good sexual expression.
2. Conservatives who appeal to "biblical authority" think that human "essence" or identity is not necessarily easily accessible, self-evident or obvious, and that the Bible discloses unanticipated aspects of human being and human possibility. Concepts such as "nature," "gender complementarily," procreative potential, and lifelong faithfulness arise *a posteriori* from a heuristic process of reading. We are thereby inducted into how we may humbly receive these other gifts of embodiment.
3. A thin account of celibacy is a common conservative aporia. Williams partially redresses it, but does not recognize that a full account of celibacy also requires an expansive vision of community friendships. If we fail to recognize the role of community friendships, it seems difficult to expect that it will be the norm for celibates to live alongside married couples in the Christian community. But once the role of these relationships is recognized, this norm is far more satisfying.
4. Williams' account may not completely avoid "sexual essentialism," which may in turn trade upon a more subtle "emotional essentialism." Evangelical moral theology need not presume either essentialism (although in practice, conservative communities do inculcate some very problematic essentialisms).
5. Some provisional observations about the Anglican Communion's current vexed situation are offered. I also observe the relevance of my argument to two recent comments by the Archbishop.

Whether or not I persuade anyone to a conservative view is less important on this occasion than the more modest task of indicating how a conservative sexual ethic can be plausible, livable, and indeed satisfying. If I achieve this goal, I hope to have assisted in the ongoing difficult discussion between Christians.[3]

3. Although all the cracks in the edifice are entirely my own, I want to acknowledge my debts to Michael Banner, Michael Hill, Stanley Hauerwas, and Oliver O'Donovan. I will not labor the point by continually referencing their ideas, but interested readers might consult: Michael Banner, *Christian Ethics and Contemporary Moral Problems* (Cambridge: Cambridge University Press, 1999) 252–68; Michael Hill, *The How and Why of Love: An Introduction to Evangelical Ethics* (Kingsford: Matthias Media, 2002); Stanley Hauerwas, "Sex in Public: How Adventurous Christians Are Doing It," in *The Hauerwas Reader*, edited by John Berkman and Michael G. Cartwright (Durham, NC: Duke University Press, 2001) 481–504; idem, "Gay Friendship: A Thought Experiment in Catholic Moral Theology," in *Theology and Sexuality:*

The Central Insight

Williams' essay makes use of the Paul Scott character Sarah Layton, a generous but lonely woman whose cynically manipulated seduction results in an aborted pregnancy and further pain. Yet in and after this sexual experience, "she had entered into her body's grace" (p. 311, citing Scott). Conservative responses have taken exception to Williams' appeal to this narrative in the development of his argument.

The usual response is to express puzzlement or disapproval that Williams has not proceeded according to biblical foundationalism, which begins (and may even end) with an interpretation of sexuality based on Genesis 1–2. To a conservative reader, Williams' approach seems at worst pretentious, and at best an idiosyncratic artifact of his sensibility as a poet and sensitive reader.

Conservatives, however, need to hear the contribution this narrative makes to Williams' account of sexual expression. By using the well-drawn character of Sarah, who is almost a worst-case example of consensual sexual involvement, Williams proceeds to explain why our moments of sexual expression, or our yearnings for them, may be accompanied by an inarticulate sense that much more is at stake than merely the presence or absence of pleasure. Since his explanation does look to the Godhead, he can claim that "much public Christian comment on these matters is not only non-theological but positively anti-theological" and "an abstract fundamentalist deployment of a number of very ambiguous texts" (p. 320). That is, a biblical foundationalist deontology seems incapable of making sexuality intelligible either in terms of our experience or in the light of our relationship to God.

These opponents surely also fail to consider the occasion of Williams' original address. He recounts Sarah's presence without belonging, expressed in her joyless detachment from community and family. There is an "appalling" mother, and half-formed connections and lost opportunities with older women whose self-identities are similarly adrift. We also meet Paul Scott's Ronald Merrick, a man whose abhorrence at his homosexual yearnings begins the eventual erosion of his soul. What must it have meant for some of those first listeners to hear a theologian recognize their experience of years or decades of silence, estrangement, longing or self-loathing? By

---

Classic and Contemporary Readings, edited by Eugene F. Rogers (Malden, MA: Blackwell, 2002) 289–305; and Oliver O'Donovan, *Good News for Gay Christians*, online: http://www.fulcrum-anglican.org.uk/news/2007/200701080donovan7.cfm?doc=179.

approaching these experiences obliquely and through the artifice of particular stories, and by asking the opening question, "Why does sex matter?" (p. 310), Williams brings hope that sexual experiences do not have to be yet more of the same and may even point to the divine grace for which all humanity longs. Abstract arguments would not inspire much hope in such a company, and would not offer much evidence that their authors have tried to notice those hidden inner worlds that a gay and lesbian community would know.

Williams' central insight is to discern (with the help of Thomas Nagel) the way the "humanity" of our sexual involvements consists in a reciprocity of desire. When one's sexual arousal and desire is gratefully received by another, and that other's reciprocal desire springs forth to be received by one's self, the cascade of giving and receiving is the culmination of one's embodied self entering "into the shared world of language and (in the widest sense!) 'intercourse'" (p. 312). The awful risk that we all know so well from adolescence and beyond is that our desire will not be received, and neither it nor by extension our self will be received as pleasing. But when all goes well, the excellence of sex lies not primarily in its physical pleasure but in the joy of this interpersonal meeting.

> For my body to be the cause of joy, the end of homecoming, for me, it must be there for someone else, be perceived, accepted, nurtured; and that means being given over to the creation of joy in that other, because only as directed to the enjoyment, the happiness, of the other does it become unreservedly lovable. To desire my joy is to desire the joy of the one I desire: my search for enjoyment through the bodily presence of another is a longing to be enjoyed in my body ... We are pleased because we are pleasing. (p. 313)

To think of this experience in terms of grace requires the grammar of theology and its account of grace. Why does sex matter so much to us? Why does it often seem much more important than a mere exercise in pleasure? Williams is to be applauded for his attempt to decode for us what we find hard to understand about ourselves, by locating sexual expression within the horizon of divine grace.

He identifies scriptural attestations of his argument both in the revolutionary mutuality of 1 Corinthians 7:4, and in the way several biblical authors use marital imagery for divine grace. We may go further and observe how these authors even situate human marriage as chronologically and ontologically subsequent to relationship between God, or God in Christ, and his people (Hos 3:1 and *passim*; Eph 5:23–33; Rev 19:7–8, 21:2). The incredibly audacious Isaiah 62:5, where "as the bridegroom rejoices in his bride, so will your God rejoice in you," is an extraordinary image of hot desire that both classical theism and modern conservatism would baulk at. Human marriage is a parable and an enactment of the joyful, ardent, and inexplicably prodigious love of God. In this connection we might also remember the long tradition of reading *The Song of Solomon* as a parable for Christ's desire and love of his people, a tradition that does not require readers to be distracted from their own bodily desires!

Williams reserves his harshest words for those versions of marriage that take no account or make a mockery of this "process and relation" of sexuality. We may well accuse the young professor of some rather heavy-handed invective against marriage. Nevertheless, the Christian pastor or theologian can only repudiate with him those reductive accounts that allow marriage and marital sex to wither into the forms he describes. Conventional heterosexual morality "simply absolves us from the difficulties we might meet" in finding grace in sexual activity "because all we need to know is that sexual activity is licensed in one context and in no other" (p. 314). Marriage serves to distance us from "the embarrassment and insecurity of desire," because procreation is "a good cause that can be visibly and plainly evaluated in its usefulness and success" (p. 318). The grace of sexuality has simply become "fenced with conditions" (p. 312). In the worst cases, "in a great many cultural settings, the socially licensed norm of heterosexual intercourse is a 'perversion'" (p. 313) because of imbalances and asymmetries in its sexual politics and processes. "[T]he facts of the situation are that an enormous number of 'sanctioned' unions are a framework for violence and human destructiveness on a disturbing scale; sexual union is not delivered from moral danger and ambiguity by satisfying a formal socioreligious criterion" (p. 316).[4]

---

4. The picture is even bleaker in the essay's LGCM/online form, a divergence that may fuel misunderstandings. A paragraph in the LGCM/online version is not in the Rogers/Hefling text: "The worst thing we can do with the notion of sexual fidelity, though, is to 'legalise' it in such a way that it stands quite apart from the ventures and dangers of growth and is simply a public bond, enforceable by religious sanctions" (LGCM, 7).

On the blessing of sexual unions, a sentence in the LGCM/online version is significantly softened in the Rogers/Hefling text. LGCM/online: "If this blessing becomes a curse or an empty formality, it is both wicked and useless to hold up the sexuality of the canonically married heterosexual as absolute, exclusive and ideal" (LGCM, 7). Rogers/Hefling: "We should

There can be no doubt that Williams is correct. Marriages regularly and tragically fail in all these ways, and Williams lays bare a core aspect of sexuality that needs to be heard, spoken, and lived. Conservative sexual ethics is not devoid of such themes, as when my mentor in ethics wrote that sexual intercourse "is an act which should incorporate and symbolize the giving of the self, and the reception of the other."[5] Yet where conservative communities fail to envision such mutual grace, their pulpits extend mere deontology while their members quietly react as Williams predicts. "It doesn't matter what I do (say) with my body, because it's my inner life and emotions that matter" (p. 314). Here we could imagine the woman who consigns herself to sex as a duty and takes refuge in her fantasies for satisfaction. "The only criterion is what gives pleasure and does no damage" (p. 314). Here we could imagine the man who primes himself with porn so that the marital bed becomes a mental movie set starring himself. Under these conditions neither can find the true presence of the other. Without news of grace, there is little option for change.

Marriage: What Conservatives Aspire to Discern

We have seen the way Professor Williams perceived conservative views on sex and marriage. They are anti-theological and abstract because they defer to constructions extraneous to theology, such as gender complementarity and natural law, and so are prone to ad hoc uses of the Bible. Hence they cannot ascertain the true meaning of sex. But what do conservatives aspire to achieve in the deployment of these stratagems?

I will begin to answer this question by way of Williams' qualified use of biblical texts. The imagery of Hosea 3:1 (p. 319) "remains strongly patriarchal, not surprisingly, but" goes on to highlight a logic of sexuality as "process and relation." "Ephesians 5, for all its blatant assumption of male authority, still insists on the relational and personally creative element . . ." (p. 319). In a milieu suspicious of the value of these texts, these concessions to modern sensibilities about gender relations are an attempt to rehabilitate the texts for use in a sexual ethic "seriously informed by our Bible" (p. 319).

---

not do it in order to create a wholly impersonal and enforceable 'bond'; if we do, we risk turning blessing into curse, grace into law, art into rule-keeping" (Rogers, 315).

5. Hill, *How and Why*, 152.

The concessions assume that we now possess a settled account of gender relations that the biblical authors have flouted, whatever other merits the texts may have. In contrast, a practice of biblical authority assumes that no account of gender relations is finally settled, and that these strange and confronting ancient Scriptures offer to every society something more that may be discerned about its gender relations.

My point is not simply that Williams' handling of the Bible fails to accord with my community's accepted hermeneutical practice. Rather, I wish to make the more substantive argument that his approach to the Bible might inadvertently deprive us of new and real insights into human being and social possibilities. I will illustrate the how this might occur by means of a digression into the discussion of gender relations.

∽

A practice of "biblical authority" attempts to read biblical texts in a way that might disclose something unexpected and unanticipated about human being. By avoiding the presumption that the texts are conventionally "patriarchal," we are freed to discover what these initially alien and confronting passages may offer. In this case, what insight might they include about men? What if, beyond a deontological prescription of how men and women should relate, something can be learnt about male power?

Male power is "inalienable" in the sense that men cannot be abstracted from the power of their bodies. This power gives men their socially influential capacities, which too often take the form of callous brutality. These claims can be inferred from Ephesians 5, which implicitly acknowledges the existence of inalienable male social power by offering a better way to enact it ("husbands, love your wives," etc., v. 25f).

Reading this passage heuristically alongside other biblical passages further discloses that inalienable social power may not be construed with Aristotle or Nietzsche as a "natural" license to dominate. In Christian thought, inalienable social power exists to serves the good of another, especially the vulnerable (cf. Mark 10:42–44; Eph 5:25; and 1 Pet 3:7). Our enquiry would also discover elsewhere in the Bible testimonies to equity between the genders, which may even have subverted their ancient contexts.

Perhaps it is their very philosophical naivety that enables biblical authors to begin to imagine the proper enaction of male power. For they bypass any attempt to describe an *esse* of men or of their power, preferring instead to imagine it enacted in love and service. Nor are "love" and "service" an over-specified description of how power may be used: a virtuous "field of operations" is established. The actual behaviors of a particular man are matters of knowledge, discernment, and freedom.

Of course, Marxism, feminism, and postmodernism have taught us to suspect that abuses of power simply take cover under the term "service." These modes of critique helpfully alert us to the false universalisms of Enlightenment rationality, but in a milieu dominated by these forms of critique, our enquiry can become bogged down in an infinite regress of suspicion. And such a regress takes us no closer to learning how we may *gladly* receive the inalienable social power of men.

In contrast, a sympathetic, inferential, and heuristic reading of the Bible has begun to give us a view of men not easily attained in our current milieu. Men are so imbued with inalienable social power that it never departs our life together, and never will for as long as there are men. Yet male power eludes a definitive specification of either its *esse* or its proper enaction. Nonetheless, we discover something about how we may gladly receive this power as the biblical authors envision it enacted virtuously, in love and service. We have not discovered a male "essence" or identity, but we have discovered a "field of operations" that seems true to reality, and elicits joyful exploration and experimentation in partnership with women. Human being and possibilities have opened up before us by our remaining open to the strangeness of these texts.

In this cameo of a different discussion, I hope to have provided some sense of how a practice of "biblical authority" consists in the search for a nexus to what at first we cannot see, but which gradually becomes recognizable and then livable. It looks for holistic tuition about the complexity of reality by remaining open to all the complexities of the Bible (and uses the Bible's deontological command set as only a first heuristic step on the long journey of wisdom). This practice supposes that the best self-awareness or God-awareness does not finally come from the analysis and articulation of our experiences. Rather, our awareness is opened to divine interrogation and guidance such as is on view, for example, in the Torah-molded prayer and reflection of Psalm 139. Similarly then, a practice of biblical authority seeks to discern whatever is not necessarily obvious about our sexual aspect.

Williams returns the mutuality of grace to centre-stage in a Christian sexual ethic, but four other concepts emphasized in the traditional account are also moved to the periphery. These are "nature," "gender complementarity," procreative potential, and lifelong faithfulness. It is beyond my scope to establish these concepts for those who do not accept their relevance. But I do hope to show why Christians who still hold to them have a plausible case. I will also suggest that the Bible offers no *esse* for these four aspects of sex, but that a practice of biblical authority inducts us in how to humbly receive them as gifts of our embodiment.

"*Nature.*" In Williams' final approving quotation of Susan Griffin, the entire discussion has been about "perception wedded to matter itself, a knowledge that comes to us from the sense of the body" and that does not deny "the power of fate and nature" (p. 320). "Nature" here means material embodiment, which cannot be effaced and whose experiences deserve a meaningful account.

To find this meaningful account, Williams directs our attention to the way embodied desire brings persons into relation. This mode of being shares some commonality with the *uncreated* relations conducted by the Triune persons, because embodied human desire is analogous to divine grace. Here is why Williams regards his approach as a properly "theological" investigation into the true character of sexual expression.

It is an approach that excludes crass appeals to "nature" as a form of law. But it also seems to imply that no other aspect of human sexual "nature" is theologically relevant if no analogy to the Godhead is evident. This implication requires further defense, if only because the sexual activities he regards as illicit (rape, pedophilia, and bestiality, p. 313) do seem to require some further account than his approach offers.

Williams submits that these activities are wrong because one party controls another without regard for the desire of another. They therefore violate the divine typology of proper human sexuality. This insight is significant, but two observations need to be made. First, by putting the fault in terms of "control," Williams implicitly acknowledges a "natural" category of embodiment—namely the power(s) of the abuser and the power differential between abuser and abused. It seems arbitrary to deny the relevance for a sexual ethic of any other aspects of our embodiment.

Second, some abusers do claim that their victims expressed desire. In such cases, Williams' diagnosis forces us to the unsafe assertion that these reports are always only ever deluded, unless we also concede that the presence or absence of desire is not the sole criterion of our judgments. It then becomes proper to wonder what other aspects of our embodiment may be at work.

"Gender complementarity," procreative potential, and lifelong faithfulness offer themselves as possible candidates in a constellation of purposes for sex that bestow meaning upon it and so also describe its "nature."

Gender complementarity. In the heuristic habit of biblical authority described above, any "theory of natural complementarity" (p. 320) can only arise *a posteriori* from the sustained reading of Scripture. Williams does not address the cumulative impact of the biblical material, where metaphors for divine desire and celebrations of sexual activity all regularly involve husbands and wives.

In the same way that hints about male power may easily be lost, so also hints about our sexual "nature" are lost if these texts are discounted as conventionally heterosexist. When we ask how we are to receive our embodiment as *gendered* people, the cumulative impact of texts from Genesis 1:26–27 onward suggests that we are to "complement" one another. Of course it is certainly true that our gendered-ness is not always expressed in terms of sexual intercourse (just as it is true that sexual intercourse does not always result in childbirth), so the *esse* of this complementarity also finally eludes us. Therefore "gender complementarity" is not a concept simply "applied narrowly and crudely to physical differentiation without regard to psychological structures" (p. 320). When Christian sexual ethics holds that Scripture inducts us into the appropriation of our gender, it thereby explores how this other proper aspect of the body may be humbly received as a gift in all our acquaintances, and especially as it pertains to our most intimate relationships.

Procreative potential. How are we to do justice to the fact that our gendered embodiment is also potentially procreative? Christian sexual ethics must explore how these inalienable aspects of our bodily existence may be humbly received as gifts. An exploration that remains open to all the data of Scripture also looks for the way scriptural texts induct us into the appropriation of our capacity for procreation.

Williams is correct to observe that the biblical presentation of marriage is not contingent upon procreation. The embodied grace of sexuality is indeed very good news for couples who grieve over infertility. However, that our church "accepts the legitimacy of contraception" (p. 320) is scant warrant by which to assert that the procreative capacity of marriage is an irrelevance.

This argument only discloses that a technological and social development has served to abstract sex from its traditional moorings in a set of human purposes for sex. The openness of marriage to children has been relegated from a central marital purpose to an optional accessory. Hence same sex unions have been able to commend themselves as an equivalent relationship because equivalently companionable. But none of these cultural developments necessarily take us any closer to a theologically informed sexual ethic.

A similar churchly logic might also accommodate the church to high divorce rates, and then proceed to deduce that "lifelong" faithfulness is an obsolete artifact of our short-lived ancestors. But is a Christian ethic really so beholden to advances in medical technology? The Archbishop clearly denies that "advances" in the technology of mass destruction should direct a Christian ethic of war.[6] Liberal and conservative Christian lassitude in this arena, and its dissonance with the vocation of the Body, is plainly exposed by Williams' position. The two arenas (war and sex) may seem incommensurable, but every arena entails a journey of discernment.

To discern that our procreative capacity may be gladly received within the "weave" of gender and sexual relations is not problematic, and should clearly inform a Christian sexual ethic in some way since it is not an unimportant aspect of the body. Indeed, in response to the appearance of contraception and the opportunity it presents for adult-centered lifestyles, we may prefer to insist that God calls married people to marriages that are gratefully open to welcoming children. (This "welcome" would also require a theological exposition, since it may be expressed not only in fertility, but also in adoption, or in hospitality, or in many other forms of interest and care.)

The logic of procreative capacity only becomes problematic when stripped of the other elements in the "weave" (as when it becomes the sole or main justification of marriage). It is equally odd to discount procreative capacity as offering nothing to the discussion about sex.

---

6. Williams, "Making Moral Decisions," in *The Cambridge Companion to Christian ethics*, ed. Robin Gill (Cambridge: Cambridge University Press, 2001) 9–11; cf. Williams, "The Health of the Spirit," in *Public Life and the Place of the Church: Reflections to Honour the Bishop of Oxford*, ed. Michael W. Brierley (Aldershot: Ashgate, 2006) 218–20.

Lifelong faithfulness. The biblical portrayal of lifelong faithfulness also inducts us into the "process and relation" of mutual sexual grace. Williams discusses how the *time* needed to discover mutual sexual grace is promoted by "unconditional," "perilous," "demanding," and "promising" public sexual unions (p. 315). But in returning to the story of Sarah Layton he asserts that liaisons outside of such unions may also result in the discovery of grace. An unfortunate caricature then follows: "an absolute declaration that every sexual partnership must conform to the pattern of commitment or else have the nature of sin *and nothing else* is unreal and silly" (pp. 315-16).

His italicized phrase is odd, for no conservative in any Augustinian tradition would seriously claim that non-married sex is entirely drained of its created good. Rather, and as Sarah's story eloquently testifies, non-married sex does not set the conditions under which our sexual nature can find its best fulfillment. It is precisely the exploitative tendency of sex without promise that compromises the discovery of grace. The poignancy of Sarah's character after her sexual encounter and once she is alone again consists, as much as anything, in what has now been lost; and people like her report that they were "used," the antithesis of any ongoing experience of grace. Williams is right to recognize here "the facts of a lot of people's histories" (p. 316), but his recognition seems fatalistic, as if we might not hope for future Sarahs to know "the body's grace" in the best possible way. Again, the validation of the body's grace makes a central aspect of sex peripheral, and so he neglects also to consider how the logic of adultery *undoes* the logic of grace.

If this comment is read as an attempt to bring safety and peace and to flee vulnerability and risk, it is hard to see where the problem lies if at the same time we have conceded—and even now defend the view—that "the body's grace" is an essential aspect of sex. Certainly no modern Archbishop would condone Sarah's seducer simply because his acts led her to glimpse the body's grace. The public "licenses" and "sanctions" of lifelong faithful marriage, for all the use of legal terms, are attempts at a kind of social clarity that brings safety to couples and to the communities that surround them. These "licenses" and "sanctions" can be inhabited with kindness, repentance, forgiveness, and joyful gladness; and to do so avoids great pain (especially for children).

The vulnerabilities, tragedies, and sexual misconnections to which Williams persistently refers can and do find some healing in lifelong faithfulness. This inference from biblical attestation, and its commendation among conservative communities, is simply the articulation of something about our sexual nature that cannot be sampled before being lived. This is an "ideal," to be sure, but hardly an unreal or silly one. Enough of humanity lives and tastes the "ideal" to make it at least plausible.

I hope to have shown the way a practice of "biblical authority" infers several interwoven themes to discern what is never entirely accessible or obvious about human sexual "nature." The four aspects I have briefly addressed, when interwoven with "the body's grace," become that complex called "marriage"—itself an elucidation of the meaning and purpose of sex.

Our cultural milieu can render us blind and ungrateful to good gifts embedded in a good created order. Scripture presumes the existence of a real moral order, but one that finally needs divine interpretation for its meaning and purposes and for the ways we may properly receive that order and enact its meaning and purpose. (We owe most of these thoughts, of course, to Augustine's pioneering lifelong journey through Scripture.)

Our "natures" are to be received under divine tutelage without us ever entirely knowing our *esse*. Such is the journey of Christian discipleship. If the project seems at times to be abstracted from our daily episodes of sexual thought, emotion, and experience, Williams also knows that his own account is similarly threatened by "abstractness and overambitious theory" (p. 312), which is the price we all pay when we try to articulate something important and irreducibly complex.

Celibacy: Another Conservative Aporia

A community's journey includes married men and women, but the journey also consists in their partnership with sexually chaste unmarried people. We should therefore examine Williams' treatment of celibacy.

If the first aporia of a conservative sexual ethic is to miss the divine symbolism of sexual intimacy, its second is the theologically thin account of celibacy often found within Protestant and Reformed sexual ethics. I will not rehearse the once-useful Reformed complaint that a "vocation of celibacy" entails an illicit proscription against marriage, for that objection would obscure the central features of celibacy that Williams helpfully observes. It is an estate not devoid of sexual desire and desiring, but where the desiring love of God may receive special attention. But is it helpful to characterize celibates as those who "see if they can find themselves, their bodily selves, in a life dependent simply upon trust in the generous delight of God" (p. 317)?

It is tempting to retort that the married are also "dependent simply upon trust in the generous delight of God." However, in his defense, it must be said that Williams' distinction does resemble that made by the apostle Paul (1 Cor 7:32-33), who contrasts the divine opportunities afforded by "un-marriage" against daily practical problems posed by marriage; and Paul also knows of the special sense in which marriage instantiates the love of God in Christ. Williams rightly draws our attention, then, to the way each vocation—celibacy and marriage—has its own way of enacting the desirous love of God.

But to describe the celibate as "dependent simply" upon God individualistically exaggerates his or her engagement with God. Such an image of the celibate resonates with modern constructions of "the single" as a loner. It therefore becomes difficult for modern "singles" seriously to hear calls to sexual chastity, because they assume that desire by God and for God is being offered as the incorporeal solution to their bodily desires, and as a cure for their sense of social disenfranchisement. To present the Christian life as consisting in the estate of either celibacy or marriage therefore seems bizarrely constrictive and unreal. Hence Williams concludes that some good sex may be had beyond marriage, and that celibacy is really an option only for the few.

But in these construals of celibacy, the mistake has been to miss the power of embodied grace in expansive networks of sexually chaste but intimate friendships. As Aelred of Rievaulx once put it,[7] friendships also require faithfulness (III.88-90) and thrive upon love, affection, security, and delight:

> Friendship involves love when there is a show of favor that proceeds from benevolence. It involves affection when a certain inner pleasure comes from friendship. It involves security when it leads to a revelation of all one's secrets and purposes without fear or suspicion. It involves delight when there is a certain meeting of the minds—an agreement that is pleasant and benevolent—concerning all matters, whether happy or sad, which have a bearing on the friendship . . . (III.51)

---

7. Aelred, *Spiritual Friendship*, trans. Mark F. Williams, (London: Associated University Presses, 1994).

Williams has sought "what sexuality might mean at its most *comprehensive*," and how sexual activity might communicate and display "a breadth of human possibility and a sense of the body's capacity to heal and enlarge the life of others" (p. 313). But the account is not in fact comprehensive, because it does not signal the many ways in which the body may heal and enlarge the life of others *through friendship*. His "failure" has been a heroic one though, for he almost-but-not-quite effectively confronts Protestant and Reformed boredom or suspicion or pity toward the chastely unmarried.

The concept of two estates, celibate and married, is made intelligible in the New Testament by a logic of "brothers and sisters" in Christ, who look forward to an eschatological experience where *all* participate as "bride" (Eph 5:23; Rev 19:7-8, 21:2). This mind-bending vision of a united collective known and desired by God accounts for Jesus' extraordinary and counterintuitive declaration of the cessation of human marriage (Mark 12:25; Matt 22:30; Luke 20:35). Yet John's heavenly vision (Rev 7:9) is also of a collective whose members have not lost their individual histories and identities. It is as if all are celibate, yet all are married to the Lamb, and intimate with each other through intimacy with him.

The celibate therefore instantiates our truest identity as people who are not finally enclosed or defined by our current temporary associations. She and he do this well when each embodies the grace of care, hospitality, and concern toward people in networks that cannot be contained by any conventional identity marker. He and she do this well when bonds of affection to the many are not distorted by those bonds that sexual expression would bring with the few. They do this well when they model for us what it is to dwell with each other, not merely as a collection of some lonely people alongside other equally lonely couples, but as a truly intimate community.

As Augustine once rhetorically put it, "what pertains more closely to a body than its sex?"[8] No sane Christian could deny what we expansively call our "sexuality," which irrespective of our marital state is a constitutive element of our embodiment. But it does not follow that "sexuality" must necessarily be erotically expressed in order that we be human and whole. We are already "bodily whole" with our "sexuality" present in our embodiment as gendered, and whether or not we enact erotic love.

---

8. Augustine, *The City of God against the Pagans*, trans. R. W. Dyson (Cambridge: Cambridge University Press, 1998) 195 (V.7). Augustine directed this comment against ancient misogynists, in defence of the good of womanhood.

A much more expansive logic and practice of Christian friendship (perhaps even with some exploration of whether "gender complementarity" is a meaningful concept in this sphere) would free us all to see how celibacy is as honorable an estate as marriage. It is equally plausible, it is authentically livable, and it is bodily whole.

Two Essentialisms

Of course Aelred has been adopted by some as a gay patron saint. On this reading, the intimacy on view in his *Spiritual Friendship* must be gay, just as self-evidently as I have used his work to help imagine networks inhabited by the chastely non-married. These different readings of Aelred reflect an impasse about anthropology. The gay reading succeeds on an assumption of sexual essentialism. (Sexual essentialism is at least the view that sexual thoughts, feelings, and attractions are necessarily central to true descriptions of human identity. At most it entails that erotic intimacy or sexual ecstasy is the pinnacle of human and relational authenticity.)

But if a human essence is not so easily available to us, the absence of any overt sexuality in *Spiritual Friendship* enables us, with much of the Christian tradition, to heuristically imagine our way into a new and unanticipated identity "in Christ." Such an approach simply recognizes what the ancients always said: that we never know ourselves as well as we think we do. In Christian thought, we are finally "known by God" (1 Cor 8:3) and in Christ we "put on a new self which will progress towards true knowledge the more it is renewed in the image of its Creator" (Col 3:10, NJB).

Is there also a sexual essentialism in Williams' essay? He signals that he is aware of the essentialist pitfall when he acknowledges that there is "something frightening and damaging about the kind of sexual mutuality on which everything comes to depend."[9] For Williams, sexuality *is* central to an understanding of the human condition insofar as thinking about sexuality leads us "into the knowledge that our identity is being made in the relations of bodies, not by the private exercise of will or fantasy: we belong with and to each other, not to our 'private' selves" (p. 317). This conclusion suggests that our personal identity is to be understood *relationally*, but it need not be taken to imply that personal identity is reducible to sexual identity.

---

9. The quoted text only appears in the LGCM/online version of the essay (LGCM, 9).

However, it is unclear why Williams' point could not also be illustrated by the embodied practices of *the church*. The mutual grace embodied in the best of married sex is also differently embodied in myriad other practices, moments, and spiritual gifts. Yet the tenor of the essay is to equate our identity with the *sexual* relations of our bodies rather than with their ecclesial relations.

For it is one thing to ask Williams' opening question, "Why does sex matter?" into the air, as it were. It is quite another to open with it in a group that has already constituted itself on grounds of sexual identity. Within such a fellowship, the way in which "sex matters" is forced to bear more freight than it is able. Sex also matters in those fellowships where grace is envisioned within networks of sexually chaste and caring friendship, but it matters alongside a very great number of other important matters. I fear then that Williams may have done his hearers a disservice if, by addressing their central question in his opening question, he renders incomprehensible for them those ways of living that are joyful, contented, aware of sexual desire, but entirely free not to express it without any fear of losing identity or wholeness.

If I may digress, I cannot help wondering if our cultural tendencies to sexual essentialism derive from another more subtle essentialism—an "emotional essentialism," where what I feel is who I am. Here I borrow and extend Diane Tice's concept of "mood purism," the view that "emotions are 'natural' and should be experienced just as they present themselves."[10] It is beyond our scope to challenge this essentialism here, but elsewhere I have begun the task of understanding, with Augustine, the way our (good) emotions can fixate upon (good) elements in an ordered moral field and thus become distorted. After divine forgiveness for these distortions and whatever behaviors have followed, our new vocation in Christ includes the reordering of our moral and emotional apprehension through the adventitious power of the Spirit, who elicits our joyful participation in such a project.[11]

---

10. Daniel Goleman, *Emotional Intelligence: Why It Can Matter More Than I.Q.* (London: Bloomsbury, 1996) 58, citing Tice.

11. Andrew Cameron, "Augustine on Obsession," in *The Consolations of Theology*, edited by Brian S. Rosner (Grand Rapids: Eerdmans, 2008); idem, "Augustine on Lust," in *Still Deadly: Ancient Cures for the Seven Sins*, ed. Andrew Cameron and Brian S. Rosner (Sydney South: Aquila, 2007); idem, "How to Say YES to the World: Towards a New Way Forward in Evangelical Social Ethics," *Reformed Theological Review* 66.1 (2007).

Of course neither essentialism is limited to gay people. Both are very prevalent in modern life, within the church and beyond it. (Perhaps homosexual life and thought is a simply a consistent articulation and expression of these essentialisms, if I may say so with no pejorative intent.)

Elsewhere, the Archbishop effectively counsels against all of our essentialist tendencies when he argues against thinking of the self "as a finished and self-contained reality, with its own fixed needs and dispositions."[12] Modern life is not limited to sexual and emotional essentialism. The various identity labels we presume to bestow always threaten to eclipse our truest vocation "in Christ."

This theological criticism of essentialism should equally be directed to those who primarily define themselves by any ideology. Sadly, conservative churches are also riddled with those false essentialisms that form the horizons within which we habitually define ourselves. Our nation, our occupation, our "family values," our passions, our preoccupations, our educational achievements, our domicile, and our familial connections all constitute some aspect of who we are—but "I consider them rubbish," said St Paul, "that I may gain Christ" (Phil 3:8). We are each called into this new identity "in Christ," and what we may discover about ourselves on this journey cannot neatly be described in advance. If it could, it would no longer be Jesus that we are following.

Twenty Years On

It is well beyond my competence to comment upon the Archbishop's recent role as mediator within the Communion over matters of human sexuality.[13] From my limited perspective, the church has informally divided a long time ago between those congregations who seek to find peace in sexually essentialist accounts of human identity, and those who seek to find their identity elsewhere. We have seen such splits in Christian history, as when Arian churches found it impossible to believe that divinity could sully itself with humanity.

---

12. Williams, "Making Moral Decisions," 5.

13. For an overview of the unfolding events, see Rhys Bezzant's essay in the present volume.

Thankfully, the right of free assembly protected by our democracies allows cultural space for each such community to assemble and attempt to find peace in its own way. Each community may have to conduct its experiment in theological anthropology over decades, perhaps even centuries. What lies ahead is the delicate political task of discerning how we might live alongside one another in relative harmony. Perhaps our divisions can stay informal, and perhaps our communities may yet find how to live alongside one another in our respective quests for peace and wholeness. Or perhaps we do well to formally name a parting of ways, for the peace that honesty and clarity can bring. I am unsure which path the circumstances demand. No one could envy the Archbishop's task of discernment in this matter.

He has made two comments during the time-frame of the dispute. I know little about their significance in context, but my argument has some relevance to each.

On the one hand, in a recent lecture[14] the Archbishop uses Romans 1:26 as a worked example for a proper hermeneutic. He takes care to insist that the example is not intended to settle controversy in the church, but to show how texts are used and may better be used. There is a debate to be had about his treatment of this text, but I want simply to question a point made in passing and another point central to his argument.

The point made in passing is that this text "is, for the majority of modern readers the most important single text in Scripture on the subject of homosexuality." I am not sure how to find or measure this majority, but I hope to have shown the way conservative appeals to "biblical authority" on human sexuality do not need to rest shakily upon this single text. A related allusion was made twenty years earlier when Professor Williams quipped, "Happily there is more to Paul than the (much quoted in this context) first chapter of Romans!" (p. 316). The ongoing suggestion that conservative sexual ethics relies upon "an abstract fundamentalist deployment of a number of very ambiguous texts," such as Romans 1:26, ignores treatments that really cannot be discounted so easily.[15]

---

14. Williams, *"The Bible: Reading and Hearing"*: *A Special Larkin-Stuart Lecture*, Trinity College, University of Toronto, April 16, 2007, online: http://www.trinity.utoronto.ca/News_Events/News/archbishop.htm.

15. See for example the excellent work by Christopher Ash, *Marriage: Sex in the Service of God* (Leicester: InterVarsity, 2003).

The central point in the Archbishop's argument is that to deploy Romans 1:26 against others evades the letter's eventual charge (in chapter 2) that the reader is also very flawed. I simply submit that every serious conservative treatment of homosexuality that I have recently heard is at pains to stress the same point. If there is anything to be learnt from the gay and lesbian community's ongoing charge of "homophobia," it is that *all* have sinned and fallen short of the glory of God (Rom 3:23). In this sense, the church is completely inclusive.

On the other hand, the Archbishop surprised many in his recent Dutch interview when he disputed the interpretation of "inclusiveness" insisted upon by particular gay Christian groups:

> [C]onversion means conversion of habits, behaviours, ideas, emotions. The boundaries are determined by what it means to be loyal to Jesus Christ. That means to display in all things the mind of Christ. Paul is always saying this in his letters: Ethics is not a matter of a set of abstract rules, it is a matter of living the mind of Christ. That applies to sexual ethics; that is why fidelity is important in marriage . . .[16]

I am unclear on the details of his dispute with that community, and do not wish to score a cheap shot by noting his dissent. Rather, I am interested in two important aspects of his response.

First, at our best (and only by the Spirit's power), conservative Christians also want to practice the Archbishop's description. We do not seek for some scriptural arsenal against gays and lesbians, but seek with them to discover and then live "the mind of Christ."

Second therefore, we begin to see what is at stake when we are also called upon to interrogate our own ideologies, habits, and emotions. We begin to see the way we are helplessly reliant upon Christ in the reordering of our own desires, sexual or otherwise. We begin to see how our own treasured essentialisms are graciously interrogated and altered in Christ. So we ask that we might join together in fellowship across our differences, subjecting all our ideologies and emotional beliefs to the power of the Spirit. The project may seem daunting and dark for each of us at times. Yet as a fellowship of friends in Christ, we will be freed into many joyful surprises as our proper identities and vocations in him become gradually but surely disclosed.

---

16. Houtman, "Not Inclusive," n.p.

8

Rowan Williams on War and Peace

TOM FRAME

Rowan Williams has been a frequent commentator on the use of armed force in support of Britain's national interests and in the preservation of Western security. In this chapter I will be dealing with his views on war and peace as an academic theologian and his contributions to political life as an Anglican bishop.

I note that Williams has never served in the armed forces in any capacity, has not been involved in the development of strategic concepts or played any part in the implementation of defense policy. His pronouncements on these matters should, in fairness to Williams, be seen as just one dimension of a busy life in which he has been called upon to address a great many diverse subjects some of which touch on his intellectual interests and pastoral ministry, and some of which do not.[1] It is, therefore, both unfair

---

1. Few bishops write consistently or extensively on war and peace. For many, the impetus comes whenever a decision is made by national governments to commit uniformed personnel to armed conflict. And when bishops write about such matters, their comments are mostly confined to the religious questions and moral dilemmas arising from the use of state-sanctioned force. While this has been largely the case for Rowan Williams, my own Episcopal experience was rather different. Serving as Bishop to the Australian Defence Force

and unreasonable to expect anyone in his situation to master every subject of public interest, including the complexities of war and peace. But in instances where Williams does claim some insights or when he strives to influence public opinion and shape government policy, there are grounds for a vigorous critique.

This essay will draw mainly on Williams' writings and newspaper reporting of his words. The first part of the chapter deals with his treatment as an academic theologian of armed conflict and its resolution (1983–89); the second part considers his public remarks and writing on actual events as a public commentator and Christian leader (1990–present).

Theology, War, and Peace

World War II ended in 1945 with an uneasy peace. As the Red Army pursued retreating German soldiers, the Soviet Union seized and maintained control of Eastern Europe and threatened even further territorial expansion in the ensuing years. The security of Western Europe was undergirded by the North Atlantic Treaty Organization (NATO) Alliance and the commitment of member nations to the preservation of individual liberties, participatory democracy, and market economies. When the Soviet Union developed and then successfully tested a nuclear device in 1949, the Cold War threatened the destruction of the planet.

Rowan Williams began to make public comments on war and peace in the early 1980s. It was a period of heightened international tension. The Soviet Union had invaded Afghanistan in December 1979 and a bitter war erupted between Iran and Iraq the following year. When US President Ronald Reagan described the USSR as an "Evil Empire" and the Soviets significantly expanded their atomic arsenal, it appeared that a nuclear conflagration was likely. Against this stark geopolitical backdrop, Williams

---

from 2001 to 2007 gave me ample opportunity to comment regularly on armed conflict, uniformed service, and Christian ethics. In addressing the many pertinent questions put to me about Australia's overseas deployments during that period (Bougainville, East Timor, Afghanistan, Iraq, and the Solomon Islands), I drew routinely upon my former career as a naval officer (1979–92), which included two years service as research officer to the Chief of Naval Staff and a further year in Defence Headquarters, and in my work as a military historian, and my continuing interest in questions relating to the prerogatives of the state and the duty of national leaders to defend the people and the property for whom they have accepted responsibility.

and Mark Collier produced a study booklet entitled *Beginning Now*.[2] It was intended for use by individuals and groups as it attempted to consider the special contribution that "the Christian tradition has to make in contemporary debates about peace and peacemaking." It explored the themes of justice and peace in both the Old and New Testaments and looked at contemporary expressions of power and recent experiences of conflict. As in all his subsequent writings, Williams drew attention to the "nature of the inner changes to which we need to open ourselves in order to become peacemakers."

The booklet was not meant to be a practical response to the Cold War and what it proposed did not hasten the resolution of superpower hostility. Its generous attitude to President Robert Mugabe, who was praised for imploring Zimbabweans to "forgive their former enemies and work together to build a new Zimbabwe,"[3] now seems a little embarrassing given the Zanu-PF party's appalling human rights record and the economic implosion of that country.

Regrettably, the booklet's prescriptions did not connect with the realities of state power nor contend with the manifest complexities of international relations. Instead it took its cue from the authors' notion of "converted imagination." Williams and Collier commented:

> We don't believe the world's problems are instantly solved by "converted imagination." We don't believe that attention and understanding will disarm the Soviet Union, and we certainly don't believe that attention and understanding should lead us to underestimate the hurtful intentions of an enemy. But faced with the current deadlock in international relations, it seems reasonable enough to ask whether we can ever find a language to speak to each other, which will somehow communicate an awareness of the other's fear and sense of poverty, a language of solidarity rather than judgement. A first step, of course, is finding the words of our own fear and poverty.[4]

This passage contains the kernels of Williams' later thinking about armed conflict. The principal problem in Williams' mind is deficient or distorted language and the prospect of grave misunderstanding leading to violence.

---

2. Williams and Mark Collier, *Beginning Now, Part One Peacemaking Theology: A Study Book for Individuals and Groups* (London: Dunamis, 1984).

3. Ibid., 59.

4. Ibid., 61.

He claimed that the language used in the conduct of international relations is impoverished or inadequate for the purpose of resolving differences. And yet, Williams' own depiction of the global tensions bore little relationship to the prevailing military or diplomatic realities.

In brief, the Soviet Union was a superpower equipped and determined to impose its will on Europe, Asia, and Africa. If unopposed, its hegemony would have been enlarged through armed aggression. The nations of the Warsaw Pact and the opposing NATO Alliance knew precisely what was at stake. There was no confusion about either aims or means. It was a clear understanding of each side's motivations and aspirations, and not impoverished language or mutual misunderstanding, that prevented war. Neither side liked the ideology of the other. These ideologies were, in fact, irreconcilable. The Cold War was essentially a collision of competing worldviews. In the end, the NATO Alliance was victorious without recourse to nuclear weapons. It was a triumph built on the larger and more diversified industrial base maintained by the United States and its allies. The Soviet economy, regulated according to communist principles, could not maintain the economic burden produced by its inefficient military establishment. Being unable to compete technologically and financially, the Soviet Union was gradually worn down politically and diplomatically and, thankfully, prevented from exerting its oppressive will on the entire world.

Although *Beginning Now* was a discussion starter rather than a detailed monograph, its shortcomings were obvious and serious. It failed to shift satisfactorily from personal dispositions to political programs; it showed little cognizance of the internal complexity of political constituencies like the nation-state; and, it did not offer a genuinely Christian critique of war but a left-wing account of international relations. (Williams had already referred to himself publicly as a socialist.)[5] The book certainly did not explain nor do justice to the conditions that created tension between nations or the racial and economic dynamics that escalated into armed conflict. This was nowhere more apparent than in its superficial treatment of the 1982 South Atlantic war fought between Argentina and Britain over the Falkland Islands, where Williams and Collier attempt to establish a perverse kind of moral equivalence between the two sides. They claim the war had started because

---

5. Rupert Shortt, *Rowan Williams: An Introduction* (London: Darton, Longman & Todd, 2003) 15.

the Argentine Junta only wanted a war in order to distract from economic and social problems at home—they needed an outside enemy because of domestic discontent. But were we [the British] not also suffering from economic problems? Was it not also a distraction for us to focus on an outside enemy instead of on our domestic problems? To what extent did Britain and Argentina come to mirror each other as "enemies"?[6]

It is hard to know where to begin a critique of this deeply flawed interpretation of the conflict. A few facts might help. Argentina was ruled by a military oligarchy that lacked a democratic mandate to rule and that felt itself unaccountable to the people. It regarded the reclaiming of the "Malvinas" (the Argentine name for the islands) as a matter of national pride although Britain had occupied them continuously since 1833. Without provocation or warning, Argentine forces invaded the Falkland Islands, which were still an internationally recognized part of the United Kingdom. Despite international condemnation and the imposition of sanctions, Argentina refused to abandon the Falklands. Britain had broad diplomatic support for its decision to thwart Argentina's decision to violate the basic principles of international law and retake the islands by force if necessary. There was bipartisan political support in Britain for the Falklands campaign. At no stage had Britain threatened to invade Argentina nor did it adopt a belligerent stance towards that country. To say the two nations "mirrored" one another is simply nonsense. There was no comparison between the intentions, aspirations or conduct of the two nations in 1982. As I will remark later, Williams rightly points to the definite need for nations to avoid hubris when self-interest can so easily be clothed with mock sincerity. But blaming oneself for the crimes of others is not the answer. *Beginning Now* was a poor piece of work.

Shortly after *Beginning Now* appeared, Williams was invited by Dr. Robert Runcie to work on what became his third book, *The Truce of God*. It would become the Archbishop of Canterbury's Lent book for 1983. It proved to be a controversial volume. In *Rowan Williams: A Short Introduction*, Rupert Shortt remarked that "despite its high Scriptural content, there were signs that the then Archbishop was taken aback by all the political salvoes. He probably found the discussion intelligent and provocative and

---

6. Williams, *Beginning Now*, 54.

a bit overblown."[7] (The book was revised and updated in 2005 to deal with various forms of post-"9/11" terrorism.)

Williams explained that in writing about "peace, internal and external," he made "no secret of the fact that I have strong convictions about the way forward to a more peaceful and less threatened world." He acknowledged that he ran "the risk of this volume being dismissed as partisan or propagandist by those who think that any expression of opinion on this subject by Christians is some sort of compromising of the non-political purity of the Gospel." While he accepted that there would be different responses to his opinions, he hoped that "some agreement may be possible about the nature of the problem and its theological and spiritual dimensions." This led him to "concentrate on this latter area rather than on the vexed questions of practical policy making." This was a prudent approach but a frustrating one as well. It was prudent because Williams effectively acknowledged the extent of his expertise and the limits of his experience. But it was also frustrating because it is in the realm of policy detail, where concrete realities need to be negotiated, that principles are often compromised to fit credible contingencies or rejected because they conflict with valid non-theological concerns. This leads to the questions: are the perspectives elucidated by Williams ever capable of being transported into policy, and do the principles he illuminates suffer irreparable harm when translated into practice? To my mind it is irresponsible to say, as I believe Williams does, that he will set out the principles while others are left to make sense of them when there is often less disagreement about the principles than there is difficulty in dealing with them in practice.

With respect to terrorism, however, Williams is clear: terrorism is always and everywhere wrong. Those committing terrorist acts are criminals who are personally responsible for their crimes. However, he notes that "when you have defined terrorism as a strategy of intimidation through indiscriminate killing, you have set a moral standard by which your own behaviour may be measured." He does not want to suggest there is moral equivalence between the acts of terrorists and Western military operations but that "the reasons for deploring one are at the very least reasons for deploring the other—whether to the same extent or not could not be quickly determined in the abstract." He draws a distinction between the Cold War

---

7. Shortt, *Rowan Williams: An Introduction*, 46.

and the post-September 11 "War on Terror," in which the West is again "being backed into certain sorts of violence against an enemy whose humanity and rationality cannot be taken for granted, with whom the only effective weapon is massive counterforce . . . we are reacting; so what we do is not our own freely chosen action. Our morally uneasy policies are forced upon us."[8]

There is, he claims, little confidence that "this strategy to combat terrorism will succeed" and this has given rise to the "conviction that nothing we do or want is going to make a difference to our fate." The fear and powerlessness provoked by the "menace of unqualified and irrational violence" serves to "reinforce our willingness to think about these matters in terms of guilt and responsibility."[9]

Williams' diagnosis is this: "we shall not understand our society and its terrors and anxieties about total war unless we grasp that behind these anxieties lies a profound sickness of spirit; and it is a sickness which only succeeds in reinforcing the structures that give rise to it in the first place." He explains that the gospel, "for a society like ours must involve a clear and accurate diagnosis of this kind of sickness . . . [T]he Gospel, by driving us to penitence, grounds this affirmation of the future in the loving will of God, remaking us through our conversion." Of what does conversion consist? It means, "in this connection, to retrieve the vision of one's own responsibility, and to learn to look in critical openness at one's own life and the shared life of society around." He says that "the Gospel frees us from fear and fantasy, from the nightmares of guilt and insecurity which paralyse our imagination and so prevent us from positive and meaningful action." Thus, discernment is crucial in determining any response to threatened violence. Williams concludes that "classical pacifism has not always provided anything like a mature analysis of power and of how power can be used non-violently; it has been weak on the details of active peacemaking and conciliation." But he is equally unconvinced by the "default position in which an innocent party is forced into threat, violence or repression by a wilfully guilty one."

But what of the church? How does it become a peaceful community or the harbinger of a more peaceful world? Williams insists that the church become "a symbol of God's purpose for a reconciled humanity; as such it works on the assumption that we do not yet know where the boundaries

---

8. Williams, *The Truce of God* (London: Canterbury, 2005) 15.
9. Ibid., 17.

of the Body of Christ might finally lie. It cannot assume that this group or that group is ultimately unreconcilable to God or to the rest of humanity." In what might be regarded as a remarkably exclusivist stance, Williams says the "church proclaims that there is one human destiny and that it is found in relation to one focal figure, Jesus." But, he hastens to add that this common destiny "cannot be worked out without 'communion,' a relation of profound and costly involvement with each other and receiving from each other. This and this alone is what saves the proclamation of Christ's uniqueness from being a piece of ideological tyranny." It is how a stranger is seen that "our common destiny can be uncovered by the grace of Christ."

But Williams is troubled by situations in which "violent resistance seems to be the only available option." He is also unsure about the actions of third-party nations (those entering a cross-border conflict between two nations in a partisan way) and concedes that "the question of what makes intervention lawful is a long and complex one." He never provides an answer although intra-state conflict has been the dominant form of warfare since 1945. To his credit, Williams struggles with the questions and the need to speak a word of peace for the First and the Third World, a word that will take concrete form in this world at this time and not just in the world to come at some indeterminate future moment. It is for these reasons that his proposals for peace have to do with the church as a prototype "global moral community" because it "claims to have been given awareness of certain basic facts about humanity" that equips it "to challenge national ethics when they become obsessed with the assumptions of rivalry and self-serving." He wants the church to "live creatively, showing that suspicion and the self-critical questioning, even the penitence, that go with it are the doors to a wider vision." This means that Christians "have a great deal of work to do in making the Church more Church-like," a prospect that Williams feels is more possible owing to the "extraordinary growth in international networks of various sorts."

Williams described his proposals as modest. He had "not tried to give authoritative answers to the problems presented daily in the newspapers" but to "suggest some tools for diagnosing a few of the things that are, as I believe, wrong at the root of the way we state some of the questions of national welfare and international security in our private and public discourse." There is no comparable systematic treatment of war and peace in Williams' later works. There is a single passing reference to armed conflict in

On Christian Theology where Williams notes that the present age is "characterised by profound conflict in many areas," within which he includes "major issues of war and defence (the legitimacy of the nuclear deterrent)."[10] He argues that "honesty compels the admission that none of these questions is likely to be 'settled' in the foreseeable future, certainly not by appeal to what is commonly taken to be the 'literal sense of Scripture.'" There are, however, two essays reprinted in *Wrestling with Angels: Conversations in Modern Theology* that deal tangentially with armed conflict: "Barth, War and the State" and "Girard on Violence, Society and the Sacred."[11]

The first essay deals with a declaration of the German Evangelical Church concerning the development and deployment of nuclear weapons. In discussing Karl Barth's thinking, Williams draws attention to the significance of the German theologian's view of the state as a means of understanding "why Barth believed the nuclear issue to be a 'confessional' matter." In his summary of Barth's thinking, Williams explains that "the state exists, not as a thing in itself, but as a means of getting things done. A political unit can look for no metaphysical, trans-historical ground: it happens to be there, and certain people happen to be born into it: it may or may not coincide with a 'nation,' and it does not in the least matter whether it does or not."

The church "unites itself with the state in what Barth . . . called the 'revolt against disorder, against the self-destruction of sin.'" But when the state "forgets its provisional nature . . . [it] ceases to be properly a state . . . [and] turns itself into a 'lordless power' and itself becomes an agent of disorder." The nuclear state "by mere possession of the means of mass annihilation, pronounces its belief that it must survive at all costs . . . and regards itself as having in principle the authority to exterminate what threatens it." Williams is drawn to Barth's line of reasoning because he "believes it goes far towards setting an agenda" for contemporary political theology. But Williams is concerned that Barth does not provide sufficient commentary on the church's contributions to policy development. In effect, what does the state need to get done and in what order? He is drawn to the need for a theology of the state expressed in functional terms although, he would want

---

10. Williams, *On Christian Theology* (Oxford: Blackwell, 2000) 57.

11. Mike Higton, ed., *Wrestling with Angels: Conversations in Modern Theology* (London: SCM, 2007).

such a theology to begin with Christology that must generate political critique because the question of God's will is "historically embodied in Jesus."

In the second essay, Williams is interested in the work of the French anthropologist Rene Girard[12] because he provides a phenomenology of violence that goes beyond Jacques Ellul's extended polemic in *Violence*[13] and Rollo May's marriage of psychoanalytic theory and sociology in *Power and Innocence*.[14] For Williams, Girard offers a "deeper grasp of the tragic in human community, and pointing towards a resolution of the tragedy from a perspective far wider than that of the immanent 'economics' of power May is concerned with." He is particularly drawn to the claim that Christ's death undermines sacred violence and the effect of such a view on atonement theory. After giving a succinct account of Girard's theories on victims, scapegoats and objectless rivalry, Williams invited his readers, prompted by Girard, to read the "specific shape of the gospel story as a story of sacral violence exposing its own absurdity." Although I am not sure of Williams' meaning here, he is plainly concerned that Girard does not raise the question of "how a community founded on the overthrow of sacral violence actually develops and works, except in rather large and bland terms." He also questions the "practical intelligibility of his project," although Girard's interpretation of Jesus' death and the political character of the kingdom of God Jesus proclaimed appealed to Williams.

Williams draws on Girard's interpretation of Cold War rivalry to present a rather unsophisticated depiction of superpower rivalry that he believed had "become a world to itself," taking the place once occupied by sacred violence. His reference to "a fetishised rivalry in the acquisition of intrinsically meaningless objects" in noting the existence of more weapons than was necessary to destroy the world, shows a serious lack of understanding of strategic concepts, weapons capabilities, and tactical warfare. There is no appreciation of the different functions of various weapons systems, countermeasures or defensive tactics. The ensuing discussion is largely philosophical rather than theological, while its basis is more ideological

---

12. Williams deals principally with Girard's *Violence and the Sacred* (London: Johns Hopkins University Press, 1977); *The Scapegoat* (London: Johns Hopkins University Press, 1986); and, *Things Hidden Since the Foundation of the World* (London: Athlone, 1987).

13. Jacques Ellul, *Violence* (New York: Seabury, 1969).

14. Rollo May, *Power and Innocence: A Search for the Sources of Violence* (New York: Norton, 1972).

and less biblical. While it might be an "account" of the Cold War, it does not deal with the complexity of its origins or its continuation. There is no mention of economics and trade, industrial capacity and technological development, diplomacy or international relations. The discussion is conducted in the abstract and with little mention of official statements. It does not credit politics with any element of sincerity or concede that other viewpoints might offer a credible explanation of why nations are drawn into conflict with each other. To believe that nations, especially democratic ones with a free press, are capable of thinking or acting consistently or collectively in a manner analogous to a natural person is unrealistic and unhelpful in identifying the fault-lines in human conflict.

The problem in this essay, as with much of Williams' writing on armed conflict, is that he does not return to the world in which conflict needs to be managed and tensions resolved. To say at the conclusion of this essay that "society will continue to stand in need of a community that offers an alternative foundational myth to that of sacred violence" does not touch nor transform the political order. Indeed, in asking "what kind of belief in such a myth is now possible in our society" and in being unsure about "what kind of participation in such a community remains" in prospect, is a concession that the foregoing discussion might fail to impart any shape or provide any substance to social discourse or interaction. To simply say "Girard's voice needs to be heard" is a rather lame conclusion.

There are scattered thoughts on war and peace in a number of other works to which Williams has contributed. Most concern the competing and complementary roles and responsibilities of the church and the state. This is an important subject because it is the state rather than the church that mandates the use of force. Williams says the "Church does not either affirm or deny 'the state' in the abstract" but only to the extent that it provides a space in which conversations about what constitutes the common good can take place.[15] State sanctioned violence is always wrong because, he says, it removes a voice from the conversation.[16] This might be unavoidable and the commission of the lesser of two evils but, according to Williams, it

15. Williams, "Mankind, Nation, State," in *This Land and People: A Symposium on Christian and Welsh National Identity*, ed. Paul Ballard and Huw Jones (Cardiff: Collegiate Centre of Theology, University College, 1979) 119–25.

16. See Williams, *Open to Judgement* (London: Darton, Longman & Todd, 2002) 44; and the discussion of this notion in Mike Higton, *Difficult Gospel: The Theology of Rowan Williams* (London: SCM, 2004) 130–31.

denies the deepest purpose of the state that the church must remind the state it must fulfill. The survival of the state at all costs is not the highest goal to which the state aspires, while the state may be resisted when it acts as though it has supreme significance. Williams believes the church should not favor endurance over integrity. This would be analogous to Israel adopting the methods of its Gentile opponents in order to survive. The nation might stand but the people would be debased. What marked them out as distinct would have been lost in the means by which it was defended. God's covenant with Israel would have survived the collapse of the nation. This truth was appreciated during the exile and celebrated when the people returned. Williams contends: "The more we seek, individually, socially and nationally, to protect ourselves at all costs from intrusion, injury and loss . . . the more we stand under Ezekiel's judgement for 'abominable deeds'— the offering of fleshly persons on the altar of stone."[17]

It is for this reason that Williams continues to insist that the possession and threatened use of nuclear weapons is unequivocally wrong. His opposition to nuclear weapons has been consistently vehement. On Ash Wednesday 1985, Williams, who was then Dean of Clare College at Cambridge University, was detained by the police after scaling the fence at RAF Alconbury, a strategic base used by the United States Air Force, in Cambridgeshire. He was a supporter of campaigns to remove all foreign nuclear weapons from British soil. He was also a critic of the Reagan Administration's Strategic Defense Initiative, also known as SDI or "Star Wars," missile defense shield.[18]

> The SDI project, which implies the possibility of an impregnable aggressive force guaranteeing lasting security, is the ultimate stage in the development of a foundational myth of "the bomb"—the ultimate security and the ultimate destabiliser at the same time. Mutual terror remains bound to an acquisitive spiral, and the tensions of conflictual mimesis remain uncontrolled.[19]

Although Williams accepts Britain's entitlement to self-defense, I could not find a single instance of Williams acknowledging publicly the need for stronger conventional defenses for Europe, any statement supporting an

---

17. Williams, *Open to Judgement*, 44.

18. Williams, *Star Wars: Safeguard or Threat? A Christian Perspective*, CANA Occasional Papers 1 (Evesham: Clergy Against Nuclear Arms, 1987).

19. Williams, *Wrestling with Angels*, 177.

increase in Britain's defense budget to offset the reduction of nuclear weapons, or a solitary instance in which he encouraged the use of armed force in either peacekeeping or peacemaking.

Williams says, in fact, he would have preferred a Soviet invasion and occupation of Britain to nuclear warfare. While Williams believes that avoiding a nuclear exchange during the Cold War "was an accident," he claims the tensions that developed were released in several "sideshows" in which First World violence was exported to Third World nations in a strategy he thinks will have dire consequences for decades to come. But with the removal of the Berlin Wall, which brought down the "Iron Curtain" in 1989, and the demise of the Soviet Union two years later, the Cold War was over and the geo-strategic balance was changed. There were new threats to peace and, like every other commentator, Rowan Williams was faced with the challenge of a proliferation in the incidence of crimes against humanity and the prospect of failed and failing states descending into chaos. As Rowan Williams left academia for the episcopate, nuclear weapons remained but their likely use receded into the background as the focus of attention shifted from Europe to the Middle East.

Wars and Rumors of Wars

On August 2, 1990, Iraqi military forces invaded Kuwait, an independent state with internationally recognized rights of territorial integrity and political sovereignty, on the pretext of assisting a "free provisional government." The UN Security Council immediately passed Resolution 660 condemning the Iraqi invasion. Resolution 661 authorized economic sanctions to be imposed on Iraq. On August 8, Iraq formally annexed Kuwait, with the Security Council declaring it null and void the next day (Resolution 662). The Security Council subsequently passed Resolution 665 authorizing Member States to deploy maritime forces to the Middle East to enforce a trade blockade. When Iraq showed no signs of withdrawing, the UN Security Council passed Resolution 678 authorizing the use of force to remove Iraqi forces from Kuwait if they were not withdrawn by January 15, 1991. While a multinational coalition, including Britain, claimed to be motivated by moral principle in seeking the liberation of Kuwait, there were selective invocations of justice and undeniable elements of self-interest.

Although most experts believed an action against Iraq in Kuwait satisfied just war principles,[20] Williams and Peter Crowe addressed an open letter to the House of Bishops of the Church of England on United Nations Day (October 24) in 1990 objecting to the proposed liberation of Kuwait by force. Their aim was to highlight British self-interest in the conditions that had led to the Iraqi invasion.

> Where were Britain and America when Iraq invaded Iran, or when Iraq used chemical weapons? Answer—supporting Iraq; because it was in our interests then that Iran should be weakened. There is a strong case for saying that Western action in the Middle East has, for the whole of this century, been dictated by self-interest, not by any concern for justice . . . Turkey is currently occupying half of Cyprus, and we [the British] are content that it should be so because we have bases in Cyprus.[21]

As he had done earlier, Williams resorted to national self-recrimination to oppose the need for armed conflict abroad. His argument was presumably that Britain and Iraq both acted on self-interest and this factor somehow nullified action on Britain's part in opposing continued Iraqi occupation of Kuwait. But we must ask: which nation does not respond to self-interest or seek to enhance the interests of its own citizens?

Williams presented no alternative to the armed ejection of Iraqi troops other than the imposition of sanctions that Saddam Hussein subsequently demonstrated made absolutely no difference to his foreign policy. Did he propose allowing Iraq to maintain its illegal possession of Kuwait on the grounds that it could not be challenged without any nation exercising some measure of self-interest? The Bishop of Oxford, Richard Harries, rejected Williams' opposition to a campaign against Iraq. He argued that "the presence of self-interest does not by itself rule out the possibility of a war being just."[22] Notably, Williams later conceded that in "the first Gulf conflict" the "case can be made, though with some awkwardness," for resorting

---

20. The respected American scholar of the just war tradition, James Turner Johnson, was in no doubt: "It is my judgment that all the just war criteria providing guidance on the justified use of force were amply satisfied in the case of the decision to use force against Iraq." See James Johnson and George Weigel, *Just War and the Gulf War* (Washington, DC: Ethical and Public Policy Centre, 1991) 30.

21. Reproduced in *Church Scene*, November 2, 1990.

22. *Independent*, October 31, 1990, 19.

to force in "honouring clear treaty obligations."[23] This involved a significant shift in attitude. By this time Williams was touted by many as a future Archbishop of Canterbury.

Williams came close to a first-hand encounter with Middle Eastern violence on September 11, 2001. He was at Trinity Church, Wall Street in New York some two blocks from the World Trade Centre when terrorist attacks were mounted on New York and the Pentagon in Washington, DC. Not long afterwards he published a short reflection, entitled *Writing in the Dust: After September 11*. Williams denied the attacks occurred because Muslims are "a problem." Nor, in his mind, was the issue "some kind of religiousness that is 'naturally' prone to violence."[24] He acknowledged "the sheer danger of religiousness. Yes, it can be a tool to reinforce diseased perceptions of reality. Muslim or not, it can be a way of teaching ourselves not to see the particular human agony in front of us; or, worse, of teaching ourselves not to see ourselves, our violence, our actual guilt as opposed to our abstract 'religious' sinfulness."

When challenged by a young man the morning after "9/11" to explain God's inactivity, Williams explained that

> any really outrageous human action tests to the limit our careful theological principles about God's refusal to interfere with created freedom. That God has made a world into which he doesn't casually step in to solve problems is fairly central to a lot of Christian faith. He has made the world so that evil choices can't just be frustrated or aborted (where would he stop, for goodness sake? He'd have to be intervening every instant of human history) but have to be confronted, suffered, taken forward, healed in the complex process of human history.

For Williams, this act of evil highlights a "frightening contrast: the murderously spiritual and the compassionately secular." He notes that the "fantastic surge of violent energy needed to plan and carry through a colossal suicide attack is, fortunately, beyond the imagination of most of us." Williams says "we face agents who don't seem to calculate gains and losses or risks as we do. It is not the deceptively comfortable Cold War notion of a

---

23. Williams, "Don't call us appeasers for hesitating at war with Iraq," *The Telegraph* (London), November 5, 2002.

24. Williams, *Writing in the Dust: After September* 11 (London: Hodder & Stoughton, 2002) 4.

balance of terror." But if the victims respond violently "our violence is going to be a rather different sort of thing. It is unlikely to have behind it the passion of someone who has nothing to lose, the terrible self-abandonment of the suicide killer which is like a grotesque parody of the self-abandonment of love." Furthermore, Western motivations are different in that "we are not acting out of helplessness, out of moral and imaginative destitution that can only feel it is acting at all when it is inflicting pain and destruction." Williams says "we (collectively) have space to calculate gains and losses. There is some space between our feelings and our choices."

While public interpretations ranged from accusations that the United States had brought the attacks on itself by pursuing an aggressive foreign policy to suggestions that the attacks were a form of apocalyptic nihilism that would lead to anarchy, sufficiently confronting that it would change the course of human history, Williams claimed that "bombast about evil individuals doesn't help in understanding anything" because "ascribing what we don't understand to 'evil' . . . lets us off the hook, it allows us to avoid the question of what, if anything, we can recognise in the destructive act of another." In situations where rage and revenge can dominate, Williams counsels a moratorium or "breathing space" on "any action that brings a sense of release, irrespective of what it achieves," and being wary of "doing something so that it looks as if something is getting done." His commitment is to "trying to act so that something might possibly change, as opposed to acting so as to persuade ourselves that we're not powerless." Williams quotes Jesus' "Sermon on the Mount," often dismissed for its passivity, as an invitation to initiative and creativity: "the world of the aggressor, the master, is questioned because the person who is supposed to take no initiatives suddenly does," and this changes the terms of the relationship and "says to the master that the world might be otherwise." It is, in effect, a decision "not to be passive, not to be a victim, but equally not to avoid passivity by simply reproducing what's been done to you. It is always something of a miracle."

Williams depicts the decision of a consortium of Western governments to invade Afghanistan and overthrow the Islamic extremist Taliban regime in November 2001 as an instinctive turning to violence "because we felt, most of us, that there really was nothing else we could do. A long program of diplomatic pressure, the reworking of regional alliances, and a severe review of intelligence and security didn't feel like doing anything. There needed to be a discharge of the tension." Williams is critical of a "violent reaction" (I would have referred to it as a "forceful response") because "it was not at all clear what would count as victory in this engagement." Capturing or killing Osama bin Laden and ending terrorism would not, Williams laments, solve the underlying problems. He concludes that both the motivation and methods of the campaign against the Taliban in Afghanistan are tainted, "because as soon as assaults on public morale by allowing random killing *as a matter of calculated policy* become part of a military strategy [Williams is mainly referring here to the use of cluster bombs], we are at once vulnerable to the charge that there is no moral difference in kind between our military action and the terror which it attacks."

Unannounced in his narrative, Williams draws a distinction between violence and force when he notes that "law itself assumes that force is justified in some circumstances to defend a community's health and survival. But that health and survival are themselves undermined when defended by indiscriminate or disproportionate means; the cost is too high. What we set out to defend has become corrupted in the process." He also sets himself against what he infers is American unilateralism in Afghanistan (although a number of nations were involved in both the invasion and the subsequent occupation of that country) when he says "there is a high price to pay for allowing one nation to act in the name of the global campaign against terror while fudging the question of how in international law the matter might be brought to conclusion." Williams asserted that "a good deal of the moral capital accumulated during the first days and weeks has been squandered."

The critical mistake, as he understood it, was to declare the terrorist attacks an act of war and to respond with a "war on terrorism." He said "clarity disappeared," presuming that some had previously existed. In noting that terrorism is a form of aberrant behavior, he doubted the wisdom and the morality of the "case for an open-ended military campaign." This led Williams to "wonder whether we have actually seen the end of war as we knew it." He notes changes to the character of armed conflict, which he refers to as "state violence," since 1945 and the "erosion of what once seemed straightforward virtues." He believes that the apprehension and punishment of terrorists and dealing with the threat of terrorism "cannot be translated into the satisfying language of decisive and dramatic conquest." He wants "us"—although the membership of that group is not clear—to "let go of the fantasies nurtured by the capacity for high-tech aerial assault," a strategy used to avoid incurring casualties.

On Rowan Williams

In seeking a different approach to dealing with international terrorism, Williams wants "our aims [to be reconceived] in terms of police action" and the "maintenance of international law." He goes on: "if we stopped talking about war so much, we might be spared the posturing which suggests that any questioning of current methods must be weakness at best, treason at worst." He concludes by addressing the experienced effects of globalization in places and among peoples who been caught up in anti-Western radicalism, and the possibility that Westerners who fear terrorist attacks might have "a door into the suffering of countless other innocents, a suffering that is more or less routine for them in their less regularly protected environments." This might provoke empathy and even sympathy leading to "a global hospitality."

Williams makes no particular claims for his reflections. He says that "writing in the dust is writing something that won't last, something exposed to dissolution . . . this isn't a theology or a program for action, but one person's attempt to find words for grief and shock and loss of one moment. In the nature of things, these words won't last, and I need to acknowledge and accept that, and hope only that they may help to take forward someone else's mourning." But he had much more to say about post "9/11" events.

A year later (Boxing Day 2002),[25] Williams claimed "the terrorist, the suicide bomber, is someone who's got to the point where they can only see from a distance: the sort of distance from which you can't see a face, meet the eyes of someone, hear who they are, imagine who and what they love." He asserted that "all violence works with that sort of distance, it depends on not seeing certain things." Then he added, "with the high-tech military methods we've got used to in recent years, there's a greater temptation to take for granted the view from a distance."

These were curious comments that defied objective analysis. He seemed to imply that terrorists and suicide bombers would recoil from their deeds if they really knew the people they were killing. But these individuals usually do know the people who will be the victims of their actions. And it is because they know them, albeit not personally or intimately, they are all the more determined to kill them. The Palestinian wearing a bomb vest who boards an Israeli bus sees the faces of all those he or she will kill or maim. It is highly personalized violence. In my view, Williams gives the

---

25. BBC Radio 4, Thought for the Day, December 26, 2002.

terrorist far too much humanity by suggesting they might act differently if their vantage point was improved. The generalization that all violence depends on not seeing things is, in my experience, simply wrong.

And he does not seem to realize the extent to which precision guided weapons have reduced the number of unintended deaths in modern combat operations. It is now possible to attack a military target while minimizing the collateral damage. This does not of itself make the deployment of these weapons right or prevent targets from being misidentified. But it means that the kinds of bombing missions that Britain mounted on Germany in 1944–45 and the United States launched against North Vietnam in 1967–70 are no longer necessary to achieve strategic or even tactical objectives. There is no moral equivalence or extension of reasoning that could place terrorism and internationally sanctioned force on any similar scale. One is always and everywhere wrong; the other can be justified in certain albeit tragic circumstances.

The dust had not long settled on New York and Washington when momentum gathered for a pre-emptive strike on Iraq, which had failed to comply with UN demands that it provide credible evidence that it no longer possessed weapons of mass destruction. As a "Coalition of the Willing" began to take shape in late 2002, Williams rejected the accusation that he was an "appeaser"—the word used to describe those opposed to war against an advancing Nazi Germany in 1938—because he "expressed misgivings about military action against Iraq."[26] He was clearly stung by the suggestion.

The two situations were, according to Williams, entirely different because the atomic bombing of Hiroshima "was the start of a process leading to the development of weaponry that made territorial struggles irrelevant. The long-distance delivery of weapons of mass destruction altered the character of war itself . . . The post-Cold War period may have seen the dissolution of this strategic assumption; but it has not taken us back to the age when nation states fought territorial campaigns." Williams could see no comparison between resisting Hitler and a desire to overthrow Saddam Hussein. He argued that "apart from the potential destabilising effect of pre-emptive action on the whole ethos of the society of states . . . the exact calculation of what weaponry might be employed by a cornered Saddam Hussein is uncertain; and so is the retaliation that might be provoked in the region from

---

26. Williams, "Don't call us appeasers for hesitating at war with Iraq."

its sole nuclear power, Israel." He went on to say that "the military option sends a destabilising message in a seriously unclear international situation; it invites a cavalier attitude to some of the principles of international law in respect of the justification of armed force." And in response to claims that the people of Iraq would be better off without Saddam, he contended that "we are not the best arbiters of the interests of others when we have interests of our own at stake."

In February 2003, with the ground invasion of Iraq involving American, British, and Australian troops imminent, Williams issued a joint statement with Cardinal Cormac Murphy-O'Connor, the head of the Roman Catholic Church in England and Wales, calling for the continuation of weapons inspections in Iraq and warning against the "unpredictable humanitarian and political consequences" of a war. By then he seems to have shifted slightly in his attitude to the war in Afghanistan, which he described in December 2002 as "at best the lesser evil," but thought an attack against Iraq could bring "real cost to our own humanity." But he opposed war with Iraq because removing even an odious regime "without reference to international law" would provoke a spiral of terrorist retaliation. "This does not depend on the sponsorship of any one state. There may also be a consolidation of anti-Western feeling and a worsening of the situation in Israel. If Arab neighbours are convinced they are excluded from the process of containment of Saddam, the results will be disastrous. If they are willing to sign up to diplomatic containment and indictment in international courts, we should work with this."[27]

Williams has not changed his views on the Iraq war that began on March 20, 2003. As someone who initially supported the case for war and publicly said it could be justified on the grounds cited by the Australian government,[28] I changed my view and publicly expressed regret at supporting the case for war when it became clear that Iraq did not possess weapons of mass destruction, did not have plans to attack its neighbors and was not giving material support to terrorist organizations. In my view, the most serious effect of the war was a diminished respect for the international

---

27. Williams, "Alternative Views: Opinion Formers Speak Out," *The Guardian*, September 25, 2002.

28. Tom Frame, "Battle hymn for a three week war," *The Australian*, February 11, 2003.

institutions that exist to arbitrate disputes. But there are no simple solutions nor fail-safe processes.

While threats appear most ominous to those at whom they are directed, the assessment of *when* a threat is fully formed or *when* a plan is completed is always liable to self-interested interpretation. As Williams has argued: "If a state or administration acts without due and visible attention to agreed international process, it acts in a way analogous to a private person. It purports to be judge of its own interests."[29] This assumes, of course, that the international process is not used to achieve objectives other than avoiding armed conflict. The United States was justified in believing that its former allies, France and Germany, were using the processes of the Security Council for self-interested purposes rather than sincerely striving to determine an international consensus on how to deal with Iraq. But, again, this did not justify pre-emptive action in Iraq. The damage done to collective security by unilateral action is serious.

In the wake of the Iraq war some commentators have suggested that the Security Council be abolished with resolutions relating to peace and security matters requiring a two-thirds majority of the General Assembly to succeed. Williams thought: "There is surely a case for a Standing Commission on Security within the UN structures, incorporating legal and other professionals, capable of taking expert evidence, which could advise on these questions and recommend UN intervention when necessary—instead of complete reliance on the present Security Council framework."

Clearly, there is scope for continuing discussion about who makes the rules governing international relations and how they are applied. The problem with Williams' proposal is the likelihood of delegates to such a standing commission being nominated by self-interested states who expect their representatives to uphold those interests in any discussions about intervention.

More recently, Williams has issued vehement denunciations of any plan to extend Western military action in the Middle East. In October 2007 he said that "when people talk about further destabilising of the region, when you read about some American political advisers speaking about action against Syria and Iran, I can only say that I regard that as criminal, ignorant and potentially murderous folly." In an interview with Britain's

---

29. Williams, "Just War Revisited," address to the Royal Institute for International Affairs, October 15, 2003, ACNS release no. 3624.

Muslim lifestyle magazine *Emel*, Williams rejected the "chosen nation myth of America" and urged the United States to initiate a "generous and intelligent program of aid directed to the societies that have been ravaged; a check on the economic exploitation of defeated territories; a demilitarisation of their presence." But he did acknowledge that political solutions to problems in the Muslim world "were not the most impressive." No-one disagreed with him on the latter point.

This World and the World to Come

It is clear from word and deed that Rowan Williams is not a pacifist. Neither is his thinking shaped primarily by the just war tradition. Admittedly, he resorts to just war principles when making a case against a particular war or the use of a specific weapon. But in my view, his depiction of the just war tradition and his description of its criteria are intended to leave little room for a just war. In any event, he is not particularly interested in judgments about the morality of wars or armed interventions. For him, the defining issues are elsewhere. The two consistent themes in Williams' writings on war and peace are the projection of individual anxieties and psychological insecurities onto international relations and the desire of human beings to secure their physical well-being irrespective of the cost to others. And yet, both themes are open to serious objection. In relation to the first, nations are not analogous to natural persons and cannot be expected to act like autonomous moral beings. This is beyond their capacity usually owing to the complexity of their internal constituencies. And concerning the second, he does not take sufficiently seriously the duty of national leaders to keep safe those for whom they accepted political responsibility when these states deprived their citizens of the entitlement to individual self-defense. But my principal objections to Williams' ideas are quite different.

Williams does not draw any systematic distinction between force and violence in any of his writings. They are not the same and this confusion blurs a number of his judgments. He does not have a good grasp of strategic concepts, international diplomacy, national security or military strategy. He does not address his remarks to the practical contingencies facing national leaders or military commanders faced with foreign policy dilemmas. He also places his commitment to non-violence ahead of the possible need to use force in order to serve the demands of justice and equity. Nor does he deal with the realities of modern conflict, particularly intra-state war, which has led to more deaths since 1945 than inter-national conflicts. Williams has a tendency to locate every participant in a conflict on a continuum of complicity that does not seem to accept that some acts can be aggressive, unprovoked, and utterly indefensible and inexcusable. To my mind, the principal problem with Williams' work is that it does not deal adequately with the world and its problems, nor provide a sufficiently clear set of principles that are needed to regulate the use of force while promoting a vision of non-violence that is practically workable. But does any of this matter?

The most acute test is whether Williams has influenced government policy. He might have shaped Christian opinion in some quarters but his writing has not altered the way in which policy is pursued. Williams seems unable to arrive at firm conclusions from which clear principles can be derived. So many things in his writings are "provisional" or a "work in progress." Williams is acquainted with the literature but appears to feel the need to consider and respond to so many discordant voices that his own proposals are so modest that they could even be missed. I am not suggesting that he is utopian, because he is not. But if Williams is not prepared to be more specific about what needs to be done, he (and the Anglican Communion he leads) will not be heard by those outside the church in the hard-headed, argumentative, and intellectual world of strategic studies where decisions affecting whole nations are made and human lives are held in the balance. While I applaud his sentiments of diplomatic moderation and welcome his attempts to make the church a prototype community of peace, Rowan Williams has spoken with conviction but not with clarity about the things that make for peace.

9

The Beauty of God in Cairo and Islamabad:

Rowan Williams as Apologist

GREG CLARKE

Pope Benedict XVI gave an address at the University of Regensburg titled "Faith, Reason and the University: Memories and Reflections."[1] Significantly, the speech was delivered on September 12, 2006, one day after the fifth anniversary of the terrorist attacks on America by al-Qaeda. The Pope began by invoking his pleasant experience of university teaching in the late 1950s, in particular the *dies academicus* where all the professors of the university gathered together, "making possible a genuine experience of universitas." The Pope described the experience in this way: "the experience, in other words, of the fact that despite our specializations which at times make it difficult to communicate with each other, we made up a whole, working in

---

1. Pope Benedict XVI, "Faith, Reason and the University: Memories and Reflections," http://www.vatican.va/holy_father/benedict_xvi/speeches/2006/september/documents/hf _ben-xvi_spe_20060912_university-regensburg_en.html.

everything on the basis of a single rationality with its various aspects and sharing responsibility for the right use of reason."

Famously now, the Pope continued in the ensuing argument to explain, through the voice of the Byzantine emperor Manuel II Paleologus, that reason teaches us there is no place for violence in the spread of religion. Violence is incompatible with the religious appeal to the reasonable soul, and not to act according to reason, the Pope concludes, is to act in a manner contrary to God's own nature.

The consequences of this address are well known. Many political leaders in largely Muslim countries interpreted the address as insulting to Islam, reading in the Byzantine emperor's fourteenth-century comments the views of Benedict XVI himself, and understanding the Pope's emphasis on reason as an assault on the Koran's teaching. Ironically, in light of the thrust of the emperor's comments (that Mohammed spread the faith using the sword), there were violent protests in some Muslim centers.

An address intended to exalt the universality of reason and the marriage of reason and faith led to confusion, misinterpretation, violence, anti-religious sentiment—and an apology just four days later, expressing sorrow over the reaction to his speech and regret that his speech concerning rational enquiry had been misinterpreted, irrationally rejected and passionately opposed.

Two years before the Pope's Regensburg address, on the third anniversary of the September 11 terrorist attacks, Rowan Williams gave an address at the Muslim university, Al-Azhar al-Sharif, in Cairo.[2] Again on a difficult date, in a place where it was unusual for a Christian authority to be given a platform, a speech was delivered concerning faith, reason, and the ethics of violence, albeit with a very different approach to the subject than that taken by Benedict XVI. The following year, Williams gave a lecture at the Islamic University, Islamabad, again defending the Christian faith. There were no uprisings after the Archbishop's addresses; although it is difficult to draw conclusions from a non-event, it is nevertheless worthwhile examining the substance and the rhetoric of the two addresses, and

---

2. Williams, "Christians and Muslims before the One God: an address given at Al-Azhar al-Sharimath, Cairo on 11 September 2004," *Islam & Christian-Muslim Relations* 16 (2005) 187–97. Reprinted in Irfan A. Omar, ed., *Islam and Other Religions: Pathways to Dialogue: Essays in Honour of Mahmoud Mustafa Ayoub* (London: Routledge, 2005) 175–80. Available online at http://www.archbishopofcanterbury.org/1053.

assessing their merit as types of public engagement.[3] What kind of thinking directs Williams' theory and practice of apologetics/public engagement? How is it that he is most usually received by non-Christian hearers with irenic respect? I will need first to outline Williams' theological aesthetics, in particular his understanding of different modes of discourse in the public sphere, before examining how such an approach was employed in the Cairo and Islamabad addresses. I conclude with some suggestions regarding a more prominent role for the eschatological dimension in the Archbishop's public speaking.

Three Styles of Discourse

Rowan Williams adopts a different approach to that taken by Benedict XVI in his theological speaking and writing. It is born from a different theological and philosophical tradition, and emphasizes the aesthetic dimension in a manner that affords less room for division among his hearers (which arises more within rational argumentation), and more hope for understanding (since its mode of operation is empathic). Williams' theological aesthetics combines elements of the poetic, the rhetorical, and the didactic. In his prologue to *On Christian Theology*, he describes a three-way interaction that occurs in theological activity between "celebratory" style, "communicative" theology, and "critical" work. The celebratory approach is found in genres not always considered primarily theological: the poem, the sculpture, the picture. Certain kinds of public speaking (for example, ecstatic utterances, story-telling, testimonials) are also often in the celebratory style. It is theological expression that emphasizes the glory of God, the impression that God makes upon the reader (or viewer, or hearer). Its primary intent is not to argue a point (although argument may be involved in a hymn or a poem), but, by attention to aesthetic elements (e.g., in a poem, by choice of rhyme, meter, line length, word selection), to "draw out and display connections of thought and image so as to exhibit the fullest possible range of significance in the language used."[4]

3. During the completion of this chapter, Archbishop Williams delivered the foundation lecture at the Royal Courts of Justice in London, and an uproar did indeed follow. It might be the subject of future thinking on the nature of Christian public engagement. His lecture is available online at http://www.archbishopofcanterbury.org/1575 (accessed 28 February, 2008).

4. Williams, *On Christian Theology* (Oxford: Blackwell, 2000) xiii.

One of Williams' key sources of theological aesthetics is the Swiss theologian, Hans Urs von Balthasar, whose enormous work, *The Glory of the Lord: A Theological Aesthetics*, links beauty essentially to Christian theology, locating it at the heart of a proper understanding of the internal relations of the Trinity and the Love that created everything that is. Williams' celebratory style of theologizing finds truth in the beautiful, and finds the beautiful to be persuasive and transforming.

For Williams, this theme has been evident in his work at least since his chapter on Augustine in *The Wound of Knowledge: Christian Spirituality from the New Testament to St John of the Cross*. Williams is attracted to Augustine's emphasis on the priority of the imagination and the heart, even in the midst of the saint's Platonic intellectualism. He expounds Augustine: "Essentially, it is the heart—or, sometimes, the 'understanding' (*mens*)—which is the subject of religious knowledge, never the discursive reason. Before ever God can be spoken of, the heart must 'imagine' or 'figure' him ... God is not known by *scientia* but by *sapientia*, the contemplative turning towards the object, not the active intellect at work on the object, organizing and analysing ..."[5]

For Williams, the aesthetic mode, the celebratory, provides an avenue of epistemic humility for the believer, one in which there is no human pride in knowledge; it is rather disquieting, affecting, difficult, and even wounding. The beautiful, as found in celebratory styles of expression such as art, song, poetry, architecture or the story, is a means by which God-controlled rather than human-controlled communication might take place: "All beauty, in some degree, pierces our blindness and deafness, leads us away from the dominating, organizing life of the intellect; in its alarming and overpowering character (and Augustine thinks here especially of spectacular "natural" beauties), it is a standing challenge to the human fantasy of a world of controlled intelligibility."[6]

This is not at all to say that for Williams discursive reason has no place in public speaking about God; instead, it is a servant not a master. The celebratory style is enhanced in its degree of articulation of beliefs by the *communicative* style. What is added is a capacity to reason with, urge, convince, woo, and shape the listener. Williams acknowledges the significance of rhetoric in theology, with its capacity to persuade and commend:

5. Williams, *Wound of Knowledge* (London: Darton, Longman & Todd, 1979) 74.
6. Ibid., 76.

"Theology seeks also to persuade or commend, to witness to the gospel's capacity for being at home in more than one cultural environment, and to display enough confidence to believe that this gospel can be rediscovered at the end of a long and exotic detour through strange idioms and structures of thought."[7]

Christian theology is not tied to a particular mode of discourse, rather it is robust enough to swap and experiment in different ways, sometimes appropriating a pre-existing mode (for instance, Scholastic appropriations of Aristotelianism) and sometimes creating new modes of discourse in an attempt to engage appropriately and powerfully with a culture. Williams considers that the communicative style requires a high level of confidence within the believer that "the fundamental categories of belief are robust enough to survive the drastic experience of immersion in other ways of constructing and construing the world."[8]

The *critical* style is that which interrogates how robust are these "fundamental categories." Williams notes that critical theology can be either conservative or revisionist, and results in either an agnosticism overall with regards to speaking about God (with "death of God" theology being one obvious such movement), or in a new kind of celebratory work, where once again the inexpressible reality of God is imaginatively expressed and re-expressed.

Williams suggests that the celebratory style is most suited to the believing community, since it assumes some shared concepts, while the communicative style is better suited to public "apologetics" (my word, not Williams') since it adopts or adapts the discourse of a group external to the Christian community; and the critical style queries the sense of the other two styles.

However, in his own writings, Williams demonstrated that a celebratory style can have great apologetic power, since its alignment with the world (when it sees beauty in its objectivity) is attractive to those with eyes to see and ears to hear. This is the approach taken in his essay, "Between the Cherubim: The Empty Tomb and the Empty Throne."[9] This reflection on the knowledge of the resurrection explicitly does not set out to prove anything about it; rather, Williams wants to point out a "convergence" of Christian

---

7. Williams, *On Christian Theology*, xiv.
8. Ibid., xiv.
9. Ibid., 183–96.

imagery, and to suggest that this is a different and appropriate way of talking about the resurrection which avoids some of the argumentative and inconclusive approaches (philosophical, historical, dogmatic) often taken by Christians seeking to communicate this aspect of the faith.

The convergence of images he notices is the cherubim in John's Gospel, one at the foot and one at the head of the grave slab, an image very similar to the cherubim who flank the mercy-seat of the ark of the covenant. In other words, the place of God's presence (the ark) is, in the resurrection narrative of John, occupied by the "absent" body of Jesus. Williams says "the space between the angels is no bad metaphor for a number of features of the tomb tradition that should concentrate our minds theologically."[10] By this iconic resemblance, the empty space begs the response of the angel to the tomb visitors: "He is not here. He has risen." This is a response that the reader is encouraged to share, not urged by historical argument (for history stops short of saying *why* the tomb was empty), nor by philosophical theology (with its concerns for the nature of the resurrection body), but by the aesthetic theology of the "visible" empty space. It could even be said that the absence is beautiful—it evokes awe and appreciation and contemplation. The surprise of seeing nothing where something (a corpse) is expected, shocks the recipient of the image into the quest for an explanation.

Williams further pursues this theological aesthetics in his lectures on art, published as *Grace and Necessity*. Discussing epistemology and ontology in relation to art, he observes that art is "grounded in what we ought to call a kind of obedience,"[11] where the artist (thinker, writer, even apologist) must work with what is provided: "What you can meaningfully say is constrained by what is given."[12] Art is the way it is, writes Williams, because reality is the way it is, "and the way reality is would be unintelligible without the doctrine of God that Christian theologians have elaborated." Art, he says, "is an acute case of knowledge in general."[13]

Art is, then, an instance of the celebratory style, for it takes what is and re-presents or reshapes it so as to appear new, fresh, and often beautiful.

---

10. Ibid., 187.
11. Williams, *Grace and Necessity* (London: Continuum, 2005) 142.
12. Ibid., 136.
13. Ibid., 169.

This is certainly distinct from a radical postmodern epistemology that sees language as creative in a less fettered way, free to play, and impossible to direct. Williams is far more interested in the possibilities of interpretation than the freedom of interpretation. He describes the relationship between human symbolic activity (speech, writing, art) and reality as "one of generation, not creation from nothing, and what can be said is not decided by an inner 'free' subject involved in endless self-reflection."[14] Using a powerful double-negative typical of his cautious optimism regarding knowledge, Williams writes that simply because there is no neat match between stimuli and their reception for the human being, "this is in no way to say that there is no truthful relation between speech and reality, or however you want to put it."[15]

Williams sees this philosophy of art as significant for theology. It provides not an argument for God's existence, but a means by which the world impresses the recipient. It is, in that way, an apologetic. Since God generates a world, kneading and honing it as a sculptor does his clay, so we see God moving into the world and becoming involved in it. This extraordinary Christian metaphysical claim (that the world is not necessary to God, but God out of love generates more than he is) provides an explanation for existence itself. The love of God means that there is a world to be explored, to be shaped and reshaped, to react to, seek to understand, and of which to express understanding. Williams has developed this concept from his reading of Balthasar, who observed the non-essential nature of the world and its inhabitants, and thus the complete freedom of the God who created it and them. "Something in the world of phenomena," writes Williams, "exceeds what is 'needed'; there is no final account of how things are that confines itself to functions."[16]

Williams' emphasis on art and culture in much of his publicly directed writing appears to relate to his understanding of apologetics. It is the *aesthetic* dimension that engages the enquirer. By this Williams seems to mean, following Maritain, that a thing is beautiful *because of* the reality that allows it to be—and that there is some sort of indirect and partially concealed pathway from that beauty to the reality that forges it. An object, full of structural integrity, clear of purpose, radiant, and consonant with the

14. Ibid., 137.
15. Ibid.
16. Ibid., 156.

physical world can be called beautiful because of its good and loving and true generation from the stuff that is given.

Consider, for example, the experience of a flavor. In "Flavors, Colors and God," philosopher Robert Merrihew Adams reaches the conclusion that it is so difficult to sustain the materialist interpretation of phenomenal *qualia*—that is, that thing which is the experience of red or the taste of sugar—that a theological interpretation becomes the less desperate expedient.[17] This agrees with Locke's claim that "The production of Sensation in us of Colours and Sounds, *etc.* by impulse and motion . . . being such, wherein we can discover no natural connexion with any *Ideas* we have, we cannot but ascribe them to the arbitrary Will and good Pleasure of the Wise Architect."[18] This is probably not quite an argument for the existence of God from flavor, but a claim that within a theistic worldview only an appeal to God's freely exerted will and pleasure satisfactorily explains the experience of flavor or any other sensation, impulse, or artistic experience. In this way, beauty and the experience of beauty directs the perceiver towards God as both the best explanation and the secret within the art itself.

An objection might be that this notion of God is too nebulous, and not associated closely enough with the Christian God. But Williams locates the philosophy of generative knowledge of God and reality precisely within the doctrine of the Triune God, whose internal relations of love for the eternal other are the grounds for selfless, love-driven not need-driven, creation of the external world. No other God or gods will do such a thing, only the Christian God. As Williams writes in a chapter on Hegel, "It is quite specifically the doctrine of God's triune being that here resolves our aporia in thinking [about the relation of God to the world]."[19]

In a book admired by Williams,[20] David Bentley Hart gives the highest place to the beauty of the Christian God as the means by which is shown what the world wishes to see: fellowship, delight, and peace:

> to speak of the beauty of the infinite is genuinely to name the Christian difference in aesthetics, a thought of the beautiful inconceivable in

17. "Flavors, Colors and God," in Robert Merrihew Adams, *The Virtue of Faith and Other Essays in Philosophical Theology* (New York: Oxford University Press, 1987).

18. John Locke, *An Essay concerning Human Understanding* (Oxford: Clarendon, 1975) 559–60 (IV.3, §29).

19. Williams, "Logic and Spirit in Hegel," in *Post-Secular Philosophy: Between Philosophy and Theology*, ed. Phillip Blond (London: Routledge, 1998) 121.

20. See Williams, *Grace and Necessity*, 160, 165–66.

terms available to non-Christian philosophy, ancient and modern alike. In the story the church tells concerning God and his creatures, beauty and infinity both are narrated as nowhere else, in such a way as to show how each belongs to the "grammar" of the other, and how both belong to a common language of delight and peace.[21]

The "infinite" in Christian theology pertains not to some abstract conception of the beautiful, but to the doctrine of the Trinity. God's triune being is the seat of beauty, and because of the role of the Trinity in creation, also the source of the creation's beauty. It is the Trinity that *is* beauty, and enables us to grasp what is truly beautiful. Hart again: "True beauty is not the idea of the beautiful, a static archetype in the 'mind' of God, but is an infinite 'music,' a drama, art, completed in—but never 'bounded' by—the termless dynamism of the Trinity's life."[22]

It may be objected that this view of "art as theological apologetics" is at the "pointy end" of public engagement, of more interest to the divinity faculty academic than the average citizen, and does not adequately account for an Archbishop's everyday defense and promotion of the Christian faith. However, it is not in the end a theoretical position but a very practical one, for it concerns effects and impressions. It concerns the particularities of engagement with God and his world. In Hart's words, "Theology should always remain at the surface (aesthetic, rhetorical, metaphoric), where all things, finally, come to pass."[23] Likewise, in public theological engagement or apologetics, what matters is the en-fleshed, en-storied, en-colored, en-sung expression and communication of what one believes about God.

This confidence in the beauty of God is what intellectually lies behind such activities as Williams' interview with UK comedian Ricky Gervais. In this interview (surely a misnomer for what ensued!), the desperate, ill-informed, and scattergun Gervais, who must be Richard Dawkins' worst publicist, bumbled through a one-sided conversation with Williams. The Archbishop barely got a word in, except to acknowledge one thing that Gervais had himself said—divine forgiveness, and the accompanying love of God for his forgiven creature, is indeed very beautiful.[24] The common

21. Hart, *The Beauty of the Infinite* (Grand Rapids: Eerdmans, 2003) 154.
22. Ibid., 177.
23. Ibid., 28.
24. Video recording available online at http://www.youtube.com/watch?v=QZGO4Y6-WTUM (accessed 28 February, 2008).

appreciation of the beauty of acts of forgiveness opened up an opportunity for theological celebration.

This small example of Williams' public engagement leads us to consider in more detail two other instances of public address where theological aesthetics shape his approach.

The Cairo and Islamabad Addresses

To examine the way in which Williams' theological aesthetics informs his public engagement, we turn to two addresses given in Muslim contexts in recent years: the 2004 address to the Islamic University in Cairo and the 2005 address at the Islamic University, Islamabad. In both contexts we might assume that the audience would not be predisposed to agree with the words uttered by an Anglican Archbishop, at least if they were words drawn specifically from creedal Christianity. How then does the Archbishop engage in these two contexts?

He appeals to beauty. In both addresses we find a variation on this theme. The 2004 Cairo address emphasizes common ethics as the means of drawing together those who believe in the One Living God, despite radical differences in their understanding of the being of that God. The 2005 Islamabad address asks the audience to imagine what it is like to live and think as a Christian. Williams outlines Christian praxis and dogma, "performing" the beautiful acts and doctrines of the Christian faith for his listeners. Assuming there is attractiveness and beauty in goodness, in peacefulness, and in truth, Williams makes his case for Christianity.

Williams' point of commonality with the Cairo university audience, in contrast with the Pope at Regensburg, is the doctrine of God. His title already assumes an association with his Muslim listeners: "Christians and Muslims before the One God." He assumes God; he does not argue for God's place within the university faculties, as Benedict XVI does. God is named in a number of ways throughout the speech, but never as Allah or Yahweh. God's power ("Almighty God") and oneness ("One Living God") are celebrated, and no battle is undertaken over God's name. Invoking the wonder and awe of a powerful God draws together his listeners, enabling the archbishop to make certain practical requests on the basis of shared submission to this figure of awe.

In claiming theological commonality at this point, Williams' intention is ethical: "I want to suggest how, despite some of our differences, we can, in the light of our belief about Almighty God, together make certain affirmations to the world about the way of peace and justice for human beings."[25]

That is not to say, however, that there is no specific identification of God in his speech. At the beginning of the speech, having asserted the oneness of God and quoted "luminous and uncompromising" words from the Qur'an saying the same, Williams immediately names the problem of the Triune God. Appealing to the locals (that is, ancient Alexandrian theologians), Williams approaches the theological conundrum of Incarnation from "their side"—he states that "God is not the name of a person like a human person." The limitations of language are acknowledged, and the terms redefined: "God" will be the name of "eternal and self-sufficient life." This life is One; but it is a life in which we can *participate* (although he does not use this word in the speech). Furthermore, he identifies God with love, not as an action of God, but as an "interaction and relation" of God. He dances around the notion of *perichoresis*, without using the term or anything like it.

Having re-filled the word "God" for his listeners, Williams makes the statement that "the disagreement between Christian and Muslim is not, I believe, a disagreement about the nature of God as One and Living and Self-subsistent." Instead, he identifies God with infinite freedom, that which is (according to Williams' own theology) beautiful. "It is essential to think of God as a life that has no limit, as a life that is free," Williams writes,[26] a concept that is only reasonable to Williams in light of the Trinity, where true freedom is found.

In six paragraphs, standing at the Cairo University, the Anglican archbishop has asked his Muslim audience to consider themselves to be untroubled by the doctrine of the Triune God, newly expressed in terms of love and life, and in fact to find in it the most beautiful expression of what they desire. He asks the listener to "adore [this God] in trust and thankfulness,"[27] accepting that words will never sufficiently grasp the infinite.

From this theological beginning, Williams' rhetorical appeal turns to personal experience and ethical reactions to the events of September 11, 2001. The Archbishop was in New York just a short distance from the World

---

25. Williams, "Christians and Muslims," 175.
26. Ibid., 189.
27. Ibid., 190.

Trade Center on the morning of the attacks; by reminding the audience of this intense, unshared experience, he is in a strong position to offer an ethically respectable response to what happened.

He chooses to invoke Jesus' teaching on loving your enemies and leaving revenge to God—without naming them as Christian teachings. Instead, he appeals to the audience as if these teachings are what can only be considered natural law: "We may rightly want to defend ourselves and one another—our people, our families, the weak and vulnerable among us. But we are not forced to act in revengeful ways, holding up a mirror to the terrible acts done to us . . . and we fail to show our belief in the living God who always requires of us justice and goodness."[28]

Williams here appeals to what is arguably a distinct teaching of Jesus, not to return evil for evil—one of Jesus' renowned reversals of human expectations. But by standing with his audience (using the pronoun "we" repeatedly), rather than indicting them or suggesting that they are somehow responsible for his "tribe's" suffering, Williams in fact models the very non-vengeance he is proclaiming. He goes on, somewhat controversially for some Christian schools of thought, to state that "whenever a Muslim, a Christian or a Jew refuses to act in violent revenges . . . that person bears witness to the true God."[29] Faith in the One Living God, in other words, is sufficient grounds for choosing the path of non-vengeance. Williams' explanation for this ethical stance is that it is a way of celebrating God, a way of seeing God's priorities—reconciliation, justice, mercy—as beautiful. He calls it "a form of adoration."[30]

It is commonly asserted that non-vengeance is one of the distinctive counter-religious teachings of the early Christian movement. Paul Barnett, for example, citing Christ's modeling of the non-vindictive way described in 1 Peter 2:23, boldly states: "Here is one of the great distinctives of Christianity (where it is true to its master). How different Peter's Jesus-paradigm is to other religions and world-views around us. We think of the unyielding and seemingly endless cycle of payback and religious pride evident in both protagonists in Israel or of the triumphalist hatred of Osama Bin Laden."[31] Nevertheless, Williams appeals to his audience that

28. Ibid., 191.
29. Ibid.
30. Ibid.
31. Paul Barnett, "Evangelism in the Post-9/11 World with reference to 1 Peter," http://your.sydneyanglicans.net/culture/thinking/1014a (accessed 30 March, 2008).

anyone who *adores* the One Living and Almighty God will behave in this (Christian) manner. Invoking the celebration of God is wagered to overwhelm the desire for vengeance, even for those who are not followers of the teachings of Jesus.

Similarly, Williams repeats the word "justice" in this section of the address, on the assumption that all of his listeners will be on the side of justice (surely no-one wittingly sides with injustice?). There is no attempt to specify the meaning of this term, resulting in a lack of clarity concerning Christian conceptions of justice and their comparison, or indeed contrast, with Muslim conceptions. Yet, a strategy of identification with the generic term, "God's justice," operates within the speech, smoothing over particularities in its efforts to draw together ethically the two religious views and appeal to the (arguably) Christian one as the beautiful one.

It is worship-driven ethics in which Williams places his hopes for peace, as he describes to his listeners the laudable process of community meetings and solidarity shown between British Muslims and Christians: "We believe that in such local ways we can, despite our disagreements, show to the world a different standard of behaviour, one that is worthy of the all-powerful and self-sufficient God we worship, worthy of him in a way that crusades and terrorism and oppression are not."

On reading the Cairo address, I was struck by an absence. Rowan Williams often speaks about the significance of identifying oneself—that is, claiming a Christian identity. He emphasizes Christ's ownership of a Christian; the name stamped on the forehead, the one-fleshness of the Christian Bride (the church) with her Bridegroom. This element of identification is missing in the Cairo address.

In contrast, another address given the following year at the Islamic University, Islamabad, is almost entirely concerned with Christian identification.[32] The Archbishop asks his largely Islamic university audience to *imagine* what it is like to be a Christian—in other words, to identify with the Christian. He explains Christian praxis—saying the Lord's Prayer, reading from a holy book, naming God as "Father, Son and Holy Spirit." He then goes on, in some theological detail, to outline a theology of incarnation,

---

32. Williams, "What is Christianity?," lecture given at the International Islamic University in Islamabad, Pakistan, November 23, 2005. Available online at http://www.archbishopofcanterbury.org/983.

obedience, atonement, resurrection, revelation, and worship, all within a forty-minute address.

Unlike the Cairo address, in Islamabad the Archbishop plainly distances himself from his listeners. In the manner of a lecture, he outlines in plain language, with little theological jargon, Christian dogma. While some have labeled the address heterodox for its descriptions of God the Father's begetting of the Son, my concern here is with technique. There are points at which he acknowledges commonalities between Christian belief and that of the Qur'an, but the majority of the lecture outlines Christian distinctives. It concludes with a call to prayer for peace, and the statement, "There are many beliefs that divide Christians from others, not least from their Muslim friends and neighbours, and this lecture will have made some of them clearly visible."[33]

This sense of identifying with Christ appears to have increased in importance in the public addresses of Rowan Williams. In a speech in 2006, he makes it explicit as the means by which Christianity can engage with pluralism:

> The question of Christian identity in a world of plural perspectives and convictions cannot be answered in cliches about the tolerant co-existence of different opinions. It is rather that the nature of our conviction as Christians puts us irrevocably in a certain place, which is both promising and deeply risky, the place where we are called to show utter commitment to the God who is revealed in Jesus and to all those to whom his invitation is addressed.[34]

It is perhaps not clear immediately that Williams has adopted a celebratory mode of engagement in this lecture. It is so concerned with the content of Christian belief and practice that it is easy to overlook the "nest" in which the lecture is cushioned. Williams asks his listener to have a vision of the Christian, in his life and beliefs. "Imagine someone watching, over a period of about one year, the things that happen in a Christian church," Williams writes.[35] Immediately, he is giving not a lecture but an imaginative drama of Christian living. He "scripts" the activities of the Christian within

---

33. Ibid., n.p.

34. Williams, "Christian Identity and Religious Plurality," *Ecumenical Review* 58.1/2 (2006) 69–75; also *Christian Century* 123.6 (2006) 29–33. Speech to World Council of Churches, Porto Alegre, Brazil, February 2006.

35. Williams, "What is Christianity?" n.p.

the church gathering, praying, uttering creedal sayings, reading the Holy Book, delivering sermons, celebrating the Eucharist. Within this dramatic framework, a great deal of Christian doctrine is communicated, but the aesthetic mode—"watch on while these Christians do what they do"— enables major differences in doctrine to be heard and appreciated without immediately drawing attention to their divisiveness.

At the end of the lecture, Williams reminds the listeners of the dramatic context as he stresses the goal of glory and adoration for the Christian believer: "What the Christian hopes and prays for is that in the end he or she will be brought by the grace of God's Spirit to see the glory of God as it is shown in the face of Jesus, and to be so united with his prayer to the Father that we never fall away. All that the observer might see in a Christian meeting for worship is directed towards this."[36]

With this statement, Williams has identified Jesus with the glory of God, providing a dramatic medium within which a Muslim listener might observe this (I presume) "blasphemy." A profoundly Christian teaching is nested within an aesthetic mode which enables empathetic reception rather than confrontation.

A Greater Eschatological Dimension?

Williams' aesthetic approach to theological speaking in public might be enhanced by a stronger eschatological dimension. It is perhaps the most muted theological theme in his public engagement, absent from his Cairo address and mere background noise in the Islamabad lecture. But a stronger connection between the aesthetic and the eschatological would seem appropriate to the way in which his theological aesthetics has developed. I wish to conclude with some preliminary explorations of how this might take place.

It can be argued that art is eschatological in nature and creativity is eschatologically driven. One of the writers dear to Williams as a young intellectual but now considered embarrassing,[37] Nikolai Berdyaev, wrote that, "The creative act, alike in its power and impotence, is eschatological—a

---

36. Ibid., n.p.

37. "I loved Berdyaev when I was seventeen and haven't been able to read him seriously since." Quoted in an interview with Rowan Williams by Todd Breyfogle, "Time and Transformation: A Conversation with Rowan Williams," *Cross Currents* 45 (1995) 308.

prefiguration of the end of the world."[38] Art captures, encapsulates, expresses, and interacts with human desires for the ultimate future. Art "proceeds from the longing for that perfect existence which is not yet, but which man, despite all disappointments, thinks must come to be when the existent has reached its full truth and reality has been subordinated to actual entities."[39] Our experience of art and nature is shaped by our expectations for the future. This seems to me a very fruitful place to try to work on the place of aesthetics in Christian public engagement, since with Barth we can say, "If Christianity be not altogether thoroughgoing eschatology, there remains in it no relationship whatever with Christ."[40]

If art is about those future desires, then there ought to be a powerful Christian apologetic that explains those desires, that responds to those desires. And if the aesthetic mode, or the celebratory style, to use Williams' own term, is a most successful means of public engagement with Christian theology, then there ought to be a major role for eschatology in such aesthetic apologetics.

There are indications in *Grace and Necessity* that the eschatological ought to play a greater role in public engagement and apologetics. Williams explains the artist's role as "imagining a world that is both new and secretly inscribed in all that is already seen," invoking a theology of new creation.[41] But this could be more specific since, in the history of art, Christian, pagan or otherwise, eschatological imagery and motifs are fundamental and inescapable.

Williams' emphasis is on the beauty of the infinite, with the infinite finding Christian definition within the Trinity. But this is always at risk of becoming a static, neo-Platonic vision of God, rather than a Christian eschatological one. For what is beautiful is often identified with what is finally, eventually, ultimately satisfying, and needs also to be identified with more historically bound concepts such as justice and peace. In Christian theology, such concepts are inextricably eschatological. Williams acknowledges difficulties in talking eschatologically outside of a Christian audience in a number of key essays in *On Christian Theology*. In his discussion of

---

38. Nikolai Berdyaev, *Dream and Reality* (London: Bles, 1950) 214.

39. Romano Guardini, quoted in Hans Küng, *Art and the Question of Meaning* (London: SCM, 1980) 51–52.

40. Karl Barth, *The Epistle to the Romans* (London: Oxford University Press, 1977) 314.

41. Williams, *Grace and Necessity*, 167.

Rosemary Ruether in "On Being Creatures," he expresses some sympathy with the criticism of a linear narrative of God's actions in the world (in other words, traditional Christian eschatology), and with the alternative view that "there is no movement to a last end, a millennium—only a confidence that, within the divine matrix, nothing is ultimately lost."[42] In seeking to come to grips with Christ's lordship in his essay, "The Finality of Christ," Williams distances himself from totalizing expressions of this lordship and searches for alternative ways of expressing the meaningfulness of Christ for all tribes and nations. He writes:

> We may still want to confess that in Christ "all things cohere," but it is possible to understand this as saying not that "in Christ all meanings are contained" but that "on Christ's judgement all histories converge" . . . A finished account of Christ as containing all meanings would make Christology non-eschatological. What we have to do is to discover how our commitment to the question Jesus poses may make itself audible and intelligible beyond the bounds of the Christian institution.[43]

It seems that in order to answer his own question here, Williams has privileged the beatific vision as the least problematic expression of the Christian understanding of the future. This vision of the glory of God in the face of Jesus ends his Islamabad address, and is the image upon which his hopes of communicating with the largely Muslim audience rest. However, might there be other images within eschatology—which, of all Christian doctrines, is most dependent on imagery—that likewise are celebratory and communicative of the Christian understanding of reality?

For example, the notion of *rest* seems to me to be an under-utilized aspect of Christian teaching in public engagement. It is a concept drawn from the seventh day of creation all the way through to the millennium and the new heavens and earth. It represents a drive which human beings of any belief system understand. It is the motif in a range of art forms, from bucolic poetry to still life drawings to ambient music. In fact, the completion of an artwork itself brings on the time of rest for its creator and is a celebration of that state of achievement and satisfaction. A theological aesthetics of rest would seem a very fruitful area for a Christian figure to engage with

---

42. Williams, *On Christian Theology*, 65.
43. Ibid., 94.

an overworked and frantically distracted public. And, as well as being a notion of common appeal across religions and worldviews, it is a distinct teaching of Jesus that true rest is found in him: "Come to me, all you who are weary and burdened, and I will give you rest" (Matthew 11:28; NIV). Furthermore, this rest is primarily eschatological in that it is only achieved following the time of judgment; until then, it remains a desire. Foretastes of such Christian rest are available in aspects of church fellowship or in marriage and friendship, and prefigurations of the final rest can be found in the kind of artistic expressions I have mentioned—a still life painting, a Chopin nocturne, a Virgil Eclogue. But the rest remains future, and ought not therefore to lethargize the Christian pilgrim.

Richard Bauckham and Trevor Hart describe such a rest as the endpoint of a journey, and the motivation for the journey: "It is the goal towards which we aim in this life; in the life to come it will have been attained. Now on the road to perfection, then we shall have been perfected. Now in motion towards our destination, then we shall come to rest. The motif of the vision of God . . . has often been understood to mean that in eternal contemplation we shall mirror the changeless perfection of God himself."[44] Bauckham and Hart emphasize the imaginative nature of Christian eschatology, especially its presentation (or revelation) in the form of visions, images, and figures in a manner analogous with fantastic literature.[45] Fantasy literature does not create its stories, characters, and imagery from nothing; rather it "is clearly parasitic upon given perceptions of what constitutes the real world."[46] It works by transforming this world into something else, and making plausible what might at first glance in this world seem impossible. This biblically-controlled fantasizing about the future does not provide distant hopes disconnected from one's current strivings in the faith, but offers visions of where one's strivings might lead. In eternity the goal is reached; in the time-bound world, eschatological imagery provides the motivation and inspiration for striving in the direction of those fantasies. There is greater room for this kind of eschatological expression in Rowan Williams' public engagement, without promoting what he fears: "an absorption in some final

---

44. Richard Bauckham and Trevor Hart, *Hope against Hope: Christian Eschatology in Contemporary Context* (London: Darton, Longman & Todd, 1999) 157.

45. Ibid., 88.

46. Ibid., 90.

'absolute.'"[47] Rather, Christian eschatology, expressed primarily in the form of images, tropes, and fantastic scenes, invites the listener on the journey towards eternity that is step-by-step and properly involved in the shaping of that future.

---

47. Williams, *Tokens of Trust* (Norwich: Canterbury, 2007) 155.

Bibliography of Rowan Williams

Primary Literature

A. Monographs

"The Theology of Vladimir Nikolaievich Lossky: An Exposition and Critique." Ph.D. dissertation, Oxford University, 1975.
The Wound of Knowledge: Christian Spirituality from the New Testament to St John of the Cross. London: Darton, Longman & Todd, 1979. American edition: *Christian Spirituality: A Theological History from the New Testament to Luther and St. John of the Cross*. Atlanta: John Knox, 1980. Revised edition: *The Wound of Knowledge: Christian Spirituality from the New Testament to St John of the Cross*. London: Darton, Longman & Todd, 1990; Cambridge, MA: Cowley Publications, 1991. Reissued as *The Wound of Knowledge: A Theological History from the New Testament to Luther and St John of the Cross*. Eugene, OR: Wipf & Stock, 1998.
Resurrection: Interpreting the Easter Gospel. London: Darton, Longman & Todd, 1982; New York: Pilgrim, 1984. Revised edition: London: Darton, Longman & Todd, 2002.
The Truce of God: Peacemaking in Troubled Times. London: Fount, 1983; New York: Pilgrim, 1983. Revised edition, Norwich: Canterbury, 2005; Grand Rapids: Eerdmans, 2005.
Arius: Heresy and Tradition. London: Darton, Longman & Todd, 1987. Revised edition: London: SCM, 2001; Grand Rapids: Eerdmans, 2002.
Teresa of Avila. Outstanding Christian Thinkers. London: Chapman, 1991; Harrisburg, PA: Morehouse, 1991. Reissued, London: Continuum, 2000.
Open to Judgement: Sermons and Addresses. London: Darton, Longman & Todd, 1994. American edition: *A Ray of Darkness: Sermons and Reflections*. Cambridge, MA: Cowley, 1995.
On Christian Theology, Challenges in Contemporary Theology. Oxford: Blackwell; Malden, MA: Blackwell, 2000.
Christ on Trial: How the Gospel Unsettles Our Judgement. London: Fount, 2000; Grand Rapids: Eerdmans, 2000.

Bibliography of Rowan Williams

Lost Icons: Reflection on Cultural Bereavement. Edinburgh: T. & T. Clark, 2000; Harrisburg, PA: Morehouse, 2002. Reissued, London: Continuum, 2003.
Writing in the Dust: Reflections on 11th September and Its Aftermath. London: Hodder & Stoughton, 2002. American edition: *Writing in the Dust: After September 11.* Grand Rapids: Eerdmans, 2002.
Silence and Honey Cakes: The Wisdom of the Desert. Oxford: Lion, 2003. American expanded edition: *Where God Happens: Discovering Christ in One Another.* Boston: New Seeds, 2005.
Areithiau a phregethau a draddodwyd gan Y Parchedicaf a Gwir Anrhydeddus Dr Rowan Williams tra'n Archesgob Cymru, Chwefror 2000-Rhagfyr 2002 [*Addresses and sermons delivered by the Most Revd and Rt. Hon. Dr Rowan Williams while Archbishop of Wales, February 2000–December 2002*]. Caerdydd: Yr Eglwys yng Ngymru, 2003.
The Anglican Way. London: Darton, Longman & Todd, 2004.
Anglican Identities. Cambridge, MA: Cowley, 2003; London: Darton, Longman & Todd, 2004.
Why Study the Past? The Quest for the Historical Church. Grand Rapids: Eerdmans, 2005; London: Darton, Longman & Todd, 2005.
Grace and Necessity: Towards a New Theology for the 21st Century. London: Continuum, 2005. American edition: *Grace and Necessity: Reflections on Art and Love.* Harrisburg, PA: Morehouse, 2005.
Tokens of Trust: An Introduction to Christian Belief. Illustrations by David Jones. Louisville: Westminster John Knox, 2007; London: Canterbury Norwich, 2007.
Wrestling with Angels: Conversations in Modern Theology. Edited by Mike Higton. London: SCM, 2007; Grand Rapids: Eerdmans, 2007.
Dostoevsky: Language, Faith, and Fiction. Waco, TX: Baylor University Press, 2008.

B. Poetry

After Silent Centuries. Oxford: Perpetua, 1994.
Remembering Jerusalem. Oxford: Perpetua, 2001.
The Poems of Rowan Williams. Oxford: Perpetua, 2002; Grand Rapids: Eerdmans, 2002.
Headwaters. Oxford: Perpetua, 2008.

C. Devotional Books

The Kingdom is Theirs: Five Reflections on the Beatitudes. London: Christian Socialist Movement, 1995. Reissued, 2002.
With Nick Aiken. *Family Prayers.* London: SPCK, 2002; New York: Paulist, 2002.
Ponder These Things: Praying with Icons of the Virgin. Norwich: Canterbury, 2002; Franklin, WI: Sheed and Ward, 2002. Reprinted, Brewster, MA: Paraclete, 2006.
The Dwelling of the Light: Praying with Icons of Christ. Norwich: Canterbury, 2003.
Daily Bible studies, in *Living Communion: The Official Report of the 13th Meeting of the Anglican Consultative Council, Nottingham 2005.* Edited by James Rosenthal and Susan T. Erdey. New York: Church, 2006.
With Wendy Beckett. *Living the Lord's Prayer.* Oxford: Lion 2007.

D. Edited Books

The Gemini Poets: Poems in Aid of the Christian Movement for Peace. Cambridge: Gemini, 1972.

With Kenneth Leech, editors. *Essays Catholic and Radical: A Jubilee Group Symposium for the 150th Anniversary of the Beginning of the Oxford Movement 1833-1983*. London: Bowerdean, 1983.

With Terry Tastard and Janet Morley, editors. *Poverty, Obedience, Chastity: A Reappraisal*. Croydon: Jubilee, 1987.

The Making of Orthodoxy: Essays in Honour of Henry Chadwick. Cambridge: Cambridge University Press; New York: Cambridge University Press, 1989, 2002.

Sergii Bulgakov: Towards a Russian Political Theology. Edinburgh: T. & T. Clark, 1999.

With Geoffery Rowell and Kenneth Stevenson, editors. *Love's Redeeming Work: The Anglican Quest for Holiness*. Oxford: Oxford University Press; New York: Oxford University Press, 2001.

John Henry Newman, *The Arians of the Fourth Century*. Vol. 4 of *The Works of Cardinal John Henry Newman*. Notre Dame: University of Notre Dame Press, 2001.

With Jim Cotter, Martyn Percy, Sylvia Sands and W. H. Vanstone, editors. *Darkness Yielding: Angles on Christmas, Holy Week, and Easter*. Sheffield: Cairns, 2001.

With Wesley Carr et al., editors. *The New Dictionary of Pastoral Studies*. London: SPCK, 2002.

E. Translations

Pascal, Pierre. *The Religion of the Russian People*. London: Mowbrays, 1976; Crestwood, NY: St. Vladimir's Seminary Press, 1976.

Balthasar, Hans Urs von. *The Glory of the Lord: A Theological Aesthetics*. Vol. 3 of *Studies in Theological Style: Lay Styles*, edited by John Riches. Co-translated by Andrew Louth, John Saward, and Martin Simon. Edinburgh: T. & T. Clark, 1986; San Francisco: Ignatius, 1986.

———. *The Glory of the Lord: A Theological Aesthetics*. Vol. 4 of *In the Realm of Metaphysics in Antiquity*, edited by John Riches. Co-translated by Brian McNeil, Andrew Louth, John Saward, and Oliver Davies. Edinburgh: T. & T. Clark, 1989; San Francisco: Ignatius, 1989.

———. *The Glory of the Lord: A Theological Aesthetics*. Vol. 5 of *In the Realm of Metaphysics in the Modern Age*, edited by John Riches. Co-translated by Brian McNeil, Andrew Louth, John Saward, and Oliver Davies. Edinburgh: T. & T. Clark, 1991; San Francisco: Ignatius, 1991.

F. Journal Articles

"The Theology of Personhood: A Study of the Thought of Chirstos Yannaras." *Sobornost: The Journal of the Fellowship of St Alban and St Sergius* 6.6 (1972) 415–30.

"The Spirit of the Age to Come." *Sobornost: The Journal of the Fellowship of St Alban and St Sergius* 6.9 (1974) 613–26.

"Christian Art and Cultural Pluralism: Reflections on 'L'art de l'icone,' by Paul Evdokimov." *Eastern Churches Review* 8.1 (1976) 38–44.

Bibliography of Rowan Williams

"'Person' and 'Personality' in Christology." *Downside Review* 94 (1976) 253–60.
"Poetic and Religious Imagination." *Theology* 80 (1977) 178–87.
"Philosophical Structures of Palamism." *Eastern Churches Review* 9.1–2 (1977) 27–44.
"Eric Gill." *Sobornost: The Journal of the Fellowship of St Alban and St Sergius* 7.4 (1977) 261–69.
"To Give and Not to Count the Cost: A Sermon Preached at Mirfield in February 1976." *Sobornost: The Journal of the Fellowship of St Alban and St Sergius* 7.5 (1977) 401–3.
"A Person That Nobody Knows: A Paradoxical Tribute to Thomas Merton." *Cistercian Studies* 13 (1978) 399–401.
With Eric Lionel Mascall. "George Florovsky (1893-1979): The Theologian." *Sobornost, incorporating Eastern Churches Review* 2.1 (1980) 69–72.
"The Logic of Arianism." *Journal of Theological Studies* 34 (1983) 56–81.
"The Prophetic and the Mystical: Heiler Revisited." *New Blackfriars* 64, no. 757 (1983) 330–47.
"Butler's Western Mysticism: Towards an Assessment." *Downside Review* 102 (1984) 197–215.
"'Religious Realism': On Not Quite Agreeing with Don Cupitt." *Modern Theology* 1 (1984) 3–24. Reprinted in *Wrestling with Angels*, 228–54.
"Violence and the Gospel in South Africa." *New Blackfriars* 65, no. 774 (1984) 505–13.
"The Resurrection of Jesus: A New Survey of the Material." *Irish Theological Quarterly* 51.3 (1985) 225–31.
"Trinity and Revelation." *Modern Theology* 2 (1986) 197–212. Reprinted in *On Christian Theology*, 131–47.
"Arius and the Meletian Schism." *Journal of Theological Studies* 37 (1986) 35–52.
"Politics and the Soul: A Reading of *The City of God*." *Milltown Studies* 19–20 (1987) 55–72.
"The Unity of Christian Truth." *New Blackfriars* 70, no. 824 (1989) 85–95. Reprinted in *On Christian Theology*, 16–28.
"Resurrection and Peace." *Theology* 92 (1989) 481–90. Reprinted in *On Christian Theology*, 265–75. Also reprinted in *Readings in Modern Theology*, edited by Robin Gill, 306–16. London: SPCK, 1995.
"Language, Reality and Desire in Augustine's *De doctrina*." *Journal of Literature and Theology* 3.2 (1989) 138–50.
"Ascetic Enthusiasm: Origen and the Early Church." *History Today* 39.12 (1989) 31–38.
"Der Literalsinn der Heiligen Schrift." *Evangelische Theologie* 50.1 (1990) 55–71. English translation: "The Literal Sense of Scripture." *Modern Theology* 7 (1991) 121–34. Reprinted as "The Discipline of Scripture." In *On Christian Theology*, 44–59.
"Penance in the Penitentiary." *New Life* 7 (1990) 25–34. Reprinted in *Theology* 95 (1992) 88–96.
"Critical Notice." (Review article of Peter Winch, *Simone Weil: 'The Just Balance'*. Cambridge: Cambridge University Press, 1989.) *Philosophical Investigations* 14.2 (1991) 155–71.
"R. P. C. Hanson's *Search for the Christian Doctrine of God*." *Scottish Journal of Theology* 45 (1992) 101–11.
"The Need for a Christian Critique of National Messianism." *Religion, State & Society* 20 (1992) 57–59.
"Saving Time: Thoughts on Practice, Patience and Vision." *New Blackfriars* 73, no. 861 (1992) 319–26. Reprinted as "A Theological Critique of Milbank." In *Theology and*

Sociology: A Reader, edited by Robin Gill, 2nd ed., 435–43. London: Cassell; New York: Cassell, 1996.

"'Good for Nothing'? Augustine on Creation." *Augustinian Studies* 25 (1994) 9–24.

"Heaven and Hell: A Modern Embarrassment." *Epworth Review* 21.2 (1994) 15–20.

"Between Politics and Metaphysics: Reflections in the Wake of Gillian Rose." *Modern Theology* 11 (1995) 3–22. This edition of *Modern Theology* is also published as *Rethinking Metaphysics*, edited by L. Gregory Jones and Stephen E. Fowl. Oxford: Blackwell; Cambridge, MA: Blackwell, 1995. Reprinted in *Wrestling with Angels*, 53–76.

"Theological Integrity." *New Blackfriars* 72, no. 847 (1991) 140–51. Revised version in *Cross Currents* 45 (1995) 312–25. Reprinted in *On Christian Theology*, 3–15.

"Theological Perspectives." *British Medical Bulletin* 52 (1996) 362–68.

"Interiority and Epiphany: A Reading in New Testament Ethics." *Modern Theology* 13 (1997) 29–51. Edition also printed as *Spirituality and Social Embodiment*, edited by L. Gregory Jones and James J. Buckley, 29–51. Oxford: Blackwell, 1997. Also reprinted in *On Christian Theology*, 239–64.

"Beyond Aesthetics: Theology and Hymnody." *Bulletin of the Hymn Society of Great Britain and Ireland* 15.4 (1997) 73–78.

"Incarnation and Social Vision—A New Look at an Old Theme." The Gore Lecture for 1989, *Theology Wales* (1998) 24–40. Reprinted as "Incarnation and the Renewal of Community." In *On Christian Theology*, 225–38.

"Prophecy Today." *Priests & People* (1998) 259–64.

"On Being a Human Body." *Chrism: The St Raphael Quarterly* 35 (1998). Reprinted in *Sewanee Theological Review* 42 (1999) 403–13.

"On Making Moral Decisions." *Anglican Theological Review* 81 (1999) 295–308. Also in *Sewanee Theological Review* 42 (1999) 147–58. Revised edition in *Cambridge Companion to Christian Ethics*, edited by Robin Gill, 3–15. Cambridge: Cambridge University Press, 2001.

"Being a People: Reflections on the Concept of the 'Laity.'" *Religion, State & Society* 27.1 (1999) 11–21.

"Tyndale and the Christian Society." 5th Annual Tyndale Society Lambeth Lecture, *Tyndale Society Bulletin* 12 (1999) 38–49. Reprinted in *Anglican Identities*, 9–23.

"Profile: Frances Young." *Epworth Review* 28.1 (2001) 10–20. Reprinted in *Wilderness: Essays in Honour of Frances Young*, edited by Rasiah S. Sugirtharajah, 1–7. London: Continuum, 2005.

"Reformed Characters: Rediscovering a Common Tradition." *Epworth Review* 28.2 (2001) 23–30.

"The Child and the Whiteness." *New Welsh Review* 51 (2000–2001) 4–16.

"Beyond Liberalism." *Political Theology* 3.1 (2001) 64–73.

"What Does Love Know? St Thomas on the Trinity." *New Blackfriars* 82, no. 964 (2001) 260–72.

"End of War." *The South Atlantic Quarterly* 101.2 (2002) 267–79. Reprinted in *Dissent from the Homeland: Essays after September 11th*, edited by Stanley Hauerwas and Frank Len-tricchia, 25–36. Durham: Duke University Press, 2003.

"Eugene F. Rogers's *Sexuality and the Christian Body: Their Way into the Triune God*." *Scottish Journal of Theology* 56 (2003) 82–88.

"Life in Christ: Thoughts on Being the Authentic Church." *Sewanee Theological Review* 46 (2003) 383–88. Revised version of Williams' enthronement sermon, Feb 27, 2003.

Bibliography of Rowan Williams

"Hooker the Theologian." *Journal of Anglican Studies* 1 (2003) 104–16. Reprinted as "Richard Hooker (1554–1600): Contemplative Pragmatism." In *Anglican Identities*, 24–39.
"Swansea's Other Poet: Vernon Watkins and the Threshold between Worlds." *Welsh Writing in English* 8 (2003) 107–20.
"The Structures of Unity." *New Directions* 100 (2003) 4–7.
"Augustine and the Psalms." *Interpretation* 58 (2004) 17–27.
"War and Statecraft." *First Things* 141 (2004) 14–18.
"Changing the Myths We Live By." *Sourozh* 97 (2004) 16–26.
"The Authority of the Church." *Modern Believing* 46.1 (2005) 16–28.
"Minding the Gaps: Thoughts on the Education of the Spirit." *Journal of Chaplaincy in Further Education* 1.1 (2005) 3–7.
"The Care of Souls." *Advances in Psychiatric Treatment* 11 (2005) 4–5.
"Formation: Who's Bringing Up Our Children?" *Sewanee Theological Review* 48 (2005) 379–87.
"Theological Education in the Anglican Communion." *Journal of Anglican Studies* 3 (2005) 237–39.
"Christian Identity and Religious Plurality." *Ecumenical Review* 58 (2006) 69–75; also *Christian Century* 123.6 (2006) 29–33. Speech to World Council of Churches, Porto Alegre, Brazil, February 2006.
"Eine Kirche, eine Hoffnung." *Ökumenische Rundschau* 55 (2006) 535–44.
"Insights of St Benedict's Rule for Cultures Today." *Origins* 36, vol. 29 (2007) 459–65.
"In God's Company: What Is the Church?" *Christian Century* 124.12 (2007) 23–27.

G. Book Chapters

"Bread in the Wilderness: The Monastic Ideal in Thomas Merton and Paul Evdokimov." In *One Yet Two*, edited by M. Basil Pennington, 452–73. Kalamazoo, MI: Cistercian, 1976. Reprinted in *Merton & Hesychasm: The Prayer of the Heart: The Eastern Church*, edited by Bernadette Dieker and Jonathan Montaldo, 275–96. Louisville: Fons Vitae, 2003.
"Three Styles of Monastic Reform." In *The Influence of Saint Bernard: Anglican Essays*, edited by Benedicta Ward, 23–40. Oxford: SLG, 1976.
"Barth on the Triune God." In *Karl Barth: Studies of His Theological Method*, edited by S. W. Sykes, 147–93. Oxford: Clarendon, 1979. Reprinted in *Wrestling with Angels*, 106–49.
"Mankind, Nation, State." In *This Land and This People*, edited by Paul Ballard and Huw Jones, 119–25. Cardiff: Collegiate Centre of Theology, University College, 1979.
"The Via Negativa and the Foundations of Theology: An Introduction to the Thought of V. N. Lossky." In vol. 1 of *New Studies in Theology*, edited by Stephen Sykes and Derek Holmes, 95–118. London: Duckworth, 1980. Reprinted as "Lossky, the Via Negativa and the Foundations of Theology." In *Wrestling with Angels*, 1–24.
"Wort und Geist." In *Das religiöse Bewusstsein und der Heilige Geist in der Kirche: Beiträge zur 5. theologischen Konferenz zwischen Vertretern der EKD und der Kirche von England*, edited by Klaus Kremkau, 77–96. Frankfurt: Lembeck, 1980. Reprinted as "Word and Spirit," in *On Christian Theology*, 107–27.

"Authority and the Bishop in the Church." In *Their Lord and Ours: Approaches to Authority, Community and the Unity of the Church*, edited by Mark Santer, 90–112. London: SPCK, 1982.
"What Is Catholic Orthodoxy?" In *Essays Catholic and Radical*, edited by Rowan Williams and Kenneth Leech, 11–25. London: Bowerdean, 1983.
"Liberation Theology and the Anglican Tradition." In *Politics and Theological Identity: Two Anglican Essays*, by Rowan Williams and David Nicholls, 7–26. London: Jubilee, 1984.
"Women and the Ministry: A Case for Theological Seriousness." In *Feminine in the Church*, edited by Monica Furlong, 11–27. London: SPCK, 1984.
"A Response." In *Essays on Eucharistic Sacrifice in the Early Church: A Sequel to Liturgical Study no. 31*. Grove Liturgical Study, no. 40, edited by Colin Ogilvie Buchanan, 34–37. Bramcote, Notts.: Grove, 1984.
"Origen on the Soul of Jesus." In *Origeniana Tertia: The Third International Colloquium for Origen Studies*, edited by R. P. C. Hanson and Henri Crouzel, 131–37. Rome: Ateneo, 1985.
"The Quest of the Historical Thalia." In *Arianism: Historical and Theological Reassessments*, edited by Robert C. Gregg, 1–35. Cambridge, MA: Philadelphia Patristic, 1985.
"Balthasar and Rahner." In *The Analogy of Beauty: The Theology of Hans Urs von Balthasar*, edited by John Riches, 11–34. Edinburgh: T. & T. Clark, 1986. Reprinted as "Balthasar, Rahner and the Apprehension of Being." In *Wrestling with Angels*, 86–105.
"Poverty." In *Poverty, Obedience, Chastity: A Re-appraisal*, edited by Rowan Williams, Terry Tastard and Janet Morley, 1–13. Croydon: Jubilee, 1987.
With James Atkinson. "On Doing Theology." In *Stepping Stones: Joint Essays on Anglican Catholic and Evangelical Unity*, edited by Christina Baxter, 1–20. London: Hodder & Stoughton, 1987.
With Richard Bauckham. "Jesus—God with Us." In *Stepping Stones: Joint Essays on Anglican Catholic and Evangelical Unity*, edited by Christina Baxter, 21–41. London: Hodder & Stoughton, 1987.
"The Nature of a Sacrament." In *Signs of Faith, Hope, and Love: The Christian Sacraments Today*, edited by John Greenhalgh and Elizabeth Russell, 32–44. London: St Mary's, Bourne Street, 1987. Reprinted in *On Christian Theology*, 197–208.
"The Son's Knowledge of the Father in Origen." In *Origeniana Quarta: Die Referate des 4. Internationalen Origeneskongresses (Innsbruck, 2.-6. September 1985)*, edited by Lothar Lies, 146–53. Innsbruck: Tyrolia, 1987.
"'Nobody Knows Who I Am till the Judgement Morning.'" In *Trevor Huddleston: Essays on His Life and Work*, edited by Deborah Duncan Honoré, 135–51. Oxford: Oxford University Press, 1988. Reprinted in *On Christian Theology*, 276–89.
"Barth, War & the State." In *Reckoning with Barth*, edited by Nigel Biggar, 170–90. Oxford: Mowbray, 1988. Reprinted in *Wrestling with Angels*, 150–70.
"The Suspicion of Suspicion: Wittgenstein and Bonhoeffer." In *The Grammar of the Heart*, edited by Richard H. Bell, 36–53. San Francisco: Harper & Row, 1988. Reprinted in *Wrestling with Angels*, 186–202.
"Christian Resources for the Renewal of Vision." In *Renewal of Social Vision*, edited by Alison J. Elliott and Ian Swanson, 2–7. Edinburgh: Centre for Theology and Public Issues, University of Edinburgh, 1989.

Bibliography of Rowan Williams

"Postmodern Theology and the Judgement of the World." In *Postmodern Theology: Christian Faith in a Pluralist World*, edited by F. B. Burnham, 92–112. San Francisco: Harper & Row, 1989. Reprinted as "The Judgement of the World." In *On Christian Theology*, 29–43.

"Eastern Orthodox Theology." In *Modern Theologians*, edited by David F. Ford, 152–70. Oxford: Blackwell, 1989.

"Does It Make Sense to Speak of Pre-Nicene Orthodoxy?" In *The Making of Orthodoxy: Essays in Honour of Henry Chadwick*, edited by Rowan Williams, 1–23. Cambridge: Cambridge University Press, 1989.

"The Incarnation as the Basis of Dogma." In *The Religion of the Incarnation: Anglican Essays in Commemoration of Lux Mundi*, edited by Robert Morgan, 85–98. Bristol: Bristol Classical, 1989. Reprinted as "Beginning with the Incarnation." In *On Christian Theology*, 79–92.

"Trinity and Ontology." In *Christ, Ethics and Tragedy*, edited by Kenneth Surin, 71–92. Cambridge: Cambridge University Press, 1989. Reprinted in *On Christian Theology*, 148–66.

"The Ethics of SDI." In *Nuclear Weapons Debate: Theological and Ethical Issues*, edited by Richard J. Bauckham and R. John Elford, 162–74. London: SCM, 1989.

"Newman's *Arians* and the Question of Method in Doctrinal History." In *Newman after a Hundred Years*, edited by Ian Ker and Alan G. Hill, 263–85. Oxford: Oxford University Press, 1990.

"Sapientia and the Trinity: Reflections on *De Trinitate*." In *Collectanea Augustiniana: Mélanges T.J. van Bavel*, edited by Bernard Bruning, Mathijs Lamberigts, and J. van Houtem, 317–32. Louvain: Leuven University Press, 1990.

"Trinity and Pluralism." In *Christian Uniqueness Reconsidered*, edited by Gavin D'Costa, 3–15. Maryknoll, NY: Orbis, 1990. Reprinted in *On Christian Theology*, 167–80.

"The Finality of Christ." In *Christology and Religious Pluralism*, edited by Mary Kelly, 21–38. London: The Sisters of Our Lady of Sion, 1990. Reprinted in *On Christian Theology*, 93–106.

"Imagining the Kingdom: Some Questions for Anglican Worship Today." In *The Identity of Anglican Worship*, edited by Kenneth Stevenson and Bryan Spinks, 1–13. Harrisburg, PA: Morehouse, 1991.

"The Bible." In *Early Christianity: Origins and Evolution to AD 600*, edited by Ian Hazlett, 81–91. Nashville: Abingdon, 1991.

"Hegel and the Gods of Postmodernity." In *Shadow of Spirit: Postmodernism and Religion*, edited by Philippa Berry and Andrew Wernick, 72–80. London: Routledge, 1992. Reprinted in *Wrestling with Angels*, 25–34.

"'Know Thyself': What Kind of an Injunction?" In *Philosophy, Religion and the Spiritual Life*, edited by Michael McGhee, 211–227. Cambridge: Cambridge University Press, 1992.

"Teaching the Truth." In *Living Tradition: Affirming Catholicism in the Anglican Church*, edited by Jeffrey John, 29–43. London: Darton, Longman & Todd, 1992.

"The Necessary Non-existence of God." In *Simone Weil's Philosophy of Culture: Readings toward a Divine Humanity*, edited by Richard H. Bell, 52–76. Cambridge: Cambridge University Press, 1993. Reprinted as "Simone Weil and the Necessary Non-existence of God." In *Wrestling with Angels*, 203–27.

Bibliography of Rowan Williams

"Doctrinal Criticism: Some Questions." In *The Making and Remaking of Christian Doctrine: Essays in Honour of Maurice Wiles*, edited by Sarah Coakley and David A. Pailin, 239–64. Oxford: Clarendon, 1993. Reprinted as "Maurice Wiles and Doctrinal Criticism." In *Wrestling with Angels*, 275–99.
"'Adult Geometry': Dangerous Thoughts in R. S. Thomas." In *The Page's Drift: R. S. Thomas at Eighty*, edited by M. Wynn Thomas, 82–98. Bridgend: Seren, 1993.
"Damnosa haereditas: Pamphilus' Apology and the Reputation of Origen." In *Logos: Festschrift für Luise Abramowski zum 8. Juli 1993*, edited by Hanns Christof Brennecke, Ernst Ludwig Grasmück and Christoph Markschies, 151–69. Berlin; New York: de Gruyter, 1993.
"The Nicene heritage." In *Christian Understanding of God Today*, edited by James M. Byrne, 45–48. Dublin: Columbia, 1993.
"Macrina's Deathbed Revisited: Gregory of Nyssa on Mind and Passion." In *Christian Faith and Greek Philosophy in Late Antiquity*, edited by Lionel Wickham and Caroline Hammond Bammel, 227–46. Leiden: Brill, 1993.
"The Paradoxes of Self-knowledge in *De Trinitate*." In *Augustine: Presbyter factus sum*, edited by Joseph T. Lienhard, Earl C. Muller and Roland J. Teske, 121–34. New York: Lang, 1993.
"Baptism and the Arian Controversy." In *Arianism after Arius: Essays on the Development of the Fourth-century Trinitarian Conflict*, edited by Michel Barnes and Daniel Williams, 149–80. Edinburgh: T. & T. Clark, 1993.
"Visible Unity." In *Returning Pilgrims: Insights from British and Irish Participants in the Fifth World Faith and Order Conference, Santiago de Compostela, 3–14 August*, edited by Colin Davey, 12–14. London: Council of Churches for Britain and Ireland, 1994.
With Philip Sheldrake. "Catholic Persons: Images of Holiness: A Dialogue." In *Living the Mystery: Affirming Catholicism and the Future of Anglicanism*, edited by Jeffrey John, 76–89. London: Darton, Longman & Todd, 1994.
"Ethik und Rechtfertigung." In *Rechtfertigung und Erfahrung: Für Gerhard Sauter zum 60. Geburtstag*, edited by Michael Beintker, Ernstpeter Maurer, Heinrich Stoevesandt and Hans G. Ulrich, 311–27. Gütersloh: Kaiser, 1995. Incorporated into "Interiority and Epiphany" (1997).
"Theology and the Churches." In *Michael Ramsey as Theologian*, edited by Robin Gill and Lorna Kendall, 9–28. London: Darton, Longman & Todd, 1995. Reprinted as "Michael Ramsey (1904–1988): Theology and the Churches." In *Anglican Identities*, 87–102.
"Between the Cherubim: The Empty Tomb and the Empty Throne." In *Resurrection Reconsidered*, edited by Gavin D'Costa, 87–101. Oxford: Oneworld, 1996. Reprinted in *On Christian Theology*, 183–96.
"Reply: Redeeming Sorrows." In *Religion and Morality*, edited by D. Z. Phillips, 132–48. New York: St Martin's, 1996. Reprinted as "Redeeming Sorrows: Marilyn McCord Adams and the Defeat of Evil." In *Wresting with Angels*, 255–74.
"God and Risk (2)." In *The Divine Risk*, edited by Richard Holloway, 11–23. London: Darton, Longman & Todd, 1996.
"Sacraments of the New Society." In *Christ: The Sacramental Word*, edited by David Brown and Ann Loades, 89–102. London: SPCK, 1996. Reprinted in *On Christian Theology*, 209–21.

Bibliography of Rowan Williams

"Angels Unawares: Heavenly Liturgy and Earthly Theology in Alexandria." In vol. 30 of *Studia Patristica*, edited by Elizabeth A. Livingstone, 350-63. Louvain: Peeters, 1997.

"Hooker: Philosopher, Anglican, Contemporary." In *Richard Hooker and the Construction of Christian Community*, edited by Arthur S. McGrade, 369-83. Tempe, AZ: Medieval & Renaissance Texts & Studies, 1997. Reprinted in *Anglican Identities*, 40-56.

"Forbidden Fruit: New Testament Sexual Ethics." In *Intimate Affairs: Spirituality and Sexuality in Perspective*, edited by Martyn Percy, 21-31. London: Darton, Longman & Todd, 1997.

"Gardens and Cities." In *Changing World, Unchanging Church? An Agenda for Christians in Public Life*, edited by David Clark, 48-50. London: Mowbray, 1997.

"Knowing Myself in Christ." In *The Way Forward? Christian Voices on Homosexuality and the Church*, edited by Timothy Bradshaw, 12-19. London: Hodder & Stoughton, 1997. Second edition: London: SCM, 2003; Grand Rapids: Eerdmans, 2004.

"Logic and Spirit in Hegel." In *Post-Secular Philosophy: Between Philosophy and Theology*, edited by Phillip Blond, 116-30. London: Routledge, 1998. Reprinted in *Wrestling with Angels*, 35-52.

"New Words for God: Contemplation and Religious Writing." In *Thomas Merton: Poet, Monk, Prophet*, edited by Paul M. Pearson, Danny Sullivan, Ian Thomson, 39-47. Three Peaks, Abergavenny, 1998.

"Origen: Between Orthodoxy and Heresy." In *Origeniana Septima: Origenes in den Auseinandersetzungen des 4 Jahrhunderts*, Proceedings of the Seventh International Colloquium for Origen Studies, August 25-29, 1997, edited by Walther Bienert and Uwe Kühneweg, 3-14. Louvain: Peeters, 1999. German translation: "Origenes: ein Kirchenvater zwischen Orthodoxie und Häresie." Translated by Peter Gemeinhardt. *Zeitschrift für antikes Christentum* 2 (1998) 49-64.

"Troubled Breasts: The Holy Body in Hagiography." In *Portraits of Spiritual Authority: Religious Power in Early Christianity, Byzantium, and the Christian Orient*, edited by Jan Willem Drijvers and John W. Watt, 63-78. Leiden: Brill, 1999.

"To Stand Where Christ Stands." In *Introduction to Christian Spirituality*, edited by Ralph Waller and Benedicta Ward, 1-13. London: SPCK, 1999.

"The Seal of Orthodoxy: Mary and the Heart of Christian Doctrine." In *Say Yes to God: Mary and the Revealing of the Word Made Flesh*, edited by Martin Warner, 15-29. London: Tufton, 1999.

"Insubstantial Evil." In *Augustine and His Critics: Essays in Honour of Gerald Bonner*, edited by George Lawless and Robert Dodaro, 105-23. London; New York: Routledge, 2000.

"A History of Faith in Jesus." In *The Cambridge Companion to Jesus*, edited by Markus N. A. Bockmuehl, 220-36. Cambridge; New York: Cambridge University Press, 2001.

"An Introduction," "Inhabiting the Ruins," "God's Plain Style," "Let a Child Be a Child," "The Shadow of the Crucifix," and "Buried Truth." In *Darkness Yielding: Angles on Christmas, Holy Week, and Easter*, edited by Jim Cotter, Martyn Percy, Sylvia Sands, W. H. Vanstone, and Rowan Williams. Sheffield: Cairns, 2001.

"Defining Heresy." In *The Origins of Christendom in the West*, edited by Alan Kreider, 313-35. Edinburgh; New York: T. & T. Clark, 2001.

"The Sermon." In *Living the Eucharist: Affirming Catholicism and the Liturgy*, edited by Stephen Conway, 44-55. London: Darton, Longman & Todd, 2001.

"Bonhoeffer and the Poets." In *Travelling with Resilience: Essays for Alastair Haggart*, edited by Elizabeth Templeton and Alastair Haggart, 197–217. Edinburgh: Scottish Episcopal Church, 2002.
"*Honest to God* in Great Britain." In John A. T. Robinson, *Honest to God*, 40th anniversary ed., 163–83. Louisville: Westminster John Knox, 2002. Reprinted as "John A. T. Robinson (1919-1983): 'Honest to God' and the 1960s." In *Anglican Identities*, 103–20.
"'Is It the Same God?' Reflections on Continuity and Identity in Religious Language." In *The Possibilities of Sense*, edited by John H. Whittaker, 204–18. New York; Basingstoke: Palgrave, 2002.
"Statements, Acts and Values: Spiritual and Material in the School Environment." In *Education! Education! Education!: Managerial Ethics and the Law of Unintended Consequences*, edited by Stephen Prickett and Patricia Erskine-Hill, 167–78. Thorverton, UK: Imprint Academic, 2002.
"Making It Strange: Theology in Other(s') Words." In *Sounding the Depths: Theology through the Arts*, edited by Jeremy Begbie, 19–32. London: SCM, 2002.
"The Cross in the 21st Century." In *Seven Words for the 21st Century*, edited by Edmund Newell, 1–10. London: Darton, Longman & Todd, 2002.
"The Deflections of Desire: Negative Theology in Trinitarian Disclosure." In *Silence and the Word: Negative Theology and Incarnation*, edited by Oliver Davies and Denys Turner, 115–35. Cambridge: Cambridge University Press, 2002.
"Theology in the Twentieth Century." In *A Century of Theological and Religious Studies in Britain*, edited by Ernest Nicholson, 237–52. Oxford; New York: Oxford University Press, 2003.
"Suspending the Ethical: R. S. Thomas and Kierkegaard." In *Echoes to the Amen: Essays after R. S. Thomas*, edited by Damian Walford David, 206–19. Cardiff: University of Wales Press, 2003.
"Historical Criticism and Sacred Text." In *Reading Texts, Seeking Wisdom: Scripture and Theology*, edited by David Ford and Graham Stanton, 217–28. Grand Rapids: Eerdmans, 2003.
"Origen," and "Athanasius and the Arian Crisis." In *The First Christian Theologians: An Introduction to Theology in the Early Church*, edited by G. R. Evans, 132–42, 157–67. Oxford; Malden, MA: Blackwell, 2004.
"Balthasar on the Trinity." In *The Cambridge Companion to Hans Urs von Balthasar*, edited by Edward T. Oakes and David Moss, 37–50. Cambridge: Cambridge University Press, 2004.
"Looking for Jesus and Finding Christ." In *Biblical Concepts and Our World*, edited by D. Z. Phillips and Mario Von der Ruhr, 141–52. New York: Palgrave Macmillan, 2004.
"God." In *Fields of Faith*, edited by David F. Ford, Ben Quash, and Janet M. Soskice, 75–89. Cambridge: Cambridge University Press, 2005.
"Holy Land and Holy People." In *Challenging Christian Zionism: Theology, Politics and the Israel-Palestine Conflict*, edited by Naim Stifan Ateek, Cedar Duaybis and Maurine Tobin, 293–303. London: Melisende, 2005.
"Analysing Atheism: Unbelief and the World of Faiths." In *Bearing the Word: Prophecy in Biblical and Quranic Perspective: A Record of the Third 'Building Bridges' Seminar Held at Georgetown University, Washington DC, 30 March–1 April 2004*, edited by Michael Ipgrave, 1–12. New York: Church, 2005.

Bibliography of Rowan Williams

"To What End Are We Made?" In *Who Is This Man? Christ in the Renewal of the Church*, edited by William Davage and Jonathan Baker, 1–22. London; New York: Continuum, 2006.
"The Forgiveness of Sins: Hosea 11:1-9; Matthew 18:23-35." In *Proclaiming the Scandal of the Cross: Contemporary Images of the Atonement*, edited by Mark D. Baker, 77–83. Grand Rapids: Baker Academic, 2006.
"The Health of the Spirit." In *Public Life and the Place of the Church: Reflections to Honour the Bishop of Oxford*, edited by Michael W. Brierley, 217–22. Aldershot, England; Burlington, VT: Ashgate, 2006.
"The Christian Priest Today," "Theology in the Face of Christ," "The Lutheran Catholic," and "True Glory." In *Glory Descending: Michael Ramsey and His Writings*, edited by Douglas Dales, 163–75, 176–87, 211–22 and 241–44. Grand Rapids: Eerdmans, 2006.
"Sermon for Easter Day." In *The Best Catholic Writing*. 2007, edited by Jim Manney, 173–80. Chicago: Loyola, 2007.

H. Pamphlets, Sermons, and Published Lectures

Eucharistic Sacrifice: The Roots of a Metaphor. Grove Liturgical Study 31. Bramcote, Notts: Grove, 1982.
With Mark Collier. *Peacemaking Theology: A Study Book for Individuals and Groups*, Beginning Now 1. London: Dunamis, 1984.
Star Wars: Safeguard or Threat?: A Christian Perspective. Cana Occasional Papers 1. Norton, Worcester: Clergy against Nuclear Arms, 1987.
Christianity and the Ideal of Detachment. Lingdale paper 12. The Frank Lake Memorial Lecture 1988. Oxford: Clinical Theology, 1989.
Violence, Society and the Sacred. Lecture delivered at St. Antony's College, Oxford, October 26, 1989. OPPS Paper 18. Oxford: Oxford Project for Peace Studies, 1989. Reprinted as "Girard on Violence, Society and the Sacred." In *Wrestling with Angels*, 171–85.
Prayer and Theological Integrity. Lecture at the Society for the Study of Theology. Oxford, 1989.
On Being Creatures. 4th Eric Symes Abbott Memorial Lecture. Westminster Abbey, 1989. Reprinted in *On Christian Theology*, 63–78.
Faith in the University. 5th Annual Lecture. Loughborough: Loughborough University and Colleges, Anglican Chaplaincy, 1989.
The Body's Grace. 10th Michael Harding Memorial Address. London: Lesbian and Gay Christian Movement, 1989. Reprinted in *Our Selves, Our Souls and Bodies*, edited by Charles C. Hefling, 58–68. Boston: Cowley, 1996. Also reprinted in *Theology and Sexuality*, edited by Eugene F. Rogers, 309–21. Oxford: Blackwell, 2002. Reprinted online: http://www.igreens.org.uk/bodys_grace.htm.
Inside Herbert's Afflictions. A lecture delivered at Trinity College, Cambridge, 1993. Printed as "George Herbert (1593–1633): Inside Herbert's Afflictions." In *Anglican Identities*, 57–72.
Mission and Christology. J. C. Jones Memorial Lecture 1994. Bryn Mawr: Welsh Members Council, Church Mission Society, 1994.

The Future of the Papacy—An Anglican View. Michael Richards Memorial Lecture, 1997. London: Catholics for a Changing Church, 2000.

Anglicans on the Fourth Gospel. Lecture delivered at the University of St. Andrew's, 2003. Printed as "Anglican Approaches to St John's Gospel." In *Anglican Identities*, 121–37. Reprinted in *The Gospel of John and Christian Theology*, edited by Richard Bauckham and Carl Mosser, 68–81. Grand Rapids: Eerdmans, 2007.

The Trinity. Edinburgh Studies in Constructive Theology. Edinburgh: Edinburgh University Press, 1998.

Room for the Spirit: Thoughts on Spiritual Values and Bodily Persons. National Society's RE Centre, Annual Lecture. London: National Society (Church of England) for Promoting Religious Education, 1999.

The Fate of Liberal Anglicanism. Lecture delivered at Westcott House, Cambridge, 2001. Printed as "B. F. Westcott (1825–1901): The Fate of Liberal Anglicanism." In *Anglican Identities*, 73–86.

The Global Economy Will Have to Confront Its Failures. Hugh Kay Memorial Lecture. Address to the Christian Association of Business Executives, November 15, 2001. Online: http://www.anglocatholicsocialism.org/williamsglobal.html and http://www.thewitness.org/agw/williams.122001.html.

"Presidential Address." Bevan Foundation's 2002 Annual General Meeting, *Bevan Foundation Review* 1 (2002) 40–42.

Faith and Experience in Early Monasticism: New Perspectives on the Letters of Ammonas. Erlangen: Universitätsbibliothek Erlangen-Nürnberg, 2002.

Has Secularism Failed? The Raymond Williams Lecture, Hay Festival, June 1, 2002. Online: http://www.churchinwales.org.uk/structure/bishops/sermonsr/r13.html.

Nations, Markets and Morals. The Richard Dimbleby Lecture, December 19, 2002. Online: http://www.bbc.co.uk/religion/religions/christianity/people/scripts/rwdimbleby.html.

Christian Theology and Other Faiths: A Public Lecture Given at the University of Birmingham on 11 June 2003 with Responses from Members of Other Faith Traditions. Birmingham, England: Centre for the Study of Islam & Christian-Muslim Relations, 2003.

"Christians and Muslims before the One God: An Address Given at Al-Azhar al-Sharimath, Cairo on 11 September 2004." *Islam & Christian-Muslim Relations* 16.2 (2005) 187–97. Reprinted in *Islam and Other Religions: Pathways to Dialogue, Essays in Honour of Mahmoud Mustafa Ayoub*, edited by Irfan A. Omar, 175–80. London; New York: Routledge, 2005.

Christian Imagination in Poetry and Polity: Some Anglican Voices from Temple to Herbert. Oxford: SLG, 2004. Also published as *Christian Imagination in Poetry*. Norwich: Canterbury, 2004.

Selected sermons and lectures by Rowan Williams as Archbishop of Wales (1999–2002). Online: http://www.churchinwales.org.uk/structure/bishops/sermonsr/index.html.

Selected sermons, lectures, speeches, interviews and articles by Rowan Williams as Archbishop of Canterbury (December 2002–present). Online: http://www.archbishopofcanterbury.org/.

I. Encyclopedia, Dictionary, and Lexicon Articles

"Ascension of Christ," "Christocentrism," "Freudian psychology," "Interiority," and "Religious imagery." In *Westminster Dictionary of Christian Theology*, edited by Alan

Richardson and John Bowden. Philadelphia: Westminster, 1983. Also published as *A New Dictionary of Christian Theology*. London: SCM, 1983.

"Dark Night, Darkness," "Deification," "Desert Fathers," "St Bernard of Clarivaux," "St Ignatius of Antioch," and "St Irenaeus of Lyons." In *Westminster Dictionary of Christian Spirituality*, edited by Gordon S. Wakefield. Philadelphia: Westminster, 1983. Also published as *SCM Dictionary of Christian Spirituality*. London: SCM, 2003.

"Jesus Christus II: Alte Kirche," and "Jesus Christus III: Mittelalter." In vol. 16 of *Theologische Realenzyklopädie*, edited by Gerhard Müller, 726-45, 745-59. Berlin; New York: de Gruyter, 1987.

"Alexander von Alexandrien." In vol. 1 of *Religion in Geschichte und Gegenwart*, 4th ed., edited by Hans Dieter Betz, 286-87. Tübingen: Mohr/Siebeck, 1998.

"Athanasius." In vol. 1 of *Religion in Geschichte und Gegenwart*, 4th ed., edited by Hans Dieter Betz, 870-73. Tübingen: Mohr/Siebeck, 1998.

"Christologie II. Dogmengeschichtlich 1: Alte Kirche." In vol. 2 of *Religion in Geschichte und Gegenwart*, 4th ed., edited by Hans Dieter Betz, 289-99. Tübingen: Mohr/Siebeck, 1999.

"Methodius von Olympos." In vol. 22 of *Theologische Realenzyklopädie*, edited by Gerhard Müller, 680-84. Berlin; New York: de Gruyter, 1992.

"Eastern Orthodox Theology." In *Blackwell Encyclopedia of Modern Christian Thought*, edited by Alister E. McGrath, 120-27. Cambridge, MA: Blackwell, 1993.

"Agennesia," and "Arius, Arianismus." In vol. 1 of *Lexikon für Theologie und Kirche*, 3rd ed., edited by Michael Buchberger and Walter Kasper, 230, 982-90. Freiburg: Herder, 1993.

"Origenes, Origenismus." In vol. 25 of *Theologische Realenzyklopädie*, edited by Gerhard Müller, 397-421. Berlin; New York: de Gruyter, 1995.

"Religious Experience in the Era of Reform." In *Companion Encyclopedia of Theology*, edited by J. L. Houlden and Peter Byrne, 576-93. London; New York: Routledge, 1995.

"Church and State." In *Dictionary of Ethics, Theology and Society*, edited by Paul Barry Clarke and Andrew Linzey, 137-40. London: Routledge, 1996.

"Jungfrauengeburt" and "Soteriologie." In *Evangelisches Kirkenlexicon: Viertier Band: S-Z*. Göttingen: Vandenhoeck & Ruprecht, 1996.

"Arianism." In *The Encyclopedia of Early Christianity*, 2nd ed., edited by Everett Fergusson, Michael McHugh, and Frederick Norris. New York; London: Garland, 1998.

"Simone Weil." In *Routledge Encyclopedia of Philosophy*, edited by Edward Craig. London: Routledge, 1998.

"Creation," and "Trinitate, de." In *Augustine through the Ages: An Encyclopedia*, edited by Allan D. Fitzgerald. Grand Rapids: Eerdmans, 1999.

"Catholicity," "Resurrection," and "Russian Christian Thought." In *The Oxford Companion to Christian Thought*, edited by Adrian Hastings, Alistair Mason, and Hugh S. Pyper. Oxford; New York: Oxford University Press, 2000.

"Incarnation 2," and "Inspiration." In vol. 2 of *The Encyclopedia of Christianity*, edited by Erwin Fahlbusch and Geoffrey W. Bromiley. Grand Rapids: Eerdmans, 2001; Leiden: Brill, 2001.

"European Theology," and "Jesus Christ." In *Dictionary of the Ecumenical Movement*, 2nd ed., edited by Nicholas Lossky, et al. Geneva: WCC, 2002.

"Mysticism," "Resurrection," and "Trinity." In *The New Dictionary of Pastoral Studies*, edited by Wesley Carr, et al. London: SPCK, 2002.
"Justification." In vol. 2 of *Encyclopedia of Christian Theology*, edited by Jean-Yves Lacoste, 843–49. New York: Routledge, 2005.
"Sin." In vol. 3 of *Encyclopedia of Christian Theology*, edited by Jean-Yves Lacoste, 1476–79. New York: Routledge, 2005.

J. Book Reviews

L'Esprit Saint dans la tradition Orthodoxe, by Paul Evdokimov (Paris: Editions du Cerf, 1969). *Sobornost: The Journal of the Fellowship of St Alban and St Sergius* 6 (1972) 284–85.

La connaissance de Dieu selon la tradition orientale, by Paul Evdokimov (Lyon: Xavier Mappus, 1967). *Sobornost: The Journal of the Fellowship of St Alban and St Sergius* 6 (1972) 359–61.

Orthodoxy, Roman Catholicism, and Anglicanism, by Methodios Fouyas (Oxford: OUP, 1972). *Downside Review* 91 (1973) 75–76.

Le Monde et L'église Selon Maxime le Confesseur, by Alain Riou (Paris: Beauchesne, 1973). *Eastern Churches Review* 8 (1976) 92–93.

"Christian Art and Cultural Pluralism: Reflections on 'L'art de l'icone,' by Paul Evdokimov." *Eastern Churches Review* 8 (1976) 38–44.

Engagement with God, by Hans Urs von Balthasar (London: SPCK, 1975). *Downside Review* 94 (1976) 153–54.

Historical Transcendence and the Reality of God, by Ray S. Anderson (London: Chapman; Grand Rapids: Eerdmans, 1975). *Downside Review* 94 (1976) 236–39.

The Wisdom of the Desert Fathers, by Benedicta Ward (SLG, 1975) and *The Sayings of the Desert Fathers*, by Benedicta Ward (London: Mowbrays, 1975). *Sobornost: The Journal of the Fellowship of St Alban and St Sergius* 7 (1976) 219–20.

"'Person' and 'Personality' in Christology." Review of *Grace and Truth: A Study in the Doctrine of the Incarnation*, by Anthony Tyrrell Hanson (London: SPCK, 1975). *Downside Review* 94 (1976) 253–60.

Living Tradition: Orthodox Witness in the Contemporary World, by John Meyendorff (Crestwood, NY: St Vladimir's Seminary Press, 1978). *Sobornost* 1 (1979) 87–88.

"D. Z. Phillips and James Richmond (Letter to the Editors)." *Theology* 83 (1980) 205-7.

Arius judaizans? Untersuchungen zur dogmengeschichtlichen Einordnung des Arius, by Rudolf Lorenz (Gottingen: Vandenhoeck & Ruprecht, 1980). *Journal of Theological Studies* 34 (1983) 293–96.

Taking Leave of God, by Don Cupitt (London: SCM, 1980); and *The World to Come: From Christian Past to Global Future*, by Lloyd Geering (Wellington: Bridget Williams, 1999). *Modern Theology* 1 (1984) 3–24.

Spirit, Saints and Immortality, by Patrick Sherry (New York: Macmillian, Albany: SUNY, 1984). *Theology* 88 (1985) 151–53.

Augustine on Evil, by Gillian R. Evans (Cambridge: Cambridge University Press, 1983). *Religious Studies* 21 (1985) 95–97.

Gnosis: The Nature and History of Gnosticism, by Kurt Rudolph (San Francisco: Harper & Row, 1983; Edinburgh: T & T Clark, 1983). *Journal of Theological Studies* 37 (1986) 202–6.

Bibliography of Rowan Williams

A Path from Rome: An Autobiography, by Anthony Kenny (London: Sidgwick & Jackson, 1985). *Theology* 89 (1986) 237-38.
Ways of Imperfection: An Exploration of Christian Spirituality, by Simon Tugwell (London: Darton, Longman & Todd, 1984). *New Blackfriars* 67, no. 799 (1986) 501-2.
Quaestiones et Dubia, by Maximus the Confessor (Turnhout, Belgium: Brepols, 1982). *Journal of Theological Studies* 38 (1987) 225-27.
The Formation of Christendom, by Judith Herrin (Oxford: Blackwell, 1987). *New Left Review* 170 (1987) 118-23.
Theology after Wittgenstein, by Fergus Kerr (New York: Blackwell, 1986). *Philosophical Investigations* 10 (1987) 344-46.
R. S. Thomas: Poet of the Hidden God, by D. Z. Phillips (London: Macmillan, 1986). *Journal of Theological Studies* 39 (1988) 653-55.
God's Decree and Man's Destiny: Studies on the Thought of Augustine of Hippo, by Gerald Bonner (London: Variorum Reprints, 1987). *Journal of Theological Studies* 39 (1988) 669.
Substance and Illusion in the Christian Fathers, by Christopher Stead (London: Variorum Reprints, 1985). *Journal of Ecclesiastical History* 39 (1988) 627-28.
The Body and Society: Men, Women and Sexual Renunciation in Early Christianity, by Peter Brown (London: Faber & Faber, 1989; New York: Columbia University Press, 1988); and *Adam, Eve, and the Serpent*, by Elaine Pagels (New York: Random House, 1990; New York: Columbia University Press, 1988). *Theology* 92 (1989) 338-41.
Being as Communion: Studies in Personhood and the Church, by John D. Zizioulas (London: Darton, Longman & Todd, 1985). *Scottish Journal of Theology* 42 (1989) 101-5.
Eunomius: The Extant Works, edited and translated by R. P. Vaggione (Oxford: Clarendon, 1987). *The Journal of Roman Studies* 79 (1989) 257-58.
Person-Exegese und Christologie bei Augustinus: Zur Herkunft der Formel Una Persona, by Hubertus R. Drobner (Leiden: Brill, 1986). *Journal of Theological Studies* 41 (1990) 264-66.
Origenes der Diamantene, by Robert Sträuli (Zurich: ABZ, 1987). *Journal of Theological Studies* 42 (1991) 336-37.
Les capitules du diurnal de Saint-Denis (Cod. Verona cap. LXXXVIII, Saec. IX), by Gilles Gérard Meersseman (Fribourg, Switzerland: Éditions Universitaires, 1987). *Journal of Theological Studies* 42 (1991) 370-72.
The Incarnation of God: An Introduction to Hegel's Theological Thought as Prolegomena to a Future Christology, by Hans Küng (New York: Crossroad, 1988). *Journal of Theological Studies* 42 (1991) 403-6.
Saints and Postmodernism: Revisioning Moral Philosophy, by Edith Wyschogrod (Chicago: University of Chicago Press, 1990). *Modern Theology* 8 (1992) 305-7.
St Peter of Alexandria: Bishop and Martyr, by Tim Vivian (Philadelphia: Fortress, 1988). *Journal of Theological Studies* 44 (1993) 352-55.
Theology in the Russian Diaspora: Church, Fathers, Eucharist in Nikolai Afanas'ev, 1893-1966, by Aidan Nichols (Cambridge: Cambridge University Press, 1989). *Journal of Theological Studies* 44 (1993) 443-46.
Structuralist Interpretations of Biblical Myth, by Edmund Leach and D. Alan Aycock (Cambridge: Cambridge University Press, 1983). *RAIN* 61 (1994) 11-12.

Liberating Sex: A Christian Sexual Theology, by Adrian Thatcher (London: SPCK, 1993). *Theology* 98 (1995) 70-72.

Scribe of the Kingdom: Essays on Theology and Culture, 2 vols., by Aidan Nichols (London: Sheed & Ward, 1994). *New Blackfriars* 76 (1995) 203-5.

Just Good Friends: Towards a Lesbian and Gay Theology of Relationships, by Elizabeth Stuart (London: Mowbray, 1995). *Theology and Sexuality* 2 (1996) 123-26.

A Big-Enough God: Artful Theology, by Sara Maitland (London: Mowbray, 1994). *Theology* 99 (1996) 59-60.

"Acting on God's Behalf." Review of *Jesus and the Victory of God*, by N. T. Wright (London: SPCK, 1996). *Church Times* (1997) 14.

"God is One and All Alone." Review of *Archetypal Heresy: Arianism through the Centuries*, by Maurice Wiles (Oxford: Clarendon, 1997). *The Times Literary Supplement* 4925 (1997) 31.

Power, Gender and Christian Mysticism, by Grace M. Jantzen (Cambridge: Cambridge University, 1995). *Theology* 100 (1997) 132-33.

Athanasius and the Politics of Asceticism, by David Brakke (Oxford: Clarendon, 1995). *Theology* 100 (1997) 140-41.

Teresa of Avila and the Politics of Sanctity, by Gillian T. W. Ahlgren (Ithaca: Cornell, 1996). *Journal of Ecclesiastical History* 48 (1997) 780-81.

Does Christianity Cause War? by David Martin (Oxford: Clarendon, 1997). *Journal of Contemporary Religion* 14 (1999) 148-50.

Das vierte Jahrhundert (Der Osten), by Rudolf Lorenz (Göttingen: Vandenhoeck & Ruprevht, 1992). *Journal of Theological Studies* 52 (2001) 364-65.

Eastern Orthodox Christianity: A Western Perspective, by Daniel B. Clendenin (Grand Rapids: Baker, 1994); *Eastern Orthodox Theology: A Contemporary Reader*, edited by Daniel B. Clendenin (Grand Rapids: Baker, 1995); and *Russian Religious Thought*, edited by Judith Deutsch Kornblatt and Richard F. Gustafson (Madison: University of Wisconsin Press, 1996). *Religion, State & Society* 29 (2001) 247-48.

Tradition and Imagination: Revelation and Change, by David Brown (Oxford; New York: Oxford University Press, 1999). *Theology* 104, no. 822 (2001) 452-53.

"A Displaced Male Orgasm." Review of *The Ordination of Women in the Catholic Church: Unmasking a Cuckoo's Egg Tradition*, by John Wingaards (London: Darton, Longman & Todd, 2001). *The Times Literary Supplement* 5154 (2002) 28-30.

"Against the Market?" Review of *Religion, Theology and the Human Sciences*, by Richard H. Roberts (Cambridge: Cambridge University Press, 2002). *The Times Literary Supplement* 5165 (2002) 3.

"Eugene F. Rogers's *Sexuality and the Christian Body: Their Way into the Triune God.*" *Scottish Journal of Theology* 56 (2003) 82-88.

Citizenship, Community, and the Church of England: Liberal Anglican Theories of the State between the Wars, by Matthew Grimley (Oxford: Clarendon, 2004). *English Historical Review* 120, no. 487 (2005) 801-3.

K. Introductions, Prefaces, Forewords, Afterwords, and Epilogues

Introduction to *Essays Catholic and Radical: A Jubilee Group Symposium for the 150th Anniversary of the Beginning of the Oxford Movement 1833-1983*, edited by Kenneth Leech and Rowan Williams. London: Bowerdean, 1983.

Bibliography of Rowan Williams

"Introductory memoir." In *A Pattern of Faith: An Exposition of Christian Doctrine*, by Geoffrey Paul Worthing: Churchman, 1986.
Foreword to *God Within: The Mystical Tradition of Northern Europe*, by Oliver Davies. New York: Paulist, 1988; London: Darton, Longman & Todd, 1988.
Introduction to *Speaking Love's Name: Some Catholic and Socialist Reflections*, by Ashley Beck and Ros Hunt. London: Jubilee Group, 1988. Reprinted online: http://www.anglocatholicsocialism.org/lovesname.html.
Preface to *The Making of Orthodoxy: Essays in Honour of Henry Chadwick*, edited by Rowan Williams, vii–xii. Cambridge: Cambridge University Press, 1989.
Foreword to *The Mysteries of March: Hans Urs von Balthasar on the Incarnation and Easter*, by John Saward. London: HarperCollins, 1990; Washington, DC: Catholic University of America Press, 1990.
Foreword to *The Transfiguration of Jesus*, by Rob Marshall. London: Darton, Longman & Todd, 1994.
Foreword to *Beloved and Chosen: Women of Faith*, by Jill Evans. Norwich: Canterbury, 1994.
Foreword to *The Mystery of the Eucharist in the Anglican Tradition*, by Henry McAdoo and Kenneth Stevenson. Norwich: Canterbury, 1995.
Foreword to *Knowing Jesus*, by James Alison. New ed. London: SPCK, 1998.
Foreword to *Discovering Holiness: The Search for the Sacred Today*, by Melvyn Matthews. London: SPCK, 1996.
Foreword to *God and Reality: Essays on Christian Non-Realism*, edited by Colin Crowder. London: Mowbray, 1997.
Foreword to *The English Mystics: An Anthology*, by Tarjei Park. London: SPCK, 1998.
Foreword to *"The Other Way"? Anglican Lesbian and Gay Journeys*, edited by Colin Coward. London: Changing Attitude, 1998.
"Afterword: making differences." In *Balthasar at the End of Modernity*, edited by Lucy Gardner, David Moss, Ben Quash, and Graham Ward, 173–79. Edinburgh: T. & T. Clark, 1999. Reprinted as "Balthasar and Difference" in *Wrestling with Angels*, 77–85.
Foreword to *Be Born in Us Today*, by John Davies. Canterbury: Norwich, 1999.
Foreword to *Strange Design: Exploring the Ways of God in the World*, by Philip Crowe. Canterbury: Norwich, 1999.
Introduction (and commentary) to *Sergii Bulgakov: Towards a Russian Political Theology*, edited by Rowan Williams. Edinburgh: T. & T. Clark, 1999.
Preface to *Healing at the Well*, by Mike Endicott. Bradford on Avon: Terra Nova, 2000.
Foreword to *Private Passions: Betraying Discipleship on the Journey to Jerusalem*, by Douglas Davies. Norwich: Canterbury, 2000.
Foreword to *Seeking the Truth in Love: The Church and Homosexuality*, by Michael Doe. London: Darton, Longman & Todd, 2000.
Foreword to *Forgive and Live*, by Una Kroll. London: Mowbray, 2000.
Introduction and Editor's Notes to *The Arians of the Fourth Century*, by John Henry Newman. Vol. 4 of *The Works of Cardinal John Henry Newman*, xiv–xlvii, 475–505. Notre Dame: University of Notre Dame Press, 2001.
With Geoffery Rowell and Kenneth Stevenson. "General Introduction: The Anglican Quest for Holiness"; and "Part 1: Introduction." In *Love's Redeeming Work: The Anglican Quest for Holiness*, edited by Geoffery Rowell, Kenneth Stevenson and Rowan Williams. Oxford; New York: Oxford University Press, 2001.

Foreword to *Anatomy of Survival: Steps on a Personal Journey Towards Healing*, by Una Kroll. London: Mowbray, 2001.
Foreword to *Literary Companion to the Lectionary: Readings Throughout the Year*, edited by Mark Pryce. London: SPCK, 2001.
Introduction to *That Mysterious Man: Essays on Augustine Baker OSB 1575–1641*, edited by Michael Woodward. Abergavenny: Three Peaks, 2001.
Foreword to *The Meaning in the Miracles*, by Jeffrey John. Norwich: Canterbury, 2001.
Foreword to *Beyond All Reasonable Doubt*, by Michael J. Meredith. New Alresfod: O, 2002.
Epilogue to *Voices of This Calling: Experiences of the First Generation of Women Priests*, edited by Christina Rees. Norwich: Canterbury, 2002.
Foreword to *Poet, Priest and Prophet: The Life and Thought of Bishop John V. Taylor*, by David Wood. London: Churches Together in Britain and Ireland, 2002.
Foreword to *Choice, Desire and the Will of God: What More Do You Want?* by John Runcorn. Peabody, MA: Hendrickson, 2003.
Foreword to *Anglicans and Orthodox: Unity and Subversion 1559–1725*, by Judith Pinnington. Leominster: Gracewing, 2003.
Foreword to *One Equall Light: An Anthology of the Writings of John Donne*, edited by John Moses. Norwich: Canterbury, 2003; Grand Rapids: Eerdmans, 2003.
Preface to *Anglicanism: The Answer to Modernity*, edited by Duncan J. Dormor, Jack McDonald and Jeremy Caddick. London; New York: Continuum, 2003.
Foreword to *The Anglican Religious Communities' Year Book*. Rev. ed., edited by Peta Dunstan and Brother Tristam. Norwich: Canterbury, 2003.
Foreword to *God, Christ and Us*, by Herbert McCabe. Edited by Brian Davies. London; New York: Continuum, 2003.
Foreword to *God's Pattern: Shaping our Worship, Ministry and Life*, by David Stancliffe. London: SPCK, 2003.
Foreword to *The Life of Antony*, by Tim Vivian, et al. Kalamazoo, MI: Cistercian, 2003.
With Walter Kasper. Foreword to *Anglicanism and the Western Christian Tradition: Continuity, Change and the Search for Communion*, edited by Stephen Platten. Norwich: Canterbury, 2003.
Foreword to *The Hare That Hides Within: Poems about St. Melangill*, by Anne Cluysenaar and Norman Schwenk. Cardigan: Parthian, 2004.
Afterword to *Blackwell Companion to Christian Ethics*, edited by Samuel Wells and Stanley Hauerwas, 495–98. Oxford; Malden, MA: Blackwell, 2004.
Introduction to *A.C.T.S. 1*, by Marcia Gibson-Watt and Penelope Bourdillon. Tregynon: Bluestone, 2004.
Foreword to *The Gestures of God: Explorations in Sacramentality*, edited by Geoffrey Rowell and Christine Hall. London; New York: Continuum, 2004.
Foreword to *Mission-Shaped Church: Church Planting and Fresh Expressions of Church in a Changing Context*. London: Church House, 2004.
Foreword to *Beginning to Preach: A Practical Guide to Preaching Well*, by Robert Beaken. London: Tufton, 2004.
Foreword to *Transforming the Ordinary: Bible Meditations for Every Day*, by John Henstridge. Oxford: Bible Reading Fellowship, 2004.
Foreword to *The Wilberforce Connection*, by Clifford S. Hill. Oxford: Monarch, 2004.
Afterword to *Trevor Huddleston: Turbulent Priest*, by Piers McGrandle, 210–14. London: Continuum, 2004.

Foreword to *Work and Prayer*, by Chris Keating. Harrisburg, PA: Morehouse, 2005.
Foreword to *Sharing God's Planet: A Christian Vision for a Sustainable Future*, by Claire Foster. London: Church House, 2005.
"Introducing the Debate: Theology and the Political." In *Theology and the Political: The New Debate*, edited by Creston Davis, Slavoj Zizek, and John Milbank, 1–3. London; Durham, NC: Duke University Press, 2005.
Foreword to *Head versus Heart and Our Gut Reactions: The 21st Century Enneagram: Mapping the Different Ways We Engage with the World*, by Michael Hampson. Wincester; New York: O, 2005.
Foreword to *Free of Charge: Giving and Forgiving in a Culture Stripped of Grace*, by Miroslav Volf. Grand Rapids: Zondervan, 2005.
Foreword to *Mister God, This Is Anna*, by Fynn and Papas. London: Fount, 2005.
Foreword to *The Gnostics: Identifying an Early Christian Cult*, by Alastair H. B. Logan. London: T. & T. Clark, 2006.
Foreword to *The Theology of William Tyndale*, by Ralph S. Werrell. Cambridge: James Clarke, 2006.
Foreword to *Power and Passion: Seven Characters in Search of Resurrection*, by Samuel Wells. Grand Rapids: Zondervan, 2006.
Foreword to *Mole under the Fence: Conversations with Roland Walls*, by Ron Ferguson and Mark Chater. Edinburgh: Saint Andrew, 2006.
Foreword to *Communion and Otherness: Further Studies in Personhood and the Church*, by John D. Zizioulas. Edited by Paul McPartlin. Edinburgh: T. & T. Clark, 2006.
Foreword to *Freddy Temple: A Portrait*, by Christopher Dobb. Kingsbury Hall, Calne, Wiltshire: Rooftop UK, 2006.
Foreword to *Strangely Orthodox: R. S. Thomas and His Poetry of Faith*, by Barry Morgan. Llandysul, Ceredigion: Gomer, 2006.
With Cormac Murphy-O'Connor. Foreword to *"Doing God": A Future for Faith in the Public Square*, by Nick Spencer. London: Theos, 2006.
Introduction to *Thou Who Art: The Concept of the Personality of God*, by John A. T. Robinson. New York; London: Continuum, 2006.
Foreword to *The Church of the Holy Spirit*, by Nicholas Afanasiev. Translated by Michael Plekon. Notre Dame: University of Notre Dame Press, 2007.
Foreword to *A Companion to Richard Hooker*, edited by W. J. Torrance Kirby. Leiden; Boston: Brill, 2008.

L. Interviews and Public Debates

"Time and Transformation: A Conversation with Rowan Williams." Interview with Todd Breyfogle. *Cross Currents* 45 (1995) 293–311.
"Quarrying for God." Interview with Roland Ashby. *Anglican Media, The Melbourne Anglican*, Australia (March 1999).
Interview with Gerry McCarthy. *The Social Edge* (March 2002). Online: http://www.thesocialedge.com/archives/gerrymccarthy/1articles-mar2002.htm.
"Living the Questions: The Converging Worlds of Rowan Williams." Interview with David S. Cunningham. *Christian Century* 119.9 (2002) 18–29. Online: http://www.encyclopedia.com/doc/1G1-86046828.html.
Interview with Paul Handley. *Church Times* (November 29, December 6, 2002).

"The Conversation." Interview with Philip Pullman. In *Darkness Illuminated: Platform Discussions on "His dark Materials" at the National Theatre*, edited by Robert Butler. London: National Theatre/Oberon, 2004.
Claire Foster and Edmund Newell, editors. *The Worlds We Live In: Dialogues with Rowan Williams on Global Economics and Politics*. London: Darton Longman & Todd, 2005.
"Belief and Theology: Some Core Questions." Interview with Rupert Shortt. In *God's Advocates: Christian Thinkers in Conversation*, by Rupert Shortt, 1–23. London: Darton, Longman & Todd, 2005.
"Schatten der Vergangenheit überwinden: Interview mit Rowan Williams, dem Erzbischof von Canterbury." *Konfessionskundliches Institut <Bensheim>: Materialdienst des Konfessions-kundlichen Instituts Bensheim* 57.2 (2006) 33–34.

M. Op-ed Pieces, Political Writings, etc.

"War in the Gulf: Can It Be 'Just'?" *Christianity and Crisis: A Christian Journal of Opinion* 50.17 (1990) 391–92. Originally published in *Manchester Guardian Weekly* 143.19 (1990).
"Whatever Happened to All the Hope?" *Church Times* (May 1, 1998) 12.
"No Life, Here—No Joy, Terror or Tears." Response to Bishop Spong's Statement. *Church Times* (July 17, 1998).
"Is Blair Still a Christian Socialist?" *New Statesman* 127, no. 4404 (1998) 36–37.
"Banking without Barclays." *The Guardian* (April 6, 2000). Online: http://www.guardian.co.uk/comment/story/0,3604,178125,00.html.
"Our Differences Need Not Destroy Us." *The Tablet* 254, no. 8328 (2000) 476. Online: http://copies.anglicansonline.org/tablet/tablet000408a.html.
"Wanted: Imaginative, Attentive, Ideological, Inspirational Mediators." *Church Times* (October 6, 2000).
"Telling that Christmas Story Like It Is." *The Guardian*, December 23, 2000. Online: http://education.guardian.co.uk/xmas2000/story/0,,416133,00.html.
"For God's Sake, Stop This Talk of War." *The Guardian*, January 21, 2002. Online: http://www.guardian.co.uk/print/0,,4339426-103677,00.html.
"War as We Know It: False Dramas, True Heroes." *Christian Century* 119.4 (2002) 7–8.
"Neighbours from Hell: Does It Have to Be Like This?" *Church Times*, April 12, 2002. Online: http://www.simonbarrow.net/terror12.
"Do Not Cling to Me." *Sojourners Magazine*, July–August 2003. Online: http://www.sojo.net/index.cfm?action=magazine.article&issue=soj0307&article=03072.

Secondary Literature

A. Monographs

Bates, Stephen. *A Church at War: Anglicans and Homosexuality*. London; New York: Tuarius, 2004.
Creegan, Nicola Hoggard, and Rowan Williams. *God's Earth: Our Home*. Wellington: Social Justice Commission of the Anglican Church in Aotearoa, New Zealand and Polynesia, 2006.

Bibliography of Rowan Williams

Cunningham, David S. *Rowan Williams the 104th Archbishop of Canterbury*. Cinncinnati: Forward Movement, 2002.

Higton, Mike. *Difficult Gospel: The Theology of Rowan Williams*. London: SCM, 2004; New York: Church, 2004.

Hobson, Theo. *Anarchy, Church and Utopia: Rowan Williams on Church*. London: Darton, Longman & Todd, 2005.

Kinzig, Wolfram, editor. *Gratiarum actio: Reden anlässlich der Ehrenpromotion des Erzbischofs von Canterbury, The Most Revd Dr Rowan Douglas Williams, durch die Evangelisch-Theologische Fakultät der Rheinischen Friedrich-Wilhelms-Universität Bonn am 11. März 2004 [Gratiarum actio: Speeches on the Occasion of the Award of an Honorary Doctorate in Theology to the Archbishop of Canterbury, The Most Reverend Dr Rowan Douglas Williams on the 11th of March 2004 by the Evangelical Theological Faculty of the Rheinische Friedrich-Wilhelms-Universität Bonn]*. Rheinbach: CMZ, 2004.

McCurry, Jeffrey. "Traditioned Creativity: Rowan Williams and the Grammars of Theological Practice." Ph.D. dissertation, Duke University, 2006.

McProud, Bryce. *Common Experience and the Accommodation of Differences: The Foundation for Unity in Rowan Williams' View of the Church*. Eugene, OR: Wipf & Stock, 2005.

Shortt, Rupert. *Rowan Williams: An Introduction*. Harrisburg, PA: Morehouse, 2003; London: Darton, Longman & Todd, 2003.

———. *Rowan's Rule: The Biography of the Archbishop*. London: Hodder & Stoughton, forthcoming 2008.

Vibert, Simon. *By Word and Spirit: Two Archbishops on the Doctrine of Revelation*. [Great Britain]: Fellowship of Word and Spirit, 2003.

Volpe, Medi Ann. "'Make Love Your Aim': Sin and the Goal of Charity in Christian Formation." Ph.D. dissertation, Duke University, 2006.

Williams, Cynwil. *Rowan Williams: Yr Archesgob*. Gwasg Pantycelyn, 2006.

Williams, Garry J. *The Theology of Rowan Williams: An Outline, Critique and Consideration of Its Consequences*. London: Latimer, 2002. Online: http://www.latimertrust.org/theology-rowanwilliams.htm.

B. Journal Articles and Book Chapters

Barton, Stephen C. "New Testament Interpretation as Performance." *Scottish Journal of Theology* 52 (1999) 179–208.

Bray, Gerald L. "A Wake-up Call to Evangelicals." *Churchman* 116 (2002) 195–99.

———. "Sex, Pleasure and the Archbishop." *Churchman* 116 (2002) 291–94.

Chapman, Mark D. "Profile: Rowan Williams." *Epworth Review* 30.2 (2003) 9–16.

Cupitt, Don. "A Reply to Rowan Williams." *Modern Theology* 1 (1984) 25–31.

Davis, Steven T. "Looking for Jesus and Still Finding Christ." In *Biblical Concepts and Our World*, edited by D. Z. Phillips and Mario Von der Ruhr, 153–62. New York: Palgrave Macmillan, 2004.

Ford, David F. "Theological Wisdom, British Style." *Christian Century* 117.11 (2000) 388–91. Online: http://www.religion-online.org/showarticle.asp?title=1976.

Gilbertson, Michael. "Controversy over the Appointment of Rowan Williams as Archbishop of Canterbury." *Anvil* 20.1 (2003) 1–6.

Goddard, Andrew. "English Evangelicals and the Archbishop's Theology." Online: http://www.fulcrum-anglican.org.uk/docs/rdwfulcrum.pdf.
Hankey, Wayne John. "Re-Christianizing Augustine Postmodern Style: Readings by Jacques Derrida, Robert Dodaro, Jean-Luc Marion, Rowan Williams, Lewis Ayres and John Milbank." *Animus: A Philosophical Journal for Our Time* 2 (1997). Online: http://www.swgc.mun.ca/animus/1997vol2/hankey1.htm or http://www.swgc.mun.ca/animus/1997vol2/hankey1.pdf.
Hauerwas, Stanley. "Ordinary Time: A Tribute to Rowan Williams." Virginia Theological Seminary commencement address, May 18, 2006. Online: http://www.vts.edu/ftpimages/95/misc/misc_31289.pdf.
Hilborn, David. "Homosexuality, Covenant and Grace in the Writings of Rowan Williams: An Evangelical Response." *Anvil* 20.4 (2003) 263–75.
Hobson, Theo. "Rowan Williams as Anglican Hegelian." *Religion & Theology* 12 (2005) 290–97.
Huebner, Chris K. "Radical Ecumenism, or Receiving One Another in Kuala Lampur." *Ecumenical Review* 57 (2005) 372–81.
Kershaw, Roger. "Islamic Terrorism and English Archbishops." *Contemporary Review* 285, no. 1662 (2004) 40–48.
Lee, Simon. "Ethics in the Dust?" *Conversations in Religion and Theology* 1.2 (2003) 210–22.
Marsh, Charles. "In Defense of a Self: The Theological Search for a Postmodern Identity." *Scottish Journal of Theology* 55 (2002) 253–82.
McCurry, Jeffrey. "Towards a Poetics of Theological Creativity: Rowan Williams Reads Augustine's *De Doctrina* after Derrida." *Modern Theology* 23 (2007) 415–33.
McGrath, Alister E. "The Writings of Rowan Williams Uncovered." August 2002.
  Part 1 online: http://listserv.episcopalian.org/wa.exe?A2=ind0208c&L=virtuosity&D=1&H=1&O=D&F=&S=&P=2410.
  Part 2 online: http://listserv.episcopalian.org/wa.exe?A2=ind0208b&L=virtuosity&D=1&H=1&O=D&F=&S=&P=2499.
Monti, Joseph. "Orthodoxy and 'The Wound of Knowledge': A Rowan Williams Sampler." *Sewanee Theological Review* 46 (2003) 269–92.
O'Donovan, Oliver. "Archbishop Rowan Williams." *Pro Ecclesia* 12.1 (2003) 5–9.
Rogers, Eugene F. "Nature with Water and the Spirit: A Response to Rowan Williams." *Scottish Journal of Theology* 56 (2003) 89–100.
Seitz, Christopher R. "Canterbury and Unity." *Pro Ecclesia* 12.1 (2003) 11–14.
Stead, Christopher. "Was Arius a Neoplatonist?" In vol. 32 of *Studia Patristica*, edited by Elizabeth A. Livingstone, 256–336. Louvain: Peeters, 1997.
Southern, Humphery. "The Impossibility of the Last Word: The Theology of Rowan Williams." *Anglicans Together* (2003). Online: http://www.anglicanstogether.org/files/LastWord.pdf
Turner, Philip. "The Archbishop and His Times: A Comment on Rowan Williams and His Circumstances." *Pro Ecclesia* 12.1 (2003) 9–11
Vaggione, Richard Paul. "'Arius, Heresy and Tradition' by Rowan Williams." *Toronto Journal of Theology* 5 (1989) 63–87.
Wainwright, Geoffrey. "Rowan Williams on Christian Doctrine." *Scottish Journal of Theology* 56 (2003) 73–81.
Weigel, George. "War and Statecraft." *First Things* 141 (2004) 18–21.

Bibliography of Rowan Williams

Wiles, Maurice. "Faith and Historical Judgement in British Arian Scholarship." In *Archetypal Heresy: Arianism through the Centuries*, 165-81. Oxford: Clarendon, 1996.

Wyatt, Michael. "Extra Leaves for the Family Table: Resources for Interreligious Conversation." *Anglican Theological Review* 88 (2006) 301-21.

C. Book Reviews

Reviews of *The Wound of Knowledge* (1980; rev. ed. 1990)

Cardman, F. *New Catholic World* 225 (1982) 45.
Cunningham, Lawrence S. *Commonweal* 119.19 (1992) 42.
Davies, Brian. *New Blackfriars* 61, no. 718 (1980) 141-44.
Faricy, R. *Gregorianum* 63 (1982) 365.
Heiser, W. Charles. *Theology Digest* 51.1 (2004) 95.
Jones, A. *Spirituality Today* 33 (1981) 373.
Louth, Andrew. *Journal of Theological Studies* 31 (1980) 650-52.
Ramsey, M. *Theology* 84 (1981) 52-53.
Tetlow, J. *America* 146 (1982) 16.
Vivian, Tim. *Cistercian Studies* 32 (1997) 279-80.
Walls, R. *Scottish Journal of Theology* 34 (1981) 550-51.
Van Der Weele, Steve J. *Calvin Theological Journal* 40 (2005) 162-64.

Reviews of *Resurrection: Interpreting the Easter Gospel* (1982)

Hearne, Brian. *African Ecclesial Review* 25 (1983) 189-91.
Hill, E. *New Blackfriars* 64, no. 751 (1983) 46.
Houlden, James Leslie. *Theology* 85 (1982) 452-53.
MacKinnon, Donald M. *Scottish Journal of Theology* 36 (1983) 131-34.
O'Collins, G. *Gregorianum* 63 (1982) 747-48.
Thornton, M. *Expository Times* 94 (1982) 91-92.
Tilley, Terrence W. *Books and Religion* 14.3 (1986) 5, 14-15.
De Waal, Esther. *Modern Churchman* 26.2 (1984) 60.
Yeago, David S. *Lutheran Forum* 23.1 (1989) 24.

Reviews of *The Truce of God* (1983, rev. ed. 2005)

Byassee, Jason. *Christian Century* 123.12 (2006) 36-39.
Cartwright, Michael G. *Books and Religion* 14.9 (1986) 7, 10-11.
Pearson, Paul M. *Cistercian Studies Quarterly* 41 (2006) 123-25.
Rodd, Cyril S. *Expository Times* 94 (1983) 226-27.

Reviews of *Arius: Heresy and Tradition* (1987; rev. ed. 2001)

Ayers, Lewis. *Anglican Theological Review* 85 (2003) 574-76.
Bauckham, Richard. *Themelios* 14 (1989) 75.
Beeley, Christopher A. *Journal of Early Christian Studies* 11 (2003) 246-49.
Bray, Gerald L. *King's Theological Review* 11 (1988) 29-30; *Churchman* 103.4 (1989) 362-63.
Chadwick, Henry. *History Today* 38.8 (1988) 55-56.

Durand, Georges-Matthieu de. *Revue des sciences philosophiques et théologiques* 72 (1988) 611–13.
Fick, W. *Revue d'histoire et de philosophie religieuses* 69 (1989) 343–44.
Flood, Gavin D. *Literature and Theology* 17 (2003) 477–78.
Gregg, Robert C. *Journal of Theological Studies* 40 (1989) 247–54.
Hall, Stuart G. *Expository Times* 99 (1988) 221.
Hanson, Richard P.C. *Journal of Ecclesiastical History* 39 (1988) 235–37.
Harmon, Steven R. *Review & Expositor* 101 (2004) 134–36.
Hugenot, Jerrod H. *American Baptist Quarterly* 21.2 (2002) 250–51.
Kearsley, Roy. *Scottish Bulletin of Evangelical Theology* 21 (2003) 246–47.
Long, Arthur. *Faith and Freedom* 43 (1990) 160–61.
Louth, Andrew. *Theology* 91 (1988) 430–31.
Markus, Robert Austin. *Times Literary Supplement* 4440 (1988) 510.
Mateo Seco, Lucas F. *Scripta Theologica* 21 (1989) 703–04.
Minns, Denis. *New Blackfriars* 69 (1988) 199–200.
Nottingham, William J. *Encounter* 64 (2003) 414–17.
Patterson, Lloyd G. "Arianism in Historical and Theological Context." *Anglican Theological Review* 71 (1989) 201–6.
Ritter, Adolf Martin. *Theologische Rundschau* 55.2 (1990) 153–87.
Russell, Norman. *Sobornost (incorporating Eastern Churches Review)* 10.2 (1988) 74–75.
Young, Frances M. *Scottish Journal of Theology* 42 (1989) 263–67.
Young, Richard A. *Perspectives in Religious Studies* 30 (2003) 126–30.
Wilkins, Margaret. *Faith and Freedom* 55.1 (2002) 87–88.

Review of "War in the Gulf: Can It Be 'Just'?" (1990)

Cunningham, David S. "Resurrection in the Wake of Way." *Christianity and Crisis* 51 (1991) 307–9.

Reviews of *Teresa of Avila* (1991)

Ahlgren, Gillian T. W. *Journal of Religion* 73 (1993) 89–90.
Egan, Keith J. *Horizons* 19 (1992) 314.
Gatta, Julia. "Mysticism and incarnation." *Sewanee Theological Review* 36 (1993) 259–63.
Gillett, David. *Anvil* 9.2 (1992) 187–88.
Louth, Andrew. *New Blackfriars* 73 (1992) 522–23.
Nichols, Aidan. *Journal of Ecclesiastical History* 43 (1992) 656–57.
Nugent, Christopher. *New Oxford Review* 59 (1992) 20–22.
Rodd, Cyril S. "First Woman 'Doctor of the Church.'" *Expository Times* 103 (1992) 160.
Sheehy, H. *Furrow* 43 (1992) 119–20.
Smith, M. *Month* 25 (1992) 68–69.
Thompson, Colin P. *Theology* 95 (1992) 60–61.
Wakefield, Gordon S. *Scottish Journal of Theology* 48 (1995) 404–5.
Welch, John. *Canadian Catholic Review* 12 (1994) 24.

Reviews of *Open to Judgement: Sermons and Addresses* (1994) and *A Ray of Darkness* (1995)

Bray, Gerald. *Sobornost* 18.1 (1996) 98.
Carl III, William J. *Homiletics* 21.1 (1996) 20–21.

Bibliography of Rowan Williams

Cunningham, David S. *Pro Ecclesia* 7 (1998) 122–23.
Gillett, David. *Anvil* 12.2 (1995) 167–68.
Habgood, John S. *Theology* 98 (1995) 72–73.
Kerr, Fergus. *Tablet* 248 (1994) 1170–71.
Seasoltz, R. Kevin. *Worship* 69 (1995) 472–73.
Stacey, John. *Epworth Review* 22.2 (1995) 177.
Webb, Joseph. *Encounter* 57 (1996) 310–11.

Reviews of *After Silent Centuries* (1994)

Jennings, Elizabeth. *Tablet* 248 (1994) 896.
Woolsey, Linda Mills. "Three Poets 'Haunted by Dreams of Eternity': Gerald Manley Hopkins, R. S. Thomas, and Rowan Williams." *Mars Hill Review* 7 (Winter-Spring 1997) 56–61.

Reviews of *Sergii Bulgakov: Towards a Russian Political Theology* (1998)

Arjakovsky, Antoine. *Ecumenical Review* 55 (2003) 285–87.
Bray, Gerald. *Sobornost* 22.1 (2000) 83–84.
Casiday, A.M.C. *Heythrop Journal* 43 (2002) 382.
Louth, Andrew. *Irish Theological Quarterly* 65 (2000) 373–74.

Reviews of *On Christian Theology* (2000)

Barnes, Michael. *The Way* 40 (2000) 391–92.
Bray, Gerald L. *Churchman* 114 (2000) 95–96.
Casiday, A.M.C. *Heythrop Journal* 43 (2002) 236.
Coble, Ann. *Journal of the Evangelical Theological Society* 43 (2000) 559–60.
Edwards, Don. *Colloquium* 35.2 (2003) 177–80.
Heiser, W. Charles. *Theology Digest* 48.2 (2001) 194.
Houlden, James Leslie. *Journal of Theological Studies* 52 (2001) 462–65.
Hughes III, Robert Davis. *Sewanee Theological Review* 44 (2001) 461–63.
Jenson, Robert W. *Pro Ecclesia* 11 (2002) 367–69.
Kelsey, David H. *Modern Theology* 16 (2000) 562–64.
Kennedy, Philip. *New Blackfriars* 81, no. 949 (2000) 143–45.
Lash, Nicholas. *Tablet* 254 (2000) 272.
Lee, J.H. *Studies in World Christianity* 7 (2001) 252–53.
Malcolm, Lois. *Dialog* 41 (2002) 315–16.
Placher, William C. *International Journal of Systematic Theology* 2 (2000) 366–69.
Plekon, Michael. *Cistercian Studies Quarterly* 39 (2004) 99–100.
Sagovsky, Nicholas *Theology* 103, no. 814 (2000) 291–92.
Tanner, Kathryn. *Anglican Theological Review* 83 (2001) 161–63.

Reviews of *Christ on Trial: How the Gospel Unsettles Our Judgement* (2000)

Anderson, Derek. *Anglican Theological Review* 86 (2004) 719–21.
Brouwer, Wayne. *Calvin Theological Journal* 39 (2004) 181–82.
Moll, Ed. *Churchman* 115 (2001) 85–86.
Skinner, Matthew L. *Word & World* 24 (2004) 450–54.

Reviews of *Lost Icons: Reflections on Cultural Bereavement* (2000)

Anderson, Derek N. *Anglican Theological Review* 85 (2003) 576–78.

Brusic, Robert. *Word & World* 24 (2004) 344-47.
Chapman, Mark D. *Modern Believing* 41.4 (2000) 60-62.
Chartres, Richard. *Journal of Theological Studies* 52 (2001) 465-67.
Ford, David F. *Theology Today* 58 (2002) 645-47.
Harvey, Nicholas Peter. *Scottish Journal of Theology* 56 (2003) 101-3.
Goodmann, James M. *Sewanee Theological Review* 48 (2004) 129-33.
Kerr, Fergus. *Tablet* 254 (2000) 793-94.
Kettle, David. *International Journal of Systematic Theology* 3 (2001) 100-102.
Leithart, Peter J. *Westminster Theological Journal* 64 (2002) 417-20.
Louth, Andrew. *Irish Theological Quarterly* 67 (2002) 79-80.
McEvoy, James. *Australasian Catholic Record* 82.2 (2005) 243-44.
McIntosh, Mark Allen. *Spiritus* 2.1 (2002) 132-34.
Nichols, Aidan. *New Blackfriars* 81, no. 957 (2000) 509-11.
Noble, Tim. *Month* 261 (2000) 450-51.
Pailin, David A. *Epworth Review* 28.2 (2001) 75-76.
Quash, Ben. *Anglican Theological Review* 83 (2001) 679-82;
———. *Studies in Christian Ethics* 14 (2001) 117-20.
Shakespeare, Steven. *Theology* 103, no. 816 (2000) 456-57.
Smith, David. *Themelios* 26.2 (2001) 108-9.
Thompson, Penny. *Contact* 136 (2001) 38-39.
Townsend, Michael J. *Expository Times* 111 (2000) 424-25.
Tranter, Stephen. *Anvil* 18.2 (2001) 151-52.
Tanner, Kathryn. *Modern Theology* 17 (2001) 410-12.

Reviews of *Love's Redeeming Work* (2001)

Power, T. P. *Toronto Journal of Theology* 19 (2003) 98-99.
Shannon, William H. *Cistercian Studies Quarterly* 39 (2004) 90-91.

Reviews of *The Poems of Rowan Williams* (2002)

Baumgaertner, Jill Pelaez. *Christian Century* 122.21 (2005) 61-65.
Doriot, Jeanne. *Cistercian Studies Quarterly* 40 (2005) 110-12.
Middleton, David. *Anglican Theological Review* 88 (2006) 479-81.
Walker, Jeanne Murray. *Christianity & Literature* 54 (2004) 93-110.

Reviews of *Writing in the Dust* (2002)

Humpherys, Jenny. *Political Theology* 4 (2003) 248-49.
Meehan, Dermot. *Furrow* 53.10 (2002) 583-84.

Reviews of *Ponder These Things: Praying with Icons of the Virgin* (2002)

Casiday, A. *Sobornost* 25.1 (2003) 102-3.
Cunneen, Sally. *National Catholic Reporter* 39.29 (2003) 22-23.
Plekon, Michael. *Cistercian Studies Quarterly* 39 (2004) 206-8.

Reviews of *The Dwelling of the Light: Praying with Icons of Christ* (2003)

Casiday, A. *Eastern Churches Review* 26.1 (2004) 105.
Cunningham, Lawrence. *Cistercian Studies Quarterly* 39 (2004) 343-45.

Bibliography of Rowan Williams

Reviews of *Silence and Honey Cakes: The Wisdom of the Desert* (2003) and *Where God Happens: Discovering Christ in One Another* (2005)

Burton-Christie, Douglas. *Cistercian Studies Quarterly* 40 (2005) 212–14.
Byassee, Jason. *Christian Century* 123.12 (2006) 36–39.
Perl, Jeffrey M. *Common Knoweldge* 11 (2005) 354–56.
Rzepecki, Arnold M. *Catholic Library World* 77.1 (2006) 54–55.
Wilson, David. *Tablet* 257, no. 8517 (2003) 38–39.

Reviews of *Anglican Identities* (2004)

Chapman, Mark D. *Expository Times* 116 (2004) 67.
Doll, Peter. *The Journal of Ecclesiastical History* 56 (2005) 593–94.
Hobson, Theo. "Rowan Williams as Anglican Hegelian." *Religion & Theology* 12 (2005) 290–97.
Nichols, Aidan. *Priests & People* 18.11 (2004) 440–41.
Pridmore, John. *The Way* 44.2 (2005) 141–43.
Quash, Ben. *New Blackfriars* 86, no. 1003 (2005) 355–56.
Webster, Peter. *Reformation & Renaissance Review* 7.1 (2005) 131–32.

Reviews of *Why Study the Past? The Quest for the Historical Church* (2005)

Byassee, Jason. *Christian Century* 123.12 (2006) 36–39.
Chadwick, Owen. *Catholic Historical Review* 92 (2006) 267–68.
Franklin, R.S. *Princeton Seminary Bulletin* 26 (2005) 345–46.
Madden, Nicholas. *Furrow* 56.7–8 (2005) 441–43.
Neff, David. "Something Old, Something New." *Christianity Today* 50.4 (2006) 104–5.
O'Loughlin, Thomas. *New Blackfriars* 87, no. 1008 (2006) 199–201.
Powell, Gareth J. *Epworth Review* 33.1 (2006) 92.

Reviews of *Grace and Necessity: Reflections on Art and Love* (2005)

Gallagher, Daniel B. *First Things* 172 (2007) 49.
Hooker, Jeremy. *Tablet* 259, no. 8597 (2005) 22.
Jasper, David. *Literature and Theology* 20 (2006) 332–34.
Lloyd, Michael. *New Blackfriars* 87, no. 1012 (2006) 665–66.
Milbank, John. "Scholasticism, Modernism and Modernity." *Modern Theology* 22 (2006) 651–71.
Marsh, Clive. *Epworth Review* 33.2 (2006) 73.
Viladesau, Richard. *Worship* 80 (2006) 188–89.

Reviews of *Tokens of Trust* (2007)

Belshaw, G. P. Mellick. *Anglican Theological Review* 89 (2007) 685–88.
Howse, Christopher. *Tablet* 261, no. 8689 (2007) 27.
Myers, Benjamin. *Princeton Theological Review* 13.2 (2007) 100–101.
Werntz, Myles. *Religious Studies Review* 33 (2007) 223–24.

Review of *Wrestling with Angels* (2007)

Richardson, Graeme. *New Blackfriars* 88, no. 1018 (2007) 742–44.

Contributors

Rhys Bezzant is Lecturer in Christian Thought at Ridley College, Melbourne. He completed an MA in German at the Universities of Melbourne and Cologne, and his MTh research focused on the revivals of eighteenth-century Austria. He is presently writing his doctorate on the ecclesiology of Jonathan Edwards at the Jonathan Edwards Center, Yale Divinity School. He is an ordained minister in the Anglican Diocese of Melbourne.

Andrew Cameron is Bruce Smith Lecturer in Ethics, Philosophy, and Apologetics at Moore Theological College, Sydney, and Chairman of the Social Issues Executive of the Anglican Diocese of Sydney. He holds a PhD in theology from King's College, London.

Greg Clarke is Director of Macquarie Christian Studies Institute at Macquarie University and a Founding Director of the Centre for Public Christianity in Sydney. He holds a PhD in English literature from the University of Sydney. His research is in theology and culture, with a particular interest in the eschatological shape of literature. His publications include *Is It Worth Believing?: The Spiritual Challenge of The Da Vinci Code*, and *Eschatology, Apocalypse and Modern Fiction: The Future of Patrick White* (forthcoming).

Tom Frame is Director of St Mark's National Theological Centre, Canberra, where he is also a professor. He was formerly an officer in the Royal Australian Navy (1979–1992) and Bishop to the Australian Defence Force (2001–2007). He is the author of twenty-two books, including *Living by the Sword?: The Ethics of Armed Intervention* and *Church and State: Australia's Imaginary Wall*.

Contributors

Michael Jensen is a doctoral candidate in moral theology at Oxford University. He is undertaking research on the Christian conception of martyrdom and its relevance for theological anthropology. He is the author of several journal articles and many reviews. He has taught theology at Moore Theological College, Sydney, and at Wycliffe Hall, Oxford, and has also worked as a school chaplain and church planter.

Andrew Moody is a research student in systematic theology at Ridley College, Melbourne. He is undertaking research on key aspects of social Trinitarianism in historical and contemporary contexts. He is a regularly published participant in public discussions on belief and society.

Benjamin Myers is a Research Fellow at the University of Queensland's Centre for the History of European Discourses. He holds a PhD from James Cook University, and he is the author of *Milton's Theology of Freedom*. He is currently writing a critical introduction on the theology of Rowan Williams, as well as a book on Karl Barth.

Matheson Russell is a Lecturer in Philosophy at the University of Auckland. He holds a PhD in philosophy from the University of New South Wales and has read theology at Oxford University. He is the author of *Husserl: A Guide for the Perplexed* and a number of essays on Heidegger. His current research is in the fields of political theology, phenomenology of religion, and theories of intersubjectivity.

Byron Smith holds honors degrees in theology, philosophy, and English literature from Sydney University and Moore Theological College, Sydney. He has served as a ministry assistant at an Anglican parish church in Sydney and has recently commenced doctoral studies in moral theology at the University of Edinburgh.

Index

Adams, Robert Merrihew, 193
Adorno, Theodor, 106
Aelred of Rievaulx, 156, 158
Affirming Catholicism, 7
Afghanistan, 164, 164n, 178, 179, 182
analogia entis, 30, 46n
angels, 139, 191
Anglican Communion/Church, xiii, xxii, 2–5, 7, 8, 13, 20, 113, 144, 176, 185
Anglo-Catholicism, xxii, 7, 12
apologetics, 188, 190–2, 194, 201
apophaticism/*apophasis,* xi, xv, xvi, 26–39, 39n, 40–46, 46n, 61, 93–95
ARCIC, 7
Aristotle, 149, 190
Arius; Arian controversy, 4n, 27, 51–53, 55–58, 62, 160
art, xxii, 25, 44n, 46, 46n, 148n, 189, 191–94, 200–203
Athanasius, x, 31, 38n, 52
atonement, 12, 16, 17, 17n, 172, 199
Augustine of Hippo, xv, 20, 32, 33, 35, 35n, 92n, 130, 154, 155, 157, 157n, 159, 189

Badiou, Alain, 107n
Balthasar, Hans Urs von, xxii, 31–33, 35n, 189, 192
baptism, xiv, 13, 112
Barmen Declaration, 53, 53n, 59
Barth, Karl, 46n, 63, 94n, 130, 137, 171, 201

Bauckham, Richard, 203
Baur, Ferdinand Christian, 71
beauty, xxii, 45n, 189–98, 201
Becker, Ernest, 123
Benedict XVI (Joseph Ratzinger), 8, 186–88, 195
Benjamin, Walter, 106
Berdyaev, Nikolai, 200, 200n
Berlinerblau, Jacques, 51n
body, xx, 11, 12, 15, 26n, 45, 104n, 115, 121, 126, 133, 135, 136, 136n, 141–49, 151–59, 191
Bonhoeffer, Dietrich, 15, 79
Brown, David, 28n

Calvin, John, 22
celibacy, xxi, 144, 155–58
Christology, xix, 12, 22, 22n, 24, 25, 70, 70n, 72, 73, 172, 202
church, x, xiii, xiv, xvii, xix, 1–24, 27n, 39–44, 47–48, 50–66, 71–77, 79, 82n, 86, 92, 103–7, 110–13, 133, 135, 136n, 153, 159–62, 169–71, 173, 174, 185, 193, 194, 198–200, 203
Cold War, 164–68, 172, 173, 175, 177, 181
Collier, Mark, 165, 166
communication, xix, 14, 15, 21, 30, 43, 75, 86, 90, 93, 95n, 96–104, 112, 113, 113n, 126, 157, 165, 186, 188–91, 194, 200, 202

Index

community, xiv, xvii, xxi, 4, 5, 11, 13, 15, 19, 43, 44, 48, 49, 53–55, 57–65, 75, 76, 78, 79, 82, 93, 94, 96–98, 101, 103–5, 106n, 108, 110–12, 116, 126, 129–37, 144–46, 149, 154, 155, 157, 161, 162, 169, 170, 172, 173, 179, 185, 190, 198
conversion, 40, 66, 73, 75–80, 82, 85, 90, 93, 99, 107, 108, 162, 165, 169
Cray, Graham, 5
creatio ex nihilo, 39, 116–18, 130, 138, 192
creation, xiv, xix, xxi, 16, 28, 30–35, 45n, 73, 75, 77, 91–94, 102, 104, 107n, 113, 115–40, 142, 146, 151, 158, 189, 192–94, 200–202
Crossan, John Dominic, 81n
Crowe, Peter, 176
crucifixion, 26, 37, 91, 93, 111, 125–27, 130, 131

Dawkins, Richard, 194
DeHart, Paul, 67n, 74n
Derrida, Jacques, 71, 81, 106
desire, xx, 34, 40, 95, 96, 99, 100, 110, 112, 120, 124, 127, 128, 142–44, 146, 147, 151, 152, 155–57, 159, 162, 184, 196, 198, 201, 203
Dionysius the Areopagite/Pseudo-Dionysius, 26, 41
discipleship, xviii, xxiii, 9, 15, 75, 85, 108, 132, 155
doctrine x, xv–xviii, 10, 38, 38n, 43, 44, 47–67, 68–72, 78, 82–84, 195, 200
Dulles, Avery, 23

ecclesiology, xiv, 1–25, 82
Edwards, Jonathan, 34
Ellul, Jacques, 172
Enlai, Zhou, 44n
eschatology, xiv, xix, xxii, 14, 16, 18, 107, 108, 108n, 157, 188, 200–204
essentialism, 144, 158–60, 162
Eucharist, 12–14, 22n, 136, 200

feminism, xviii, 71, 77, 77n, 83, 117, 150
forgiveness, xiv, 19, 39n, 85, 120, 127, 128, 154, 159, 165, 194, 195

Frei, Hans, 74
friendship, 3, 9, 144, 156–59, 162, 199, 203

gender, xxi, 7, 142, 144, 148–53, 157, 158
Gervais, Ricky, 194
Girard, René, 171–73
Goddard, Andrew, 44n
grace, xix, xx, 10, 12, 13, 17, 18, 20, 64, 67, 70, 75, 77, 85, 93, 94, 95n, 104, 105n, 107, 113, 117–19, 125–34, 141–48, 151, 152, 154–57, 159, 162, 170, 200
Gregory of Nyssa, 28n, 121n
Gregory Palamas, 26
Griffin, Susan, 151

Harnack, Adolf von, 80
Harries, Richard, 176
Hart, David Bentley, xxii, 193, 194
Hart, Trevor, 46n, 203
Hegel, G. W. F., xv, xviii, xix, 27n, 28n, 35n, 36, 86–95, 101–6, 108, 109, 193
Heidegger, Martin, 98
heresy, 38n, 50, 51n, 53–58, 61–64
hermeneutics, xviii, 25, 36, 70, 71, 73, 80, 81n, 149, 161
Higton, Mike, vii, 26n, 37n, 173n
history of doctrine, 47–53, 55, 59, 62, 64
Hobson, Theo, 1n, 6
Hodgson, Peter C., 87n, 91n
Holy Spirit, xiv, 5, 11, 13, 14, 19, 21–24, 34, 36, 41, 43, 44n, 45n, 52, 92, 104, 118–20, 122, 131, 137, 138, 159, 162, 198, 200
homosexuality, xx, 3, 142, 145, 160–62
Honneth, Axel, 96n
humanity, xiv, xix, xx, 12–15, 29–31, 35, 42–45, 93, 94, 104–6, 113, 115–18, 125–27, 131, 133, 135–40, 144, 146, 155, 158–60, 169, 170, 175, 181, 182
Hussein, Saddam, 176, 181

IARCCUM, 7
identity, x, xvii, 12, 21, 24, 30, 36, 49, 50, 53, 58, 59, 61, 63, 64, 66, 67, 75, 78, 80, 92, 103–5, 110, 111,

236

117, 119, 120, 128, 129, 131, 132, 144, 150, 157–60, 198, 199
Ignatius of Antioch, 126n
imitatio dei, 116, 121, 126
incarnation, xix, 10, 12, 13, 16, 19, 21, 28, 31, 38n, 39, 44, 45, 68n, 69, 70n, 73, 91–93, 95n, 126, 134, 137, 138, 196, 198
Iraq, xxi, 164, 164n, 175, 176, 181–83
Irenaeus of Lyons, 41
Islam, 113n, 178, 187, 198
Israel, ancient, 80, 92, 174
Israel, state of, 180, 182, 197

Jeremias, Joachim, 81
Jesus Christ, ix, xiv, xvi, xviii, 6, 12, 14, 15, 17–21, 25, 27–30, 35–38, 39n, 41–46, 60, 63, 69–73, 75, 76, 78–84, 92, 104n, 110, 115, 116, 118, 125, 126, 128, 130, 134, 136, 138, 157, 160, 162, 170, 172, 178, 191, 197–200, 202, 203
John, Gospel of, 18, 23, 42, 75, 191
John of the Cross, xv, xix, 16, 27n, 33, 35, 35n, 44, 45n
Johnson, James Turner, 176n
judgment, xiv, xvii–xix, 12, 17n, 21, 37, 39, 40, 50, 53, 56, 63, 68, 70–73, 75–77, 81–4, 93, 94, 104, 110, 174, 202, 203
justice, xix, 2, 32, 86–89, 99, 101, 102, 104, 107, 112, 113, 136, 165, 175, 176, 185, 196–98, 201
justification, x, xiv, 16–18, 96, 122

Kant, Immanuel, 70, 94, 106n, 109
Käsemann, Ernst, 65
Kenosis; kenoticism, xv, xix, 31, 34, 86, 91, 103, 104, 105n, 107, 113, 119, 120, 133, 134, 137, 138
Kerr, Fergus, 131n
krisis, xvi–xviii, 71, 72, 82–84, 85

Laden, Osama bin, 179, 197
Layton, Sarah, 142, 145, 154
Lévinas, Emmanuel, 94
Lindbeck, George A., xvi, 48–50, 62, 64, 74, 76

Locke, John, 193
Lossky, Vladimir, xv, 7, 22n, 26, 27, 30, 37n, 39n, 40n
love, xv, xix–xxiii, 9, 23, 29–36, 39n, 40, 42, 44, 45, 46n, 75, 91, 92, 103–6, 110, 113, 115, 117, 118, 120, 121, 126, 128, 130, 131, 134, 135, 138, 142, 143, 147, 149, 150, 155–57, 169, 178, 180, 189, 192–94, 196, 197
Luther, Martin, 10, 20, 41, 93, 130
Lux Mundi, 12

MacIntyre, Alasdair, 58
MacKinnon, Donald, 30n
Macquarrie, John, 2
Maritain, Jacques, 192
marriage, xx, 142, 143, 146–48, 152–58, 162, 203
Marx, Karl, 89n
Marxism, 71, 77n, 150
May, Rollo, 172
McCormack, Bruce, 137
McGrath, Alister E., 24
Milbank, John, 65
Moberly, R. C., 38, 73n
Moltmann, Jürgen, 28n
Mugabe, Robert, 165
Murphy-O'Connor, Cormac, 182

Nagel, Thomas, 146
NATO, 164, 166
negotiation, xvi, xvii, xix, 49, 57, 58, 60, 61, 64, 85, 86, 88n, 89, 94–105, 108, 112, 113n, 118n, 168
New Testament, xix, 11, 20, 23, 43, 46n, 71–73, 83, 84, 157, 165
Nicaea, 39, 43n, 51–54, 57
Nicene Creed, 48n, 54, 59, 76
Nietzsche, Friedrich, 107, 149

O'Donovan, Oliver, 2, 109, 110, 144
orthodoxy, xv–xvii, 38, 49, 50, 53–67, 80, 92, 107n

Paleologus, Manuel II, 187
Pannenberg, Wolfhart, 69
parables, 78–81, 83, 147

Index

Pauw, Amy Plantinga, 23
peace, xiv, xxi, xxii, 14, 85, 106, 107, 136, 154, 160, 161, 163–65, 168–70, 173, 175, 183–85, 193–96, 198, 199, 201
pluralism, 43, 199
politics, x, xiii, xviii, xix, xii, 40n, 50, 56, 58, 77, 85–87, 89, 92, 95, 98n, 99, 102–4, 108, 110, 112, 113, 115, 117, 136, 138, 147, 161, 163, 164, 166–68, 171–73, 175, 182–84, 187
post-liberalism, xvi, 74, 82
postmodernism, xvi–xviii, 11, 16, 27, 71, 71n, 72, 86, 87, 87n, 94, 106, 150, 192
prayer, xix, xx, 13, 16, 20n, 75, 133–35, 150, 198–200
procreation, 144, 147, 151–53

resurrection, xix, 12, 19, 21, 28, 60, 63, 78, 79, 83, 107n, 113, 125, 139, 190, 191, 199
revelation, 6n, 14, 17, 18, 24, 27, 36–38, 44n, 47, 48, 83, 93, 156, 199, 203
Rose, Gillian, xviii, xix, 87n, 88n, 102, 102n, 103, 105n
Ruether, Rosemary, 202
Runcie, Robert, 167

sacraments, xiii, xiv, 12–14, 17, 20, 24, 111, 126, 129, 142
same-sex relationships, 2, 142
Scott, Paul, 145
Scripture, 17n, 18, 20, 22–24, 43, 52, 53, 57, 71, 73–75, 77, 79, 82, 84, 108, 133n, 138, 139, 142, 146, 149, 152, 155, 161, 162, 167, 171
self, xix, xx, 4, 72, 78, 86–92, 103, 109, 110, 124, 125, 127–29, 131, 132, 134, 145, 146, 148, 158, 160
September 11 attacks, xxi, 168, 169, 177, 180, 186, 187, 196
sex, sexuality, xx, xxi, 2, 3, 66, 141–62
Shortt, Rupert, 12n, 26n, 167
sin, xx, 17, 24, 42, 45n, 46, 117, 124, 125, 127, 129–32, 136, 139, 154, 162, 171, 177
social Trinitarianism, 23, 32, 133n
social contract theory, 98n

Sölle, Dorothee, 131n
spirituality, xix, xx, xxiii, 20, 25, 26, 34, 41, 66, 84, 93, 115–40, 159, 168, 177, 189
Spong, John Shelby, 45n
suffering, x, 19n, 29, 91, 93, 131, 132, 167, 177, 180, 197

Tanner, Kathryn, 49, 50, 62, 63
Tendenzkritik, 71, 72, 77, 82–84
Teresa of Avila, 16, 128, 134
Thomas Aquinas, xv, 32, 33, 35, 92n, 118
Tice, Diane, 159
Torrance, Thomas F., 47–50
tradition, xvii, xxii, 7, 26n, 43, 47, 50–67, 70, 113, 126, 165
Trinity, x, xv, xviii, xix, 21, 23, 24, 25–46, 92, 117, 119, 120, 133n, 137, 138, 189, 194, 196, 201

union with Christ, 16, 17, 45n, 134

via negativa/negative theology; see 'apophaticism/*aphophasis*'
violence, 14, 88, 89, 102, 103, 107, 123, 130, 147, 165, 169–73, 175, 177–81, 184, 185, 187, 197
war, xxi, xxii, 98n, 109, 112, 153, 163–85
Wiles, Maurice, xi, xvii, xviii, 38n, 68–72, 74, 78, 82, 83
Windsor Report, 2, 3, 8, 11
Wittgenstein, Ludwig, xvi, 48, 56, 97n
Word of God, xix, 20, 22, 79, 120n

Zizioulas, John, 14, 22n

www.ingramcontent.com/pod-product-compliance
Lightning Source LLC
Chambersburg PA
CBHW031726230426
43669CB00007B/256